THE TEMPLE SCROLL

Also by Yigael Yadin

The Art of Warfare in Biblical Lands
The Message of the Scrolls
Masada
Bar Kokhba
Hazor

THE TEMPLE SCROLL

The Hidden Law of the Dead Sea Sect

YIGAEL YADIN

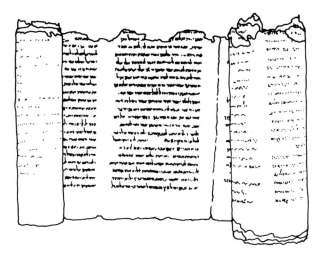

Random House  New York

Editor: Moshe Pearlman

Library of Congress Cataloging in Publication Data

Yadin, Yigael, 1917–
  The Temple scroll.

  Bibliography: p.
  Includes index.
    1. Temple scroll—Criticism, interpretation, etc.
  2. Fasts and feasts—Judaism.   3. Temple of Jerusalem (Jerusalem)   I. Title.
  BM488.T44Y33 1985   296.1′55   84–45773
  ISBN 0–394–54498–6

Manufactured in Great Britain

23456789
First Edition

Contents

Preface

The manuscript of this book was completed in March 1984, and the proofs were ready three months later. Professor Yadin and I were about to go over them together when, on 28 June 1984, he suffered a massive heart attack and died within minutes. He was sixty-seven.

A remarkable man and a remarkable scholar, he was born in Jerusalem and brought up with a sense of history instilled in him by his archaeologist father. It inspired his generalship when he was in the army, and later it directed his genius to the illumination of his people's past.

When he was Chief of Operations in Israel's War of Independence in 1948–9 and subsequently, at the age of thirty-two, Chief of the General Staff, he drew upon his student researches into the varied tactics employed in biblical battles fought in the very land he was now defending. They had an urgent relevance to a commander in 1948 meeting invasion from all directions, for the key encounters in successive centuries usually took place over the same high ground, mountain passes and strategic routes, their military importance undiminished in our own times.

I was on Yadin's staff during that war and, as we drove to the battlefronts, he would point out the mounds we were passing that held the remains of cities and villages mentioned in the Bible, and speak with excitement about the prospect of one day undertaking his own archaeological excavations.

After he left the army and completed his doctoral studies, his rise in the world of scholarship was rapid. He became an international authority in two fields: biblical archaeology and Dead Sea scroll research. His prodigious contribution to both sprang from wide knowledge, a capacious memory and a questing and analytical mind. In addition, he possessed a rare detective-like ability to discern hidden clues in a word or fact recalled from an ancient document or earlier dig that shed light on the text or excavation on which he was engaged.

An example of his flair for logical deduction was a discovery derived from the biblical record that Solomon built three chariot cities at 'Hazor, and Megiddo, and Gezer'. At Hazor, his first spectacular dig, Yadin uncovered the Solomonic gatehouse, with its distinctive design of three chambers on each side of the entrance corridor. A similar gate had been found earlier at Megiddo. In excavating Gezer some eighty years ago, however, British archaeologist R.A.S. Macalister had made no mention of such a structure. Yadin reasoned that Solomon's engineers would surely have followed a standard plan, and he felt certain, therefore, that Gezer must have had a gate like the other two.

Yadin accordingly made a fresh study of Macalister's detailed report of his dig. He soon spotted the design of a building that had been erroneously ascribed to the second century BC and called a 'Maccabean castle'. The error in dating was understandable, for at that time archaeology was still in its infancy. What Yadin had detected in the plan was the three-chambered western half of a characteristic tenth century BC Solomonic gate. Ten years later, when another archaeological team excavated at Gezer, the other half of the gate came to light, thus confirming Yadin's theory.

Yadin also had a gift for intuitive 'hunches'. This is well illustrated by his solution to a puzzle in the biblical account of David's capture of Jerusalem. The Bible relates that the Jebusite defenders lined their ramparts with 'the blind and the lame'. Josephus, the first-century AD historian, observed that this strange act was a gesture of derision and contempt. Modern scholars considered this explanation implausible. David and his men had already acquired a formidable military reputation, and the Jebusites must have watched their approach with the gravest anxiety.

Yadin found a clue in a second millennium BC Hittite text relating to the ceremony at which the troops were sworn in. A 'blind woman and a deaf man' were paraded before them, and the officiating priest warned that they would be similarly afflicted if ever they showed disloyalty. Yadin suggested that the frightened Jebusites used the same symbolic rite to deter the Hebrews by instilling in them the superstitious terror that they too would be stricken by the same handicaps if they attacked the maimed.

Yadin's theory, now generally accepted, is given added weight by the rest of the biblical passage. When his forces doubtless hung back, David promised a most uncommon reward to the first man who 'getteth up ... and smiteth the Jebusites, and the lame and the blind': that man 'shall be chief and captain'. It was David's tough, brave nephew Joab who defied the curse.

These attributes of insight and intuition added a dimension to the quality of all Yadin's scholarly work, and is apparent throughout his detailed textual analysis of the Temple scroll. Moreover, an articulate man of great charm, he possessed the ability to present abstruse scientific facts and theories in simple non-academic language readily understood by the layman.

Yadin was not one to rest on his record of achievement. After a stint in politics as Deputy Prime Minister, he returned to his post at the university and was also planning further archaeological excavations in the land he loved, the land of the Bible. However, I think he was content to have crowned his Dead Sea scroll research with his work on the Temple scroll, which he regarded as the most important of all those unique documents.

Moshe Pearlman
Jerusalem, November 1984

PART ONE

THE ACQUISITION

1 The Million Dollar Proposal

A letter out of the blue from a stranger; secret meetings in Geneva, Beirut and Amman; a million dollar proposal; the hint of a clandestine connection with the Royal Court of the Hashemite Kingdom of Jordan; furtive transactions between Bedouin tribesmen and an antiquities dealer; and an exciting message during a crucial discussion by the Ministerial Defence Committee of the Israel Cabinet in the midst of the Six Day War – these were elements in a tortuous process which led to the acquisition of a priceless treasure of antiquity. This, after nine years of decipherment and study, turned out to be what I have called the Temple scroll, written in the second century BC, secreted in a Dead Sea cave two hundred years later to save it from the Roman conquerors, undisturbed for nineteen centuries, discovered in a well-preserved state, presented for sale by a Virginian clergyman, but eventually acquired in quite another way.

This may well be the most important of all the Dead Sea scrolls discovered so far. The discovery of those momentous documents sent shock waves throughout the world of biblical and historical scholarship, challenging the conventional notions of the influences that shaped early Christianity, and adding greatly to our knowledge and understanding of the history of the Bible text, the Talmud and the development of traditional Judaism. It was as though a miraculous tele-time-scope had suddenly zoomed through a two-thousand-year screen to provide a dramatic close-up of the scenes in the Holy Land during the final centuries of Jewish independence and the birth of Christianity.

The scrolls had belonged to the library of a devout Jewish sect called the Essenes. They had quarrelled with the Jewish religious establishment in Jerusalem for being too lax in carrying out the laws and injunctions of the Torah, the Law of Moses, according to the Essene interpretation. They had accordingly gone to dwell as a separate and isolated community at a place now called Qumran on the north-western shore of the Dead Sea, at the edge of the Judean desert, where they could follow their own stern rules of religious conduct, waiting for their 'return' to Jerusalem 'at the End of Days'.

Some of the scrolls and fragments discovered in the Qumran caves were Hebrew Books of the Bible, such as Genesis, Exodus, Deuter-onomy, the prophets Isaiah, Jeremiah and Ezekiel, and, among the Writings, Psalms and Proverbs. These are at least one thousand years older than the earliest previously known Hebrew biblical texts. Others were manuscripts of biblical commentaries. The biblical Books show that the standard text in use today was known and used two thousand years ago; yet at the same time other texts were current which differed somewhat in detail, and such biblical texts appear in other scrolls and fragments also found at Qumran. They are similar to the Septuagint, the third–second-century BC Greek translation of the Bible from the original Hebrew. It is evident, therefore, that at the time of the writing of the Qumran scrolls, the canon of the Hebrew Bible had not yet been finalized.

The remaining Dead Sea scrolls are of particular interest from the historical point of view, for there had been no knowledge of their existence until their discovery in our generation. They are original works of the Essene sect, and one of the most spectacular revelations of these sectarian books, including the Temple scroll, is that many of the customs and beliefs hitherto accepted as distinctly Christian in-novations, or Greek influences on Christianity, had in fact existed in the second and first centuries BC among this section of the Jewish community, who had sought to preserve the 'purity' of Judaism by adhering strictly to the Law of Moses. It was very possibly the leader of this Jewish sect who composed the Temple scroll, and he was clearly a man of formidable erudition, as I gathered from my studies. Some of the ideas of his sect were subsequently adopted by other Jews who broke away from their religion and fathered Christianity.

The Temple scroll is a remarkable work of prodigious significance. No less remarkable is the manner in which it reached my hands – seven years after I was apprised of the existence of 'scrolls' in a letter dated 1 August 1960. I knew virtually nothing of this particular scroll throughout those seven years, and only during my subsequent nine years of studying its text did I discover its full meaning and impor-tance.

The letter I received was from a Virginian clergyman, unknown to me, whom I shall call Mr Z, as he was most anxious to remain anony-mous. He wrote as follows: 'I have been in discussion with your good friend, Dr William F. Albright, of Johns Hopkins University. He suggested I write to you. This letter is highly important and must be kept in strict confidence.'

He went on to say that 'After many months of negotiation, I am

able to negotiate with you important authentic discoveries of Dead
Sea scrolls. These were discovered at the same time and in the same
place as those you obtained from Archbishop Samuel.'

This was a reference to four Dead Sea scrolls which had been in the
possession of Mar Athanasius Samuel, head of the Syrian Orthodox
Christian Church of St Mark in the Old City of Jerusalem when the
Old City was under Jordanian occupation. He had left Jerusalem for
the United States early in 1949, taking the scrolls with him and
hoping to sell them for several million dollars. He had tried to do so
for the next five years, but found no takers at that price. In 1954 he
sold them to me, on behalf of the State of Israel, for a quarter of a
million dollars, under odd circumstances. They now joined the three
scrolls my father had acquired under more unusual circumstances in
1947, so that Israel was now in possession of all seven complete or
substantially complete scrolls that had been discovered in a Dead Sea
cave. Since this was public knowledge, it was understandable that
anyone with additional scrolls to offer should approach me.

Continuing his letter, Mr Z wrote that the scrolls he was proffering

can be authenticated by you, and it is my understanding from Dr Albright
that you have many financial contacts here in the United States. As a
member of the clergy, I feel that these scrolls rightfully belong in Israel. I
have in my possession the most complete scrolls in history. I have been
dealing directly with a trusted link in Jordan. We can proceed on one basis
only: no publicity can be released in any way, shape or form, as lives would
be involved.... Dr Albright, you and I are the only ones who are aware of
this letter. It is so important that this be kept confidential. I would be able
to negotiate this with you upon word from you.... I prefer to make the
transaction in Geneva.

This letter lay on my desk in Jerusalem, unread, throughout the
month of August. I was away in Moscow, attending a congress of the
International Oriental Society which I had been asked to address.
Curiously enough, the subject of my lecture was my discovery of
ancient documents at archaeological excavations I had conducted six
months earlier (March 1960) only a few miles south, it transpired, of
the cave in which the Temple scroll had originally been secreted. My
manuscripts, however, were of quite a different nature. They had been
written some two hundred and fifty years later by a Jew with a
different outlook from that of the Dead Sea sect. These documents
were despatches sent by Bar Kokhba, leader of the Jewish revolt
against the Romans in AD 132.

It was only upon my return from Moscow that I read Mr Z's intriguing letter, and I lost no time in cabling a reply, expressing interest
and seeking further information. I wished to know whether the 'subjects of your letter' were already in his possession, how many there
were, where I could see them, and the approximate price he was asking.

He cabled me two weeks later stating that he had just returned from the Middle East and was sending me 'full details'. And, indeed, a few days thereafter I received a long letter, dated 16 September 1960, telling me that 'I received your wire two weeks ago, the day I left for the Middle East', and now, upon his return to Virginia, giving me the following information:

I've been in long negotiations in Jordan concerning the scrolls. I am able to report to you at this time that I have the sole and exclusive contact with Mr X. [Here he mentioned the name of an antiquities dealer in Jordan.] If we can proceed on a secretive basis, I can guarantee to get all the scrolls in the hands of Israel within the next few months.

It will be recalled that at that time, what has become widely known as the West Bank, as well as East Jerusalem, including the Old City, had been annexed by Jordan. The Jordan–Israel border on the north-western shore of the Dead Sea lay just south of the caves where the major Dead Sea scrolls had been found (including the seven acquired by my father and myself), and just north of the area in which I and other Israeli archaeologists had carried out excavations. Though Jordan and Israel had signed an armistice agreement in 1949 – I happen to have been one of the signatories of its first draft, agreed with King Abdullah at his winter palace in Shuneh – Jordan had refused to follow it up with peace negotiations. Mr Z, seeking to arrange a deal between myself and an antiquities dealer living in an area controlled by Jordan, had to tread very warily.

Mr Z's letter went on to say that 'John Allegro [a British scholar engaged in scroll research] mentioned in the United Press a few weeks ago that there were five scrolls in the hands of the Bedouin.... However, I can report to you, and this must not be published, that there are ten scrolls, one is in bronze, several are in gazelle skin and goat-skin, and one is in pure gold.'

I did not quite know what to make of this: it seemed too remarkable to be true, and if there were indeed such a bounty of scrolls I would surely have heard of it through the scholarly grapevine. There was, after all, contact through neutral countries between scholars (all foreign) working in Jordan and their counterparts in Israel. Moreover, the reference to the scroll 'in pure gold' aroused my scepticism. However, I was jerked to attention by the contents of the next paragraph and above all by what was attached to it:

I am sending you a picture of a piece 5 inches by 15 inches that I have, which I could release here in the States. It is about the size of some that are on display in the Rockefeller Museum. [This museum is located in East Jerusalem, and the Jordanian Department of Antiquities exhibited there a number of scroll fragments found near the Dead Sea.] We have had to pay a considerable amount of money [for this piece of scroll], much more than expected in this negotiation, since dealer X knows the real value. I can send this piece to you at once for about $20,000. Of the other scrolls I can deliver, one is 10 inches by 14 feet on gazelle skin, that came out of Cave 1, discovered twelve years ago at the same time as the ones you have from Archbishop Samuel. I can deliver about four more by November 15th. These will cost in the neighbourhood of one million dollars a piece. He [dealer X] is a very hard person to deal with, and through many many months of negotiations we have the exclusive rights. This is the only way that these scrolls can get in the hands of Israel. If you desire to work with me on this, I will proceed without publicity.... The political situation in Jordan is very restless at this time, so we are making sure of every step. Please let me hear from you at once so that we may proceed with caution and certainty.

Enclosed with the letter was the photograph.

One million dollars for a scroll! The figure was astronomical. But what *is* the price for something that is priceless? And priceless to whom? Presumably, in the jargon of the marketplace, 'whatever the traffic will bear'. But the 'traffic', in the case of the biblical and sectarian Dead Sea scrolls, was meagre, for they were considered priceless only by impecunious scholars, who were not often able to secure the financial backing of their governments, university foundations, or even more wealthily endowed trusts. Archbishop Samuel had found this to be true even of foundations in the United States, and had finally sold them to me for a fraction of the sum he had originally set. Admittedly, even this sum was substantial, and I was able to acquire his scrolls only because the Government of Israel had guaranteed the payment – which fortunately was largely covered later by a generous benefactor. But the Government had not known this at the time, and had been ready to risk the entire cost itself because of Israel's passionate interest in ancient Hebrew documents which could shed light on the early history of Israel, the Bible and the Talmud.

With this experience, which was assuredly known to both Mr Z and dealer X, it was most likely that Israel would be interested in their offer, but even the Israeli Government would be hard put to pay their prices. I accordingly wrote to Mr Z on 27 September 1960 telling him that the sums he wanted for the scrolls were 'fabulous', compared to what I had paid for similar items in the past and to what I had been offered only recently. I understood, I told him, that the prices mentioned were those quoted by dealer X, but knowing the way of commerce in the Middle East, I was confident that he would settle for 'a more realistic price'.

As to the scroll fragment of which he had sent me a photograph, 'I'm willing to buy it,' I wrote, 'but again, not for the price quoted, since ... it is in a rather poor state of preservation. From what I know of the value of such items ... a price of $6–7,000 would be fair.'

Though one would never dream of paying a huge sum for a complete scroll on the basis of a photograph alone, I thought it reasonable to risk a modest amount for this fragment. If indeed it proved to be genuine – and from my study of the photograph it indeed looked genuine – there would be no loss. It might also give me some indication of Mr Z's veracity about the other scrolls he had mentioned – though I could not exclude the possibility, if the fragment *were* genuine, that it was to serve as bait in an elaborate million-dollar confidence trick.

So, on the same day as I wrote to Mr Z, I also sent a note to my esteemed friend, Professor Albright. This formidable American scholar, perhaps the outstanding biblical archaeologist of the century, had been helpful, albeit indirectly, in enabling me to purchase the four scrolls from Archbishop Samuel. And Mr Z, in his first letter, had told me he was approaching me on the recommendation of the professor. I said this in my note to Albright, told him of Mr Z's proposal, and asked his opinion on the reliability of the man and the seriousness of his offer.

Albright replied without delay. He had not met Mr Z, but had spoken to him on the telephone, and he seemed to be 'a good deal of a promoter. I did suggest that he write you, since in this sort of thing the most improbable leads are sometimes worth while.' Albright had first heard of him through an intermediary 'who is also a promoter and, like Mr [Z], must be treated with great caution'. However, Albright continued,

there can be no doubt that there is a lot of material now in the hands of the Bedouin, and other places; but the prices which have been quoted are certainly much too high. Since you ... have avenues of indirect approach which are much closer to Beirut and Jordan than anyone here, I doubt whether you can get anything useful through Mr Z. However, one never knows.

Albright's reply was followed a few days later by a fat manila envelope from Mr Z. Inside was a letter dated 3 October 1960 and, to my astonishment, wrapped in a cloth napkin was an inscribed fragment of a leather scroll, the original of the photograph he had sent me earlier. I was amazed that this had been entrusted to the mail.

There were also surprises in the letter. After stating that he was 'enclosing the scroll piece as per your letter for which you said you would pay $7,000', agreeing that 'the state of preservation is not too good', he went on to deal with what I had said about the inflated prices he was asking for the complete scrolls. I had to take into account, he wrote, that these scrolls

are desired by many people if certain barriers can be removed. You may be interested to know that Prime Minister Majali [of the Hashemite Kingdom of Jordan], who was assassinated a few days ago, had agreed to give a government permit for the removal of such scrolls for the sum of $30,000. However, he was assassinated before this could be worked out. Negotiations are presently on with the xxx [and here he mentioned a high dignitary in

A fragment of the Psalms scroll sent by Mr Z through the mail.

Jordan who may still be alive, so I will not refer to him by name].... If these details can be worked out, people will be standing in line all over the world for these scrolls.

What he was hinting at, of course, was that with the widespread interest in the Dead Sea scrolls since the 1947 discovery of the first ones in an area under Jordanian occupation, and the subsequent high prices they commanded, certain high officials in the Government of Jordan could be induced to issue permits for scrolls to be sold and taken out of the country.

Referring to a remark in my first letter, Mr Z wrote: 'I do not know what offers you have had recently, but you do not have the offer of the ten scrolls which are completely allocated to me.' He then proceeded to talk of one particular scroll which, he said – erroneously as it transpired – had been found in the same cave – Cave 1, as it was later designated – as had those which I had acquired from Archbishop Samuel. If we could make a deal on this one, he wrote, he was sure we could 'work out all the details' on the other nine. 'This one, that I can deliver to you within thirty days, is in the best condition of any of the discoveries. It is 10 inches by 14 feet.' (This, too, proved inaccurate.) 'I would be able to negotiate with you on the price of this scroll, but I do not feel that it could be sold in any way for less than half a million dollars. It is on gazelle skin. It is in the finest condition of any of the scrolls found.' (It subsequently emerged that the sole subject of our exchange had been this one scroll. There had been no others.)

Then came details of how we could conclude the deal.

I will notify you by wire in time for you to meet me in Geneva, Switzerland, at the Hotel Richmond on October 31st, so you can examine the scroll and we can discuss the finances at that time. If we can get together on this, then I can deliver you more within a thirty days' period. I realize definitely that you know the field very well, and I respect your judgement. However, this has come down to real high financing, as you realize. Please let me have your feelings in the matter about the first scroll at once, as I expect to be in Geneva the end of the month.

The letter ended with his asking me to make out a cheque for $7,000 in his name for the parchment fragment he had enclosed; whetting my appetite with 'a slight possibility that there are fifteen scrolls in all'; assuring me that he has 'the situation under control', and that he would do his best 'to co-operate' with me 'on a realistic price, considering the tremendous value'.

When I unwrapped the fragment sent by Mr Z, held it in my hand and looked closely at the writing, my mind flashed back to a Jerusalem evening towards the end of November 1947 when I had first heard my father talking about a similar piece of a Hebrew Dead Sea scroll, the secrets of which he was trying to fathom. My father was Elazar Sukenik, professor of archaeology at the Hebrew University of Jerusalem (as I was to become several years later). At the time I was Chief of Operations of Haganah, the Jewish underground defence force during the British mandatory period in Palestine. (My Hebrew code name in that underground force was Yadin, and I adopted it after the establishment of the State of Israel in May 1948.)

It was my father who had been the first to recognize the genuine antiquity of the Dead Sea scrolls, to perceive their significance, and even to suggest that the Qumran sect was none other than the Essenes. He was indeed the first scholar committed to Dead Sea scroll research.

He had glimpsed the fragment he was telling me about in circumstances more unusual and risky than those surrounding my acquisition. At the beginning of the last week in November 1947, he had gone to lecture at the university and found an urgent message from an Armenian friend asking him to telephone as quickly as possible. Palestine at the time was in a state of turmoil. The United Nations General Assembly was expected any day to vote upon a resolution that would partition the country into a Jewish State and an Arab State upon the termination of the British Mandate. The Arabs were opposed to the resolution and, if it were passed, outbreaks of violence could be expected. Tension was high in Jerusalem, with its mixed population, and the British authorities had erected security barriers separating the two communities. Individuals could cross from one zone to the other only with a military pass. My father lived in the Jewish sector, his friend in the Arab sector.

The Armenian was an antiquities dealer and, when my father telephoned him, he said he needed to talk to him on a matter too important for discussion on the telephone. They had to meet, and meet quickly, with no time to secure a pass. My father accordingly said he would come to the barrier between the two zones and talk across the barbed wire.

RIGHT A fragment of a Dead Sea scroll shown to the late Professor E.L. Sukenik across a barbed-wire fence. It was the first ever seen by a scholar, and proved to be part of the Thanksgiving scroll.
LEFT Professor Sukenik studying the ancient text. He was the first scholar to recognize the antiquity and importance of the Dead Sea scrolls (© *Fred Csasznik*).

Thus it was in this strange situation, my father on one side, his friend on the other, that the Armenian, after a preliminary greeting, drew from his briefcase a scrap of parchment, and, without a word, held it up for my father to see. Peering at it through the looped barbed wire, my father could make out the letters of ancient Hebrew writing, not unlike the script on first-century stone ossuaries he had come across in his archaeological excavations in the Jerusalem area. But he had never seen such writing on leather. He looked up at his friend with unabashed excitement and curiosity, and the Armenian, pleased by my father's unspoken but obvious reaction, told him how he had come by the fragment.

It had been brought to him the previous day by an old Arab antiquities dealer from Bethlehem, who said some Bedouin had come to him with several parchment scrolls which they wished to sell. They claimed to have found them in a cave near the Dead Sea shore, not far from Jericho. Since the Arab dealer did not know whether they were genuine, he had brought them to the Armenian, who in turn had approached my father. The fragment he had just displayed was from one of the scrolls, and he sought my father's judgement on whether it was authentic. If it was, would my father wish to buy the scrolls for the Museum of Jewish Antiquities of the Hebrew University?

My father told me later that he had had a momentary thought that this was possibly the work of a forger. But as he continued to peer, his hunch became stronger that this was no forgery but the real thing, and on the basis of the fragment alone he decided to risk buying the scrolls for the university. He asked his Armenian friend to proceed at once to Bethlehem and bring more samples of the scrolls, and to telephone him on his return. My father in the meantime would try to get a military pass so that he could visit the Armenian at his store and examine the parchments more closely.

The Armenian telephoned on 27 November 1947 to say that he had the additional samples, and my father, armed now with his pass, rushed over to see them. He sat in the dealer's store and tried to decipher the writing, finding it good and clear, and resembling even more closely than the first sample the lettering on the stone ossuaries. He was now more convinced than ever that these were fragments of genuine ancient scrolls. He and the Armenian resolved to go to Bethlehem the following day, 28 November, to start negotiating with the Arab dealer for their purchase.

The evening of that day, 28 November, was when I had called on my father in Jerusalem, and listened to him on the subject of the scrolls. As a senior officer in the Haganah, with headquarters near Tel Aviv, I had come to Jerusalem to check on the preparedness of the Jewish population against possible Arab attack. After spending several hours touring the city with the local Haganah commander, I went to visit my parents before returning to Tel Aviv. My father was in his study when I arrived, and as he glanced up from the parchment and saw me, his eyes glowed with excitement, and without any preliminaries he shot the question: 'What shall I do? Shall I go to Bethlehem? I must. First thing in the morning. What do you say?'

I assumed he had made an important archaeological discovery – he was always in a state of exhilaration when this occurred – but I could not guess what it was this time. Only a short while before he had returned from a lecture tour in the United States, and had not yet resumed his excavations. So what could he have discovered? Having little time to unravel the mystery – I was due back at headquarters – I asked my father to sit down and begin from the beginning.

What had happened came out with a rush as my father began talking, the words tumbling over each other as he told me of the Armenian, the Bethlehem Arab, the Bedouin, the fragments, and above all of the scrolls from which they had been detached – scrolls which he felt were within his grasp. He was confident that he would succeed in securing them as a perpetual Jewish heritage, particularly because of the symbolic timing: chance had brought them to his notice at the very moment when, if the UN resolution went through, Jewish sovereignty in Palestine would be restored after almost two thousand years – the very age of the scroll fragments he had been privileged to see.

I confess that, as I listened, problems of defence receded from my mind, and I found myself transported in time and place from the Jerusalem of 1947 to the Dead Sea's Qumran of long ago. My father, his account completed, brought me back sharply to his opening question: should he go to Bethlehem? This was to have been the day he was to go with the Armenian to see the Arab dealer and initiate the process of buying the scrolls. But he had not gone. He explained:

I'm afraid I have been very foolish. I was so excited when I got home yesterday that your mother asked me what it was all about. I told her, and I was silly enough to add that I was going to Bethlehem today.... You should have heard her reaction. She said I was crazy even to think of making such a dangerous journey entirely through Arab territory at such a time. And so I had to put him off. But I cannot, I cannot sit here doing nothing. What shall I do? Shall I go?

What was I to tell him? As a student of archaeology myself, I felt that the opportunity of acquiring such priceless documents could not be missed. As a soldier I knew well the dangers of my father's travelling to Arab Bethlehem. As a son I was torn between both feelings. In the end I advised him not to go. The UN resolution was to be put to the vote that night and, if carried, Arab attacks might begin immediately. With that I left him and returned to headquarters.

LEFT The scroll of The War of the Sons of Light against the Sons of Darkness, a military manual for the war at 'the End of Days', one of the three scrolls acquired by Professor Sukenik.

RIGHT The Thanksgiving scroll before it was unrolled, another of the three scrolls acquired by Professor Sukenik. The text, similar to psalms and written in the first person, may have been composed by the founder of the Qumran sect, the 'Teacher of Righteousness'.

It was more than a month later that I passed through Jerusalem – a group of kibbutzim in the area were under heavy attack from the Arab Legion – and I again saw my father. Only then did I discover that the morning after I had left him, he had slipped out of the house without telling my mother, gone to Bethlehem with the Armenian, seen the Arab dealer and concluded the arrangements for buying the three scrolls he was offered. It transpired that late at night on 28 November, a few hours after I had advised him not to go, he had heard the news on the radio that the vote on the UN resolution had been postponed until the following night. Since he had it fixed in his mind that the attacks would be launched immediately *after* the vote, he decided to seize the chance of going next day. It had been a worrying journey, through hostile territory in an Arab bus to and from Bethlehem. (The Armenian had told him later that he had been scared stiff by the responsibility he assumed in taking his Jewish friend on such a risky mission.) But it passed without incident. My father had been just in time. A few hours after his return to Jerusalem, on the night of 29 November, the resolution was carried and there was dancing and jubilation in the streets of Jerusalem, despite the awareness that the morrow could bring widespread attacks. It did, and contact between the Jewish and Arab sectors was virtually suspended.

Two months later, however, an acquaintance from the Arab sector managed to get in touch with my father and asked for an urgent meeting. At his mention of 'scrolls', my father agreed to take the risk, and when they met, the man produced four scrolls and asked if my father wished to buy them. He was a Christian Arab, a member of the Syrian Orthodox community, and he said the scrolls belonged to the head of his Church, Archbishop Athanasius Samuel. The Archbishop had bought them from Bedouin of the Ta'amira tribe. (It was men of this tribe who had sold the three scrolls to the Bethlehem dealer, from whom my father had bought them.) After a brief examination, my father judged that the four scrolls were genuine, that they were of the same origin as the three he already possessed, and that one of them was another Isaiah scroll, in better condition than the one he had. He told the Archbishop's emissary that he would be willing to buy them for the Hebrew University, but would like to take them home for a more careful examination. The emissary agreed, and they arranged to meet a few days later to initiate negotiations for the purchase.

The next meeting, however, proved short and inconclusive, the emissary indecisive. He finally suggested a meeting the following week at which he would be accompanied by the Archbishop, to be held, tentatively, at the Yugoslav Consulate. He would confirm time and place later. With deep regret my father returned the scrolls, and they parted.

It was the last my father saw of the scrolls and of the emissary. The confirmation never arrived and the meeting never took place. Months later my father received a message to say that the Archbishop had decided not to sell. It subsequently transpired that the emissary had been sent to my father to learn whether the scrolls were indeed genuine, and when my father had expressed his willingness to buy them, the Archbishop had his answer. He was then advised by American scholars that he would get a much better price in the United States – and that was where he eventually took them.

My father died early in 1953, and on going through his papers I found that upon learning that the four scrolls had been put beyond his reach, he had written in his journal: 'Thus the Jewish people have lost a precious heritage.' He was not to know that, by fortuitous circumstance, they were to end up in Jerusalem, together with the three he had himself acquired.

In the following year, towards the end of May 1954, I had been invited by Professor Albright to lecture at Johns Hopkins University in Baltimore on the first three scrolls in the possession of the Hebrew University. They were the Book of Isaiah and two non-biblical scrolls composed by the Essenes – The War of the Sons of Light against the Sons of Darkness; and the Thanksgiving Scroll. My father had worked on these documents until his death, and I, at the request of the Hebrew University, undertook the decipherment and study of the War scroll upon completing my term as Chief of the General Staff of the Israeli Army and resuming my archaeological career. The subject of my lectures to universities in the United States was thus the product of our joint studies.

In an informal chat with Professor Albright after my Johns Hopkins lecture, I learned that Archbishop Samuel had dropped his price for the scrolls from several million to 'around half a million dollars', and even at that figure he had still found no American takers. Asked whether there was a chance I might be able to buy them for Israel, the professor thought it was 'a possibility', and promised to find out the Archbishop's address. I told him this was unlikely to help me, for there could be difficulties if I approached the Archbishop directly. Agents from one of the Arab countries might try to prevent him from selling the scrolls to Israel. He had already been denounced as a smuggler and traitor by Jordan, and he would be reluctant to court further trouble.

I bade farewell to Albright and left for New York, thinking throughout the flight of what he had said about the 'possibility' that the scrolls might yet be secured for Israel.

A few days later, on 1 June 1954, my attention was drawn by a journalist friend, Monty Jacobs, to a tiny advertisement in that day's issue of the *Wall Street Journal* headed 'The Four Dead Sea Scrolls'.

It read: 'Biblical Manuscripts dating back to at least 200 BC are for sale ... ideal gift to an educational or religious institution by an individual or group.' A box number was given for replies.

I could barely believe what I was reading, so soon after my talk with Albright. It seemed to bear out what he had said about the Archbishop's difficulties in selling the scrolls: he had now resorted to an advertisement in the press. I had no doubt that these were the very scrolls which the Archbishop's emissary had shown to my father in Jerusalem more than six years earlier, in February 1948. After failing to fulfil their promise to sell them to my father, the Archbishop and his emissary had been in touch with the American School of Oriental Research in Jerusalem, headed at the time by Professor Millar Burrows of Yale. In January 1949, when the Archbishop arrived in New York with the scrolls, he was persuaded to allow the American School to publish facsimiles of the three scrolls edited by Professor Burrows and his colleagues (even though the Yale Divinity School, which had considered buying them, had finally decided not to).

I promptly replied to the *Wall Street Journal* advertiser expressing interest, though I had little hope that the Archbishop would respond when he saw my name at the end of the letter. I therefore consulted with a New York businessman, a relative of mine, about getting someone who was not associated with Israel to make a similar enquiry about the advertisement. He accordingly arranged with his banker to write to the box number 'on behalf of one of our customers', seeking further details of the scrolls and the procedure for examining them. My own letter was never acknowledged; but the banker received a reply a few days later signed by 'Charles Manoog, Trustee for 4 DSS' (Dead Sea Scrolls). On 11 June, after intensive negotiations conducted by my go-between and Manoog, who said he was acting on behalf of 'Archbishop Athanasius Samuel, of St Mark's Monastery, Head of the Syrian Orthodox Christian Church in Jerusalem', it was agreed that the scrolls would be sold to us for a quarter of a million dollars. The lawyers of both parties would now set out the contract of sale and, when all was ready, the Archbishop would be present at the signing ceremony.

It was only then, as I recall, that I suddenly realized I did not have the money. I was confident, however, that we could find a generous donor among our New York Jewish friends. But this could take time, and I was reluctant to wait, for each day increased the risk of our identity being exposed and the consequent possible intervention by one of the Arab States. However, I could raise a loan from our friends, if it could be secured by a guarantee from the Israel Government. I therefore cabled the Prime Minister's office in Jerusalem, and within forty-eight hours received the reply: 'Prime Minister and Minister of Finance are delighted with the wonderful opportunity. Orders for suitable guarantee have been despatched. *Mazal Tov.*'

On 1 July, one month after the advertisement had appeared, the Archbishop and Mr Manoog met with my representative in New York's Waldorf-Astoria Hotel, with the lawyers of both parties present. The scrolls were in the hotel vault, and there they were examined at my request by my friend, Professor Harry Orlinski, who was also engaged in scroll research. (It was arranged that he would introduce himself as Mr Green.) I awaited his verdict in my hotel room, and he telephoned me as soon as he had completed his task: all was well. He followed it up with this statement:

I examined this afternoon the 4 DSS which formed the subject of negotiations ... with the representative of the Archbishop Samuel of the Syrian Church, Jerusalem. I made a detailed inspection of the scrolls and compared them with the official reproduction published by the American School of Oriental Research ... edited by Professor Millar Burrows. I am satisfied that the scrolls ... are the authentic 4 DSS referred to and reproduced in the above mentioned work by Professor Burrows and that they are complete.

He added the reservation that 'the right hand fragment of the first page' of one of the scrolls was missing. I instructed my representative not to hold up the proceedings because of the missing piece if the Archbishop promised to send it on. He agreed, and was as good as his word.

Shortly thereafter I was fortunate to be introduced to Mr Samuel Gottesman, the New York industrialist and benefactor, and he was generous enough to contribute the major part of the cost of the scrolls. He was prompted to do so primarily because of his understanding of their importance, and of his interest in Israel and in Jewish history and culture. He was also impressed by a letter I had received from Professor Albright after I had telephoned him about the purchase.

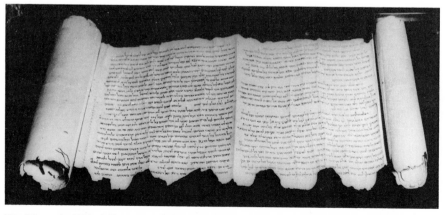

The Manual of Discipline, one of the most important of the sectarian scrolls, prescribing the rules for the Dead Sea sect at Qumran, the earliest known monastic community.

Albright had written: 'In my opinion the price you mentioned over the telephone is a bargain. . . . Quite aside from the unique value of the three principal scrolls' – which Albright had seen, as they had been published in facsimile – 'is the importance of the [fourth scroll]'. This, it will be recalled, was the one that the Archbishop had not allowed Professor Burrows to publish. But a fragment from it had been detached, and from that it was known that the language was Aramaic. Thus, Albright's letter continued, the importance of this scroll, 'which has not yet been unrolled', lay in the fact that it 'will provide a fairly lengthy text in Jewish Aramaic during the last two centuries of the second Temple period [end of the second century BC to the latter half of the first century AD]. Its importance for the history of Biblical Jewish religious literature is also very great.'

The Government of Israel decided to mark the acquisition of the scrolls by establishing in Jerusalem a special Shrine of the Book to house these and other ancient documents, and also to serve as a centre for biblical and scroll research for scholars all over the world.

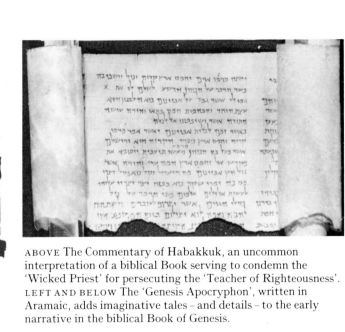

ABOVE The Commentary of Habakkuk, an uncommon interpretation of a biblical Book serving to condemn the 'Wicked Priest' for persecuting the 'Teacher of Righteousness'. LEFT AND BELOW The 'Genesis Apocryphon', written in Aramaic, adds imaginative tales – and details – to the early narrative in the biblical Book of Genesis.

Upon the death of Samuel Gottesman, his children took it upon themselves to build the centre in memory of their parents. It now stands
on its own as one of the most remarkable pavilions in Jerusalem's
Israel Museum, its prized exhibits the first seven Dead Sea scrolls and
the scroll that is the subject of this book.

2 Stalemate

I had never been without hope that those seven would be joined by
additional scrolls, and this hope was heightened when I received the
first letter from the Virginian clergyman, Mr Z, and more so when he
sent me the fragment of leather. By then, 1960, the possibilities had
become wider. The find of the seven in a Qumran cave in 1947, the
first full-length scrolls to be discovered, sparked the search for further
scrolls in other caves in the area, both by the local Bedouin, who had
found the first documents by chance, and by scholars, who carried
out systematic excavations.

The Bedouin would sell their Qumran discoveries to a dealer 'under
the counter', for unauthorized private possession of local antiquities
was illegal. Finds by scholars would also become the property of the
Jordan Government's Department of Antiquities. In neither case,
except by special arrangement with the government, were the scrolls
permitted to be taken out of the country, in accordance with Jordanian regulations – though there were ways, hinted at in Mr Z's letters,
in which these could be circumvented. (Similar prohibitions are common in most countries where antiquities are found.) Thus, the sale by
dealers of scrolls acquired from Bedouin was usually furtive, since the
potential buyers were non-Jordanians. In many cases it might be
years before a propitious moment occurred for the dealer to make a
highly profitable sale, and it would be worth his while to wait for that
moment (though the result was often damage to the scroll by being
kept without protection against humidity and insects).

As for the scholars, those who have made discoveries so far have
all been foreigners – there are as yet no reputable Jordanian archaeologists or scroll researchers – and they have usually been given the
right to publish photographs and the fruits of their research, but not
to keep or remove the scrolls. They had to work on the scrolls in the
place where these were kept – the Archaeological Museum (Rockefeller Museum) in East Jerusalem, which was then, like Qumran,
within Jordanian occupied territory.

By the time Mr Z wrote to me, there had been two further important finds of scrolls in the Qumran area. The 1947 finds of our seven
scrolls had come from what was later called Qumran Cave 1. In 1954

the scholars had found a large quantity of scroll fragments, as well as considerable portions of scrolls, in Cave 4. And in 1956 the Bedouin had made a more significant discovery in Cave 11 of several scrolls which were rumoured to have been virtually intact. It was not known whether all had been delivered to the government Antiquities Department, or whether some had found their way to a private dealer and were being held for a later secret sale. All that was known to the scholarly public was what the scholars working in Jordan had published, and there was little enough of that by 1960.

It seemed feasible to me that Mr Z's talk of 'scrolls' in his communications may have been a reference to the batch of finds in Caves 4 and 11. What was not feasible was the possibility that these were up for sale, even furtively. On some of them, scholars were still in the midst of their research. However, in his letter of 3 October 1960, which had been accompanied by the scroll fragment, Mr Z had made specific mention of one particular scroll which he said he could let me have 'within thirty days' at a cost of half a million dollars, and the availability of a single scroll was not beyond the bounds of possibility.

I therefore decided to reply to this letter without delay to show my continued interest, even before a thorough examination of the fragment which might give me an indication of whether he indeed had access to Dead Sea scrolls.

I wrote to him on 9 October, telling him I would be sending him a $7,000 cheque for the piece of scroll he had enclosed; but as for the 14-foot scroll for which he was asking $500,000, I feared he was overestimating my prospects of raising such a sum. True, I was optimistic about finding a generous donor, but the basis on which I was prepared to negotiate was the sum I had paid to the Archbishop for his four scrolls. Those, I reminded Mr Z, were of the highest importance, and one of them was 25 feet long and in excellent condition. It was therefore pointless to meet him until he could confirm that this basis was acceptable to the owner.

He replied quickly, in a letter dated 29 October sent from New York, telling me he was on his way overseas and asking whether I could see or get in touch with him at Naples, his first stop. He was then flying to Beirut, and on to the Jordanian part of Jerusalem, and from there back to Geneva. There was no reply to my proposal that the sum I had previously paid for scrolls should be the basis of the price for this one. His only reference to it was a doubtful story that I had acquired those scrolls at a bargain price: 'Archbishop Samuel told me he found out later that Mr Gottesman [the donor who had contributed the major portion of the $250,000 paid to Samuel] would have paid two million dollars' for them. He added that there were more scrolls he could deliver, and that there were other buyers who were 'very interested', including 'a museum in Switzerland that has the money'.

*   *   *

After this disappointing reply, I let the matter rest for a while, but it remained in my mind as I applied myself for most of the month to a study of the fragment I had bought from him for the Shrine of the Book. Since it was encrusted with grime, I had it photographed by infra-red. On the basis of on the result, I was able to complete the decipherment by the end of November. I then took it to James Bieberkraut, the expert who had helped my father in the past, for further cleaning and infra-red photography, and was able to improve on my reading and understanding of the fragment. It became clear to me that it was part of a scroll from Qumran, and this strengthened my feeling that dealer X, with whom Mr Z claimed to be in touch, might indeed be in possession of ancient documents. This fragment was assuredly of scientific importance to scroll researchers, and I contemplated publishing my findings in one of the learned journals. But when I eventually met Mr Z, he begged me to postpone publication for several years, and I did so, never imagining the sensational circumstances under which it was to appear.

Meanwhile, the exchange of correspondence between Mr Z and myself continued. Since he paid frequent visits to the Arab countries of the Middle East which prohibited communication with Israel, we had arranged that if he wished to get in touch with me from there, he could write or cable me through a friend in London.

I tried to fathom from his letters what was really going on between him and his contacts in Jordan. He seemed to be rather gullible, accepting at face value the stories he was told by dealers and government officials. It was evident, however, and this was confirmed when I met Mr Z, that he had indeed held talks with officials, some of them at very high levels in the government and the royal court, who had given him to understand that apparently even scrolls in the Museum of Antiquities could be available for sale. This explained why the number of scrolls he kept offering me varied from letter to letter after his return from each trip to the Middle East. It reached a peak, with a figure of more than twenty scrolls, in the letter he sent me on 11 February 1961 from the Excelsior Hotel in Beirut. It opened with 'I have some good news', to soften his report that, on the single scroll which he had mentioned in earlier letters, dealer X had 'decided to wait until Easter or 1 April'. But he continued with this startling information:

However, I have worked with top men in the Jordanian Government and we are able to deliver twenty to twenty-five [scrolls], the entire lot, within three weeks' time, even the ones in the Museum. They have a high figure on them – fifteen million dollars. . . . Some of them are still in the original jars, the way they were found. I will keep you posted on the big developments. . . . We must give a three-year guarantee of silence to protect all concerned.

What was I to make of this extraordinary information? I had little doubt that he was writing in good faith, and that he had indeed heard that this huge batch of treasured scrolls was available for purchase. He might have been told this directly by a corrupt official or at second or third hand by dealer X. And whoever told him may well have believed it was possible.

I had little time to ponder or even reply to this letter, as I was about to embark on a second archaeological search of caves in the Judean desert south of Qumran. Again I was fortunate to discover exciting objects and writings from the second-century period of Bar Kokhba, including a well-preserved bundle of documents comprising the personal archives of a certain Babata, a woman who belonged to Bar Kokhba's entourage. I wrote to Mr Z about these finds, and added that I had heard rumours of his efforts to interest others in the purchase of scrolls.

I found his reply upon my return from the Judean desert. In this letter, dated 29 May 1961, he denied the reports I had received and assured me that he had been dealing with me alone. Then came the down-to-earth admission that, although he had spoken of varying numbers of scrolls at different times, the one item that was positively available was a single scroll.

I've been dealing fourteen months on this situation [he wrote]. I have appreciated your frankness and I have felt that we understood each other. I have sifted through all the reports and all of the alleged finds. There is only one [scroll]. I can tell you on good authority that there is only one remaining. Only one. This is the one I held in my hands and no one else in the world will get it but me. As you recall, there were eight in the original discovery. This one was kept behind. Regardless of the rumours you may hear, these are the facts.

He may have believed these 'facts', though I presumed they were merely a cover-story suggested by the dealer to obscure the traces of how the scroll had reached him. However, I now felt that this scroll did exist, that it was in the hands of dealer X, and that he had told Mr Z he could try his luck at finding a buyer.

The next item in Mr Z's letter was the price. 'I have one desire to see this scroll in Israel where it belongs. [Dealer] X will deliver it now for $100,000 in cash. The worst that can happen is that in the final moments X will refuse. The $100,000 would then be returned to the donor with my responsibility of paying 6 per cent interest on this money.' He followed this with details of how the refund would be guaranteed if the project fell through.

My hopes of securing the scroll rose. I now believed it was available, that the price of $100,000 was reasonable, and that Mr Z could deliver. I wrote to him on 10 June that I was discussing the matter with my friends and, if things were as he described in his letter, we would find a mutual language.

A few days later I left Jerusalem for London on a sabbatical leave, and communication was now simpler. The first letter I received there was the most encouraging of all, for enclosed in the envelope, like the other I had received months earlier in Jerusalem, was a piece of inscribed leather. This one, however, had bits of English postage stamps stuck on the back for strengthening, and it was further protected with silver paper and cardboard. Mr Z wrote that he had been to Bethlehem and had

completed things with dealer X. There has always been the big question: is the scroll genuine? This was the hold-up at this end. After nine hours of discussion with X, he let me have a small piece of the scroll.... I will need two things from you by return mail. One, a letter from you stating what these few words [on the fragment] say, and also what you think this is and the time period. The entire scroll is 9 inches wide and about 15 to 18 feet long. Two, with your letter to me, please return this piece of parchment as it must go back to the scroll. I want to finish this business at once.... This has taken one and a half years, but now it will be settled.

I cabled an acknowledgement at once, and then picked up the enclosed piece of leather with even greater excitement than I had felt with the first fragment, for this was part of the very scroll I hoped to acquire. It had no encrustation, and I was able to read it even without infra-red photography. The language was Hebrew, beautifully written, and I sensed a recognition of the hand of the scribe. He had almost certainly belonged to the school of scribes who had written some of the seven Dead Sea scrolls with which I had become so familiar. From the content, although I could discern phrases associated with such biblical terms as 'the high priest' and the 'ordination sacrifice', it was clear that the sentences were not identical with any in the known biblical text.

After a brief examination of the fragment and its writings, and after photographing it, I returned it to Mr Z, as requested, on 21 August, together with replies to his questions. The fragment, I wrote, seemed to be part of a genuine scroll of the Dead Sea type. The inscription was in Hebrew, written by a good scribe, but there was not enough of it on the piece to tell whether it was from a known apocryphal work or a document composed by the Dead Sea sect. I had to reserve my final judgement both because the fragment was too small, and, since he wanted it returned quickly, because I had not had enough time to consult the pertinent sources.

I then gave him the name of a friend in the United States, Barney Barnett, a lawyer, to whom I said I was writing in the hope that he could make contact and reach an agreement with Mr Z. I added, however, that 'the fragment leads me to conclude that the scroll is not intact – its lower part is eaten away – and I am therefore worried by its state of preservation. But I agree with you that it is high time to conclude the matter.' I ended by informing him that I would be in the United States in October and November lecturing to universities, and we would no doubt be in touch.

For obvious reasons, I was cautious in this letter; but I had no need to suppress my enthusiasm when I wrote to Barnett, and I told him so, sending him a copy of what I had written to Mr Z. That letter, I wrote, 'in no degree expresses my excitement at what I saw in the fragment.... The script is one of the finest we have yet seen' and 'there is no doubt of its authenticity.... It is definitely not a biblical text, and it might therefore be of the utmost importance to the study of the Dead Sea sect.'

I went on to tell Barnett that although it was true, as I had written to Mr Z, that the lower part of the fragment was eroded, it could well be that the whole scroll was in a good state of preservation. If that were so, and if the measurements he had specified were accurate, then, I wrote, 'it may be one of the finest scrolls discovered so far, and it is our duty to the world to retrieve it from the dealer, and our duty to the Jewish people to restore it to its historical home in Israel.'

I ended my letter to Barnett by imploring him to do all he could to secure the scroll before it was lost to us. I told him to regard the price quoted by Mr Z, $100,000, as the maximum, 'but provision must be made to ensure that the money is retrievable if the "merchandise" is not up to expectation'.

Eight days later, on 29 August 1961, after the excitement of handling the scroll fragment and being quoted a reasonable price for the scroll, hopes plummeted. Encouraged by the judgement in my letter that the fragment seemed to be from an authentic scroll, Mr Z now informed me that because of his expenses, as well as other offers he had received, the price for me would now be $750,000 – an immediate down payment of $150,000 and the rest upon delivery of the scroll.

In a furious cabled reply I said that if things remained as stated in his letter, 'you can rule me out as a customer'.

I next heard from Mr Z when I arrived in New York for my lectures, and found a letter from him dated 10 October. The tone was quite different. He now asked me to state my final price for the scroll, and excused himself by blaming dealer X, who 'has been impossible. ... I am sorry I ever started.... Unless I can work something with you, I am going immediately to King Hussein and expose this character. I've lost. I might as well close the book on the whole deal. What will you pay as the last and final dollar? Please contact me at once.'

I did so, feeling that there was now a distinct possibility that we might secure the scroll, and for a sum closer to $100,000 than the varying inflated figures he had been quoting. What followed were weeks of complex discussions with attorneys and wearisome negotiations over price. We also had to work out a detailed agreement specifying the intricate procedure for the handing over of the scroll, examining it for authenticity, and transferring the money. The total amount to be paid was $130,000, and we secured a loan from the Government of Israel and Jerusalem's Shrine of the Book, which would be repaid, I hoped, by a generous donor. Of this sum, $10,000 was to be paid as an advance.

The negotiations ended in a six-page agreement, which included a letter from Mr Z to my representative, Mr Barnett, stating: 'You have arranged for the deposit of $120,000 with the Chase Manhattan Bank and you have given me the sum of $10,000 in cash, the said total sum of $130,000 representing the full purchase price for the scroll if it is purchased.' It goes on to say that Chase Manhattan would pay the full amount to Mr Z if the following conditions were met:

1. I, Mr Z, deliver to you a scroll approximately 12 inches wide and 15 feet long, which matches the fragment which I previously delivered to your expert [namely, myself].

2. The fragment which I provisionally delivered to your expert had been removed from the scroll and had constituted an integral part thereof.... The scroll is of the type known as a 'Qumran Scroll' and is in a suitable state of preservation; all the foregoing to be to the complete satisfaction of your expert.

The complete document of agreement, also addressed to Mr Barnett, was signed on 17 November 1961 by Mr Z on behalf of himself and of the dealer X. It stated that

I have heretofore furnished to Professor Yigael Yadin a fragment taken from a scroll which ... is believed to be of the type known as 'a Qumran Scroll', heretofore found in the vicinity of the Dead Sea.... The scroll is at present in the possession of X [the dealer in Jordan]. You desire to purchase the scroll provided that its authenticity [as hereinafter defined] is verified and the scroll is in a suitable state of preservation.

The clauses that follow cover the procedures for verification of the genuineness and state of the scroll, and Mr Z then states that he will 'deliver or arrange for the delivery of the scroll to Professor Yigael Yadin ... within ten days from the date hereof'. In consideration of this understanding, I was to advance him the sum of $10,000, and, he continues, 'if the scroll is not delivered as aforesaid or is not purchased by you, I will forthwith refund to you the sum of $10,000 upon the return to me of the fragment.... Professor Yadin may conduct such tests in and upon the scroll as he and his sole judgement may determine to be necessary.'

The remainder of the agreement included provisions for the authentication of the scroll by Professor Albright. Upon the signing of this document, the fragment was to be handed over to me. I would match it against the scroll whenever I took possession, and this would help with its verification. Mr Z would now travel to Jordan to complete the deal.

I met him a week later upon his return. To my chagrin, he brought not the scroll, but the story of his meeting with the dealer. 'X wants bigger sums now,' he said. 'He needs the scroll to show the Bedouin what to go on looking for ... he also has to pay them more.' Mr Z stressed that the scroll was still with dealer X – 'he did not sell it to anyone else. But he does not trust all our arrangements with the bank, nor does he like our contract.' Mr Z claimed it had finally been agreed that one of X's sons would go to Beirut 'within approximately three weeks' bringing the scroll with him, and another son would fly to Geneva, with arrangements for the simultaneous exchange of the scroll for the money.

I parted from Mr Z feeling sorry for him. I thought that despite his promotional tactics, he had acted with a certain degree of good faith, but had been strung along by the shrewd dealer X. For myself, I was sorry to see the scroll slipping beyond my grasp, a scroll I was almost certain existed and was genuine.

A letter sent me by Mr Z on 1 December did nothing to raise my spirits. Dealer X was now demanding $200,000, he wrote, and if the two of us could go to Geneva with a firm offer for that sum, 'I am sure we can get the scroll.' He then urged me to take good care of the fragment I had received (at my request) upon the signing of the agreement, when he had been given the $10,000 advance against the purchase of the scroll. 'The piece you have is the key. Don't lose it.... In order to work in good faith on both sides, since you have the all-important piece, I will hold the $10,000.'

Further letters from Mr Z continued to arrive throughout January and February 1962, ranging in tone from hope to despair. In one depressing note, he rues the day he met dealer X. 'It has been a tragedy.... X is not ready to settle. He is crazy. He thinks he is going to get half a million.... He now insists that I do not sell the fragment you have. However, I want you to keep faith in me. You keep that piece from the scroll.'

In a letter to attorney Barnett of 12 May 1962, he regrets that he cannot yet deliver the scroll, but still believes he will be able to do so 'one day'. He wrote again to Barnett one week later saying he was determined to get the scroll from dealer X and he was not giving up. He cited 'troubles between Lebanon and Jordan' which made it difficult to move from one country to another; nevertheless he would like to make yet another effort, and he asked for more money. 'Yadin should keep the piece he has. I am sending a note to X stating I will go to the King if he doesn't settle.'

That was the last I have about him in my records. All trace of Mr Z and the $10,000 vanished. The only 'mementos' left to me of the undulating exchange with this strange clergyman from Virginia, Mr Z, were two fragments of scrolls. The first was the one he had sent me in Jerusalem for which I had paid $7,000. The second, which I had received later in London, was part of the scroll I had hoped to acquire. It was this second one that was to play an important part five years later in the successful retrieval of the precious scroll.

However, the first scroll fragment was also to figure in a surprising development in the field of Dead Sea documentary scholarship, though not immediately, as I had other scientific preoccupations. Most of my time was taken up with the decipherment, study and partial publication of the documents I had discovered at excavations in the caves of Bar Kokhba. And from the end of 1963 until the spring of 1965 I headed the huge archaeological expedition on the rock of Masada, overlooking the Dead Sea, which yielded the dramatic remains, including ancient scrolls, of that historical site. These, too, required long and concentrated study and decipherment, with little thought for anything else.

Nevertheless, 'the scroll that got away' was never far from my mind, and I would follow the literature on Qumran developments in the scientific journals devoted to scroll research with considerable eagerness. But there was no word about this scroll. Nor was it ever mentioned in the stories I heard at first or second hand from scholars who had visited Jordan to work on the Dead Sea documents. For some reason, the existence of this scroll was known (apart from the lawyers) only to Mr Z, dealer X and myself.

From time to time, as a relaxation from the work in which I was engaged, I would take up the first fragment I had bought from Mr Z to see if it held further data I might have missed. It was quite short, and I had already studied and deciphered it, but had not published my findings, as Mr Z had requested me not to. One day in 1963, looking through the latest issue of a German archaeological journal, I came across an article by a noted American scroll scholar, my colleague Professor J.A. Sanders, which turned out to be his preliminary publication of a Dead Sea scroll. He had been working on it, unrolling and editing it, since 1961 in the Rockefeller Archaeological Museum. It was a Psalter, consisting of thirty-eight biblical psalms, interspersed with a number of apocryphal psalms which had been excluded from the canonical Book of Psalms. This Psalter had been among the scrolls discovered in 1956 in Qumran Cave 11, and the article I was reading was illustrated by photographs of parts of the scroll, published for the first time. As I examined them, I was struck by the likeness of the script to that on my fragment. Indeed, they were identical. This suggested that the fragment could well be part of that scroll. However, I decided to wait until the publication of the complete scroll before reaching a final conclusion.

This occurred in 1965, with the appearance of the splendid official volume by Sanders called *The Psalms Scroll of Qumran Cave 11*, published by Oxford's Clarendon Press. A study of this volume left me in

The entrance to Cave 1 of Qumran, where the first seven Dead Sea scrolls were discovered (© *David Harris*).

The two jars containing the
scrolls bought by Professor
Sukenik from the Bethlehem
antiquities dealer. Such jars,
unique to Qumran, may have
been produced for the specific
purpose of storing scrolls. The lids
served as models for the dome of
the Shrine of the Book.

The complete Isaiah scroll, one of four scrolls bought by the author from Archbishop Athanasius Samuel. The text contains some variants of the 'traditional' biblical text.

Professor Sukenik noticed that the Hebrew writing on the Thanksgiving scroll was similar to the script on 1st century BC stone ossuaries he had excavated in the Jerusalem area. An example of that script appears on the tombstone of the secondary burial in the Herodian period of King Uzziah. It reads: 'Here were transferred the bones of Uzziah, King of Judah. Let none open it.' (© *Israel Museum, Jerusalem*)

The Shrine of the Book in Jerusalem's Israel Museum houses the complete Dead Sea scrolls, including the Temple scroll. Its outstanding architectural features are the white dome (shaped like the lid of a Qumran jar) and the black basalt wall, symbolic of the Sons of Light and the Sons of Darkness respectively (© *Israel Museum, Jerusalem*).

no doubt that the fragment in my possession was indeed part of Sanders's scroll. I was even able to fit it into a place that was missing in his scroll. How it ever came into the hands of the dealer who had sold it to Mr Z and he to me was a mystery. But I could guess how it had become detached. Sanders wrote, and showed in photographs, that four fragments had peeled off from the beginning of the scroll proper. My fragment had obviously been a fifth, and a study of the content showed clearly its correct position within the scroll: it came immediately after the four fragments and immediately before the 'intact' scroll. The last verses on my piece of leather were the opening lines, up to verse 12, of what is numbered Psalm 105 in our Bible. These verses, and a further eleven, were missing from the same Psalm in Sanders's scroll, the text of which starts with verse 24 of Psalm 105! The missing eleven, verses 13 to 23, had without doubt been on the perished end part of my fragment and the perished beginning of Sanders's scroll.

At that time the President of Israel was Zalman Shazar, himself a biblical and Hebrew scholar, and he would hold regular meetings in the presidential residence of the Jerusalem Bible Study Circle. Towards the end of December 1965 he invited me to use that forum to announce the existence of this fragment and talk about it, and the date set was 1 January 1966. I felt that Dr Sanders should be the first to know about it, and from me, not the newspapers. I therefore cabled him on 31 December telling him I had in my possession a fragment of 'his' scroll, giving its content by psalm number, and its place in his scroll.

I then prepared my findings for publication in the scientific journal of the Hebrew University Bible Project called *Textus*, and it appeared there in 1966. At the same time I wrote to Sanders offering him all the photographs and necessary data which he might wish to incorporate in a forthcoming second edition he was getting ready for the press. And indeed, in this volume, *The Dead Sea Psalms Scroll*, published by Cornell University Press in 1967, he managed to include the fragment in a postscript together with a photograph I had sent him. Accompanying it was a kind mention of my cable to him on the eve of my announcement, and the following item which had appeared in the 2 January 1967 issue of the *New York Times*:

Professor Yigael Yadin, Israel's leading archaeologist, announced tonight the acquisition of a fragment of a Dead Sea scroll containing portions of the Psalms. The Israeli fragment, Professor Yadin said, fits between several fragments and part of a larger scroll belonging to Jordan. The Jordanian manuscript contained 38 of the Psalms of the Bible. The Israeli fragment contains parts of three additional psalms and some are missing verses of a Psalm in a larger scroll.... The fragment was purchased in 1960 from an anonymous American who requested that publication be withheld for several years.

An infra-red photograph of the Psalms scroll fragment before cleaning (see picture on page 14). The tetragrammaton, written in the Paleo-Hebrew script, is clearly discernible in Lines 1, 2 and 3 in the right column; Line 9 in the middle column; and Lines 4 and 7 in the left column.

To this, Professor Sanders had added:

One can imagine the shock the news conveyed. I was totally unprepared for such a development as I had carefully checked all the materials that had been brought from Qumran Cave 11 into the Palestine Archaeological Museum in Jerusalem, Jordan, and knew that only four of those fragments belonged to the scroll. I knew also that all the Cave 11 yield had been under lock and key, by order of the trustees of the Museum, since 1956 when the cave had been found until the Fall of 1961 when I began the task of unrolling and editing the scroll.

A number of essential questions remain unanswered, especially the crucial one of how the fragment got from the Museum (or the cave) into the hands of the 'anonymous American'. Prof. Yadin, who is not only one of the world's leading scholars but also a generous, thoughtful gentleman, informed me in subsequent correspondence what he knew with the exception of the information [the name of Mr Z] which he was bound, by promise to the anonym, not to reveal.

As I mentioned earlier, I did not know then, I still do not know, nor do I believe that the 'anonymous American', Mr Z, ever knew how the fragment came into the hands of dealer X. But there is reason to suppose that when the dealer, who had acquired the scroll from the Bedouin, sold it to the Palestine Archaeological Museum (a purchase made possible by the generous donation of Mrs Elizabeth H. Bechtel of San Francisco), he had kept back one fragment and held on to it. This, as we were to see, was his occasional practice.

Thus, the scholarly problem with the first piece of scroll I had bought from Mr Z had been successfully resolved after five years. But there was no such resolution with the second fragment. I could read the ancient Hebrew script and understand the meaning of the words, but I could not know to what they referred unless I was given the context. The context would be provided by the scroll itself, of which Mr Z had assured me this was a part; but the prospect of ever securing it, which came to mind whenever I picked up the fragment for an occasional re-read, seemed dim indeed. As one wag put it later, it took a war to get it.

3 The Treasure

The war was the Six Day War of June 1967.

During that war I served as co-ordinator between the Prime Minister, the Minister of Defence and the Chief of Staff, and the military events drove all thought of the scroll from my mind.

I had been asked by Prime Minister Levi Eshkol to perform this function because of a key change in government personnel on the eve of the war. In the previous weeks, President Nasser of Egypt had carried out a series of hostile acts against Israel, the gravest of which had been a blockade of the Gulf of Eilat. This, had it been left unchallenged, would have doomed Eilat, Israel's southern port and outlet to the Red Sea, as well as stifling the development in the Negev. It would have severed Israel's maritime ties with East Africa and the Far East. Indeed, it was largely to break that blockade eleven years earlier that Israel had launched the Sinai Campaign, capturing the whole of Sinai. Israel had withdrawn from Sinai only after receiving written assurances from the United States that a renewal of the Egyptian blockade would be recognized as an act of war, and Israeli action would be considered justified. Now, with its renewal in May 1967, the Israeli Government was active diplomatically but took no military action, beyond mobilizing the reserves. In the weeks that followed, with further provocation by Egypt, and the signing of a military pact by Egypt, Syria and Jordan, there was profound anxiety among the Israeli public over what they felt was the hesitancy and lack of forthrightness on the part of the government. There was a popular demand that Premier Eshkol, who also held the Defence portfolio, should relinquish it and appoint Moshe Dayan in his place. I was among those who persuaded the Prime Minister to follow this course, and when he agreed, he asked me, as a former Chief of Staff, to be his military adviser. It was to be my task, he explained, now that he was no longer in direct charge of defence, to be in close touch with Defence Minister Dayan and the Chief of Staff, so that I could brief and advise him on the operational plans and developments. He was particularly concerned, he told me, about Dayan's tendency 'to behave in an unconventional manner'.

War broke out five days later, on Monday 5 June. Early that morning, Israel had sent messages through third-party diplomatic channels to King Hussein of Jordan urging him to stay out of the war. His answer was given by his artillery, which shelled the Jewish part of Jerusalem. (One shell narrowly missed the Shrine of the Book.) Jordan had joined Egypt and Syria in the hostilities. After two days of bitter battles, the Israeli Army beat back Jordan's Arab Legion and captured the Jordanian-occupied sector of Jerusalem, including the Old City and the Rockefeller Museum of Antiquities, as well as Bethlehem; and Israel's forces were chasing the Jordanian Army across the West Bank to the eastern side of the river Jordan.

That night, Wednesday 7 June, I had just stretched out for a nap, when I was struck by the thought that dealer X, with whom Mr Z had been associated seven years earlier, might well now be within Israel's jurisdiction. After brief talks with the Prime Minister, the Minister of Defence and the Chief of Staff, a Lieutenant-Colonel Goren of the Intelligence Corps was put at my disposal for tracing the dealer and, if possible, the scroll. I briefed him about the dealer and his probable whereabouts, about the Dead Sea scrolls in general and the particular scroll I had hoped to acquire, and gave him a detailed description of the leather fragment to which it was alleged to have belonged and which was in my possession.

By the afternoon of the following day, Thursday 8 June, the dealer had been found. Told by Lieutenant-Colonel Goren that he was interested in a scroll of which I had a fragment, the dealer took him to his home, and there, from a primitive cache beneath the floor tiles, he unearthed a paper-wrapped shoe-box which, he said, contained the scroll, and handed it to the officer. He also gave him a cigar box, saying that it held some detached fragments.

Hurrying back to GHQ, Goren was told that I was at an urgent meeting of the Ministerial Defence Committee. It was, indeed, a crucial evening meeting. We had just completed the capture of the whole of Jordanian-occupied territory west of the river Jordan, from Jenin in the north to Hebron and beyond in the south. We were now holding vital discussions on what to do about Syria. While we had been engaged with Egypt and Jordan, we had maintained only a holding operation on the northern front, despite persistent Syrian attacks. With Egypt and Jordan routed after four days of fighting, the Defence Committee had now met, expecting to order Northern Command into action to drive the Syrians from the Golan Heights. This would free our eastern Galilee kibbutzim and other farm villages from the frequent Syrian shelling to which they had long been subjected. To the surprise of his colleagues, Dayan argued against the move at that time, and the discussion became very heated. (He changed his mind during the night, and the attack was launched early in the morning.) In the midst of this discussion, a clerk came in and handed me a note telling me that Lieutenant-Colonel Goren awaited me in the outer office.

Since I was at the meeting as the Prime Minister's adviser, with no voting powers, I waited until I had heard the major arguments on both sides, offered my own judgement, and then left quietly to find out the results of Goren's investigation. To my astonishment, he handed me the parcel, saying simply: 'I hope this is the scroll you want.'

I carefully removed the wrapping, found a shoe-box marked 'Bata', and opened it. Inside was a wrapping of towel, and inside the towel

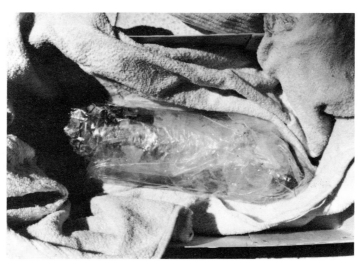

LEFT The 'Bata' shoe-box in which the Temple scroll had been kept by antiquities dealer X, a former cobbler.
RIGHT Inside the box, the scroll had first been wrapped in a towel and then had been given an additional protective wrapping of cellophane.

a wrapping of cellophane, and inside that was a scroll. Its upper part was damaged, as though it had dissolved. With it inside the cellophane was a wad of several pieces of thin leather. (Later, when I began work on the scroll, I called this Wad Y. It proved of immense importance.)

The cigar-box, labelled 'Karel I Elegant', contained fragments which had also become detached from the scroll. Many were in a shocking condition, crumbled and macerated. But again, one large chunk of pieces stuck together, later called Wad X, was to be of crucial value in indicating the number and sequence of the columns of writing at the beginning of the scroll.

(Upon further enquiry some time later, the dealer admitted the existence of yet additional fragments of this scroll, and he handed them over. He had hidden them behind family photographs in his own home and in his brother's house. These, too, turned out to be

The cigar box containing the damaged wads of fragments. All were subsequently detached, their writing recovered and deciphered, and each fragment was inserted in its proper place in the scroll.

very important, containing vital sections of three columns. As for the fragment I had obtained from Mr Z, this was eventually integrated into the scroll in its proper place.)

There was no question of my unrolling and examining the scroll on the spot as soon as I received it from Lieutenant-Colonel Goren. Unrolling alone would be a careful and lengthy process, requiring the services of an expert experienced in the techniques of handling such fragile matter. All I could do was look and lightly touch – ancient artefacts, particularly scrolls and papyri, have been known to disintegrate, literally crumble into dust when dropped or roughly handled after being secreted for centuries. I was able, however, to see something of the writing on the fragments, and this made me certain that here was indeed the scroll I had believed I was on the verge of buying from Mr Z.

I had spent some time inspecting this documentary treasure, while life and death discussions were proceeding in an adjacent room. The boxes were put away for safekeeping, and I returned to the meeting of the Defence Committee. Not until the six days of fierce battle were over was I able to retrieve the scroll and apply myself to the task of probing its mysteries. It was to take me nine years.

Under Jordanian law, as we have seen – and as in many countries, including Israel – all antiquities found in the country automatically become the property of the State. Only professional archaeologists, usually sponsored by a recognized institution of higher learning, are granted permits to carry out scientific excavations. By arrangement in certain cases, the government may allow the institution to keep some of the discoveries. If an unauthorized person finds an ancient artefact or scroll, he is required to notify the authorities, and, if they consider it of sufficient interest, they may acquire it and pay him

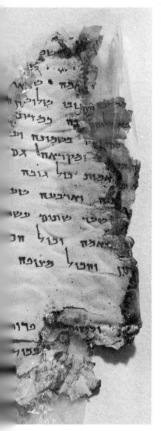

LEFT The group of fragments stuck together in Wad Y, with
what remained of Column 5 at the top.
CENTRE Wad X, with its portions of the all-important
injunctions for the 'Days of Ordination'. Line 6 contains the
words 'the baskets of bread', which may have been the
central element in the sect's celebration (see page 59).
RIGHT One of the fragments that dealer X had hidden
behind the family photograph. It contains part of the text
on the First Fruits Feast. It, too, was eventually fitted into
its correct place in the scroll.

compensation. Disagreement over the size of the payment is settled
by arbitration. Failure to notify the authorities renders the finder
guilty of illegal possession, which carries the penalty of imprisonment
and confiscation of the antiquity.

Thus, under this law, the scroll hidden and held illegally by dealer
X for several years would have been confiscated by the Jordanian
Government had they known about it, and in addition to this punishment he would probably have been given a jail term. With the West
Bank now held by the Israel Army, the Israeli Military Government
applied Jordanian law to the territory and officially confiscated the
scroll, though dealer X paid no further penalty. On the contrary, he
later applied to the Israeli Government for compensation, presenting
his case through an Israeli attorney, and the Government agreed to
consider his request, even though, apart from the illegality of his
concealment of the scroll, he had kept it under dreadful conditions
that caused extensive damage to its upper portion. Negotiations were
begun over the amount he was to receive, in which the Attorney
General for the West Bank and I myself were eventually involved.
They ended with dealer X being paid the sum of $105,000 – roughly

the figure that had been agreed with Mr Z. One of the reasons prompting this decision was to encourage others who might be concealing Qumran scrolls – and doing them irreparable damage by keeping them in unsuitable hiding-places – to bring them forth.

The scroll was acquired by the Government of Israel for the Shrine of the Book in the Israel Museum, but the major part was contributed by the British businessman and benefactor, Sir Leonard Wolfson. He happened to have been in Jerusalem at the time, and when we talked about the scroll, I mentioned incidentally that it was written in exquisite Hebrew. To my surprise – for though we had been friends for years I had not known it – he said he remembered the Hebrew he had learned as a child and could still read it, and he wondered whether he could see the scroll. I promptly took him to the Israel Museum, extracted the document from the safe, and sure enough he was able to read the better-preserved parts of the script. Before long, we received a cheque for $75,000 from the Wolfson Foundation, and the Shrine of the Book decided it would be exhibited as the Wolfson Scroll, in addition to the title that was descriptive of its contents, the Temple Scroll.

I mentioned earlier that the sudden thought of this scroll had struck me out of the blue during the night of the third day of the Six Day War when my mind was wholly absorbed with the battles just fought and the battles yet to come. However, this was not my only concern with scrolls in those days. I had received a telephone call that very morning from General Rehavam Ze'evi, who was then Deputy Chief of Operations, telling me that our troops who had broken through the Jordanian lines in Jerusalem after tough combat had now reached the Rockefeller Museum, only a few yards away from the north-eastern corner of the Old City which had not yet been captured. There was still fighting in the area, and he and the Jerusalem Command were worried lest the Museum and its contents, particularly the scroll collection, might be damaged. He asked me to ensure that someone responsible should proceed at once to the spot and see to it that all the ancient documents and fragments were placed in safes. I was proud that General Ze'evi, though under minute-to-minute pressure from the battle events on all three fronts, should nevertheless have given thought to the safety of universal cultural treasures.

From GHQ in Tel Aviv I promptly telephoned my wife Carmella in Jerusalem and asked her to call two of my colleagues, Professor Nahman Avigad, who was also engaged in scroll research, and Dr Avraham Biran, Director of Antiquities, explain what was required, and put them in immediate touch with the Jerusalem military command. I knew that even reaching the Museum would not be easy. Only a few hundred yards away, and not many hours earlier, the battle at a site later called Ammunition Hill had been one of the bitterest and

bloodiest of the war. Even the capture of the Rockefeller area had not
been easy, and it was still under mortar and artillery fire. The Jordan
Arab Legion had used the Museum as a military post, much as the
Syrians and the PLO did with the museum in Beirut during the war
in Lebanon in 1982.

Indeed, even travelling in an armoured half-track, Avigad and
Biran were able to get to and enter the Museum only after several
hours, for the information that it was in our hands had apparently
been premature. However, once inside, they were pleased to discover
that the thousands of fragments were in a safe.

I cannot refrain from adding the following related episode that
occurred the same day, which my wife told me when she telephoned
that evening. She said that a young Israeli soldier, weary, sweaty,
battle-grimed, knocked at our door and, without any preliminaries,
said:

I would like to inform your husband that we have just occupied the Rockefeller Museum. But there is still fighting in the area and soldiers are battling
for their lives. They may unwittingly cause damage to the exhibits and the
scrolls. Someone in authority must come and see what can be done. ... I was
given a short leave as my wife is about to give birth, and I am on my way
to the hospital now, but I thought it my duty to come here first.

I met him when the war was over, was glad to hear that his wife and
baby were doing well, and thanked him wholeheartedly for his
public-spirited action – and thoughtfulness – when he had just
emerged from combat. He was a true soldier of the People of the
Book.

Incidentally, when Avigad and Biran had entered the Rockefeller
Museum, it was the first time Israeli scholars were able to see its Dead
Sea documents. Until then, when this eastern sector of Jerusalem was
under Jordanian occupation, no Israeli was allowed access to the
Museum or its contents. Moreover, no Jewish scholars even from other
countries were permitted to be members of the international team
engaged in examining and studying the scrolls in East Jerusalem. I
am happy to say that Israel did not retaliate in kind. After the war,
I was authorized by the Government of Israel and the Shrine of the
Book to inform the Dominican scholar Father Roland de Vaux, who
was principal editor of the Museum's scrolls and fragments, that he
and his team would be permitted to continue with their research. We
set two conditions. One was that they were to proceed quickly with
the publication of the thousands of fragments they had had at their
disposal for so many years. By then, 1967, they had published very
little of the material, and this had been a great loss to the scientific
world. There had been no Jordanian scroll scholars who were familiar
with the nature of their work and who might therefore have been
prompted to prod them. Now that we were in control, we wanted
that rectified. Our second condition called for a change in the title of

the official series of publications of what little *had* been allowed to see the light of scientific day. They had been called 'Discoveries in the Judean Wilderness of Jordan'. We wanted some reference to the fact that the studies were now continuing under Israeli auspices.

I consider this to have been a very generous gesture on the part of the Israeli Government to the team of foreign scholars, and I regret that it has not always been acknowledged in their publications. Even more regrettable is the fact that their material is not reaching the scientific world as quickly as it should, as promised and as expected.

Though I was much concerned with other problems during the historic final days of the war, and the weeks that followed, my heart was primarily with the scroll in the shoe-box. What could it be? When could it have been written. Second century BC? First century BC? First century AD? What light might it shed on the turbulent physical and spiritual events of those centuries? What more would it tell us of the fascinating Dead Sea sect which had not been revealed in the other scrolls? Would it confirm or call in question the theories we had developed from our study of these earlier documents?

As to its physical condition, my immediate feeling when I had opened the box brought by Lieutenant-Colonel Goren had been a mixture of elation and disappointment. The upper part of the scroll was very soggy and parts of it seemed to have dissolved. One side was more seriously damaged than the other. It had probably been closest to the source of the damp – not in the cave where it had lain for centuries, but probably in the dealer's unsuitable cache where it had been kept for only a few years. This had given the top of the scroll an uneven, wavy edge, as we found when it was eventually unrolled.

The encouraging feature at my first encounter was that two thirds of the scroll seemed to be intact, and that it was probably very much longer than the different measurements – 12 and 15 feet – given to me at various times by Mr Z. I gathered this when I noticed how tightly the document had been rolled. The true length would be known only when it was completely unrolled, and Mr Z, or dealer X, had offered a rough estimate based no doubt on the diameter of the rolled scroll and without counting the 'turns'. But observing the tightness of the rolling, the number of 'turns', and making a ready reckoning of their circumferences, I was convinced that they had erred on the short side.

As for the wads of fragments that had become detached from the scroll and which Goren had brought me in the cigar box, even a cursory examination showed that the Hebrew letters on the back of one of the fragments appeared in mirror-image. They were back to front, and read from left to right instead of Hebrew's right to left. It was evident at the time, and confirmed when the entire scroll was

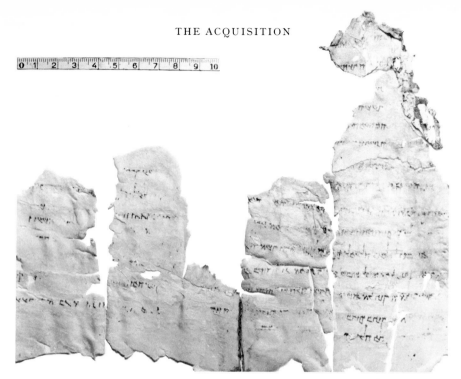

Tight rolling and humidity occasionally caused some of the writing to peel off from its column and become transferred in mirror-image to the back of the next column 'wrapped' round it.

unrolled, that in these cases, since the document had been rolled so tightly, and perhaps also because of humidity, the text of one column of writing had become transferred to the back of the next column which had been 'wrapped' round it, and parts of the original column had been left blank. This 'transfer' of the writing to the back of the succeeding column occurred with considerable frequency not only in the detached fragments but also in the scroll itself. When, after several years, I reached the stage of scientific publication, we printed these columns in reverse, and the transferred mirror-image words now appeared precisely as they had in their original columns, and, together with what remained in those columns, yielded the text of the scroll.

These were only my preliminary observations, and they were thrust to the back of my mind until the war ended two days later. Only on 13 June did I feel sufficiently free to consider the immediate practical task of unrolling the scroll. I had of course thought of entrusting this delicate work to James Bieberkraut, but he was now too old and infirm to tackle what promised to be the longest of all the Dead Sea scrolls. The only other name that came to mind was that of Joseph Shenhav, known to Israeli archaeologists as Dodo. I had been impressed by his skills when he served as chief of restoration and reconstruction at my archaeological excavations at Hazor and Masada, having received special training in this work at several European centres. He had also made a special study of the preservation of ancient scrolls. He was now director of the laboratories at Jerusalem's Israel Museum, but as a reservist had been called up for the war and would not be demobilized for another few weeks. Since my own appointment by the Prime Minister continued for a while, the waiting period was considerably eased by our general preoccupation with the post-war political opportunities.

With Dodo's return to civilian life and his ready response to my invitation, he converted one room in his house into an improvised laboratory for the unrolling of the scroll. Nothing sophisticated was really required, simply a hermetically sealed chamber in which the degree of humidity could be regulated. Dodo accomplished this by following the comparatively primitive but ingenious technique developed by H. J. Plenderleith of the British Museum: a boiling kettle of water, and a hygrometer to gauge the humidity. This softens the leather and makes it more flexible. The expertise lies in sensing, by close observation and touch, just how much or little humidity is necessary to give the hard, fragile and frayed leather the exact degree of flexibility that will make possible its unrolling without disintegrating, and without ruining the writing. One can never tell in this process and with so delicate a scroll what will happen when one begins to unroll tightly rolled leather which has been hidden for ages, or detach the fragments in a wad.

I arranged for Aryeh Volk, the senior photographer at my archaeological dig at Masada, to photograph each stage of Dodo's progress, and his results were immensely helpful to me later in the decipherment of the text. I, too, took many colour photographs. Dodo asked Mrs Ruth Yekutiel of the Israel Museum to assist him in the delicate work.

The easiest to deal with was Wad Y, the one that had been round the scroll together with the cellophane wrapping. As the fragments were carefully detached, they were marked by a serial number so as to fix the exact position of each. Only when the scroll proper was unrolled did we discover that these fragments contained the remains of the opening columns of the scroll's text. (A column in a scroll is the equivalent of a page in a book.) The rolling of the scroll in antiquity had started from the end and finished at the beginning, so that with the unrolling, the first columns to appear were the starting columns of the text.

These Wad Y fragments were parts of columns that had been rolled so tightly that letters and even whole words of one column had become transferred in mirror-image to the back of the leather containing the succeeding column. With the rolling of the scroll from the end towards the beginning, it was possible to determine that the order of the fragments in the wad was indeed the original order of the columns of writing. Thus, the inner fragment held a later column – in this case

Column 5 – than the outermost fragment, which held the first. But since the back of this outermost fragment contained blurred signs of letters which may have been imprinted on it from at least one preceding column, we designated it Column 2. This assumption was supported by my later studies of the content of the scroll.

The second wad we tackled was the one that had been brought to me in the cigar box, and which we subsequently marked Wad X. Here, too, we numbered the fragments serially as they were separated, and these turned out to contain the main existing portions of Columns 6 to 13. Again, there were instances where the entire text of one column appeared in mirror-image on the back of the succeeding one, with the writing side of the first fragment left completely blank. Thus, the remnants of Column 8 (shown in the accompanying photographs) were preserved only on the back of Column 9.

A blank Column 8, with its text in mirror-image transferred to the back of Column 9.

Separating the fragments in Wads X and Y, recovering their writing, and establishing their order in the scroll, proved the easiest of our tasks. The main challenge, apart from the corpus of the scroll, was posed by the small wads and individual fragments remaining in the cigar box and inside the cellophane wrapping. How and where did they fit together, and into the text of the scroll? Fortunately Dodo, who is also a superb sculptor, had an eye for this challenging work.

He had shown a special skill at the excavations at Hazor and Masada in piecing together the potsherds we had dug up. He now applied himself to a similar task with these small wads, managing to match the fragments by registering the shapes of the ragged edges, without even reading the texts.

Dodo's 'working title' for this group of wads was 'The Domino', and it became our current usage. He had to use several techniques in the separation process. The fragments in reasonably good condition were detached by submitting them to the usual humidification of 75 to 80 degrees centigrade. In some cases, the scalpel was used – very delicately. The more stubborn ones were treated by the emergency process of softening them at an almost 100-degree humidity for several minutes, followed by another few minutes of refrigeration. But even this could not be done in several instances where such separation might have damaged the writing.

Following the detachment of all the fragments it was possible to separate by one or other of these techniques, what was left of the Domino was a black, amorphous, macerated mass of leathers. I estimated that they contained the remnants of probably another two or three columns of writing, which could not be discerned by the naked eye, let alone deciphered. What we did, therefore, was to photograph

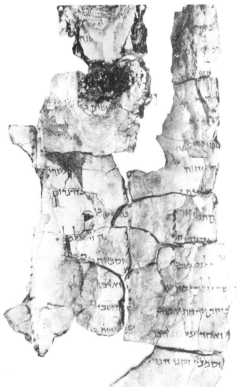

ABOVE Dodo performing 'plastic surgery' on the 'Domino' group of fragments.
LEFT The pieced-together jigsaw puzzle of the 'Domino' wads of fragments.

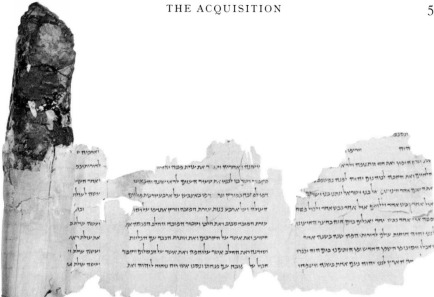

Unrolling the scroll.

the mass in various ways to try and retrieve as many of the remaining letters as possible. We photographed back and front, with the usual lighting and with the lighting behind the object, with both regular and very sensitive film and, of course, in infra-red and colour. Although only a few words became distinguishable, this variety of photographs was to furnish me later with enough data to determine that parts of the Domino fitted into some of the fragments in Wad X, and also told me something about a column in Wad Y. Those Domino fragments, which had been successfully separated and were in relatively good condition, turned out to belong to later columns in the scroll, from Column 15 onwards.

Compared to the stubborn and protracted task of separating the fragments – some took days, some weeks – the process of unrolling the main body of the scroll was less arduous. Most of it responded to the normal humidification of 75 to 80 degrees. But there were parts that did not. We could see at the outset, by looking through the bottom of the roll, that portions of the middle had also suffered damage. The dampness had apparently penetrated the inside of the scroll, and this was confirmed when we had unrolled a good part of the scroll and came upon the damaged leather. We subjected it to the emergency process, but it was ineffective. We had no other course but to photograph it in the various ways we had employed with the Domino, and we were able thereby to retrieve substantial sections of the writing. Anyone viewing the scroll today in the Shrine of the Book would see very little text on this damaged section. But in my scientific publication of the Temple scroll, I was able to offer the photographic retrieval of many parts of the lost script. I should add that in this restoration we were aided by the Criminal Investigation

Department of the Police Force, who used more sophisticated equipment to photograph the damaged section.

Dodo, at times, had to use plastic surgery on the scroll, cutting the columns lengthwise and rejoining them after separation. This proved an intricate operation, carried out effectively over several months with patience and dexterity. So concerned were we that what we had already achieved might be endangered by this subsequent treatment of the columns that we photographed each stage before taking the next step. Thus, in the scientific publication for the specialist, we published several photographs of the same column, as only by studying them all can the preserved text be deciphered.

Slowly, slowly, the unrolling proceeded and, eventually, there before us lay the open scroll. The top part, as we had seen even when the scroll was still rolled, had been badly damaged, with portions missing. The edge was an uneven wavy contour, with some 'valleys' deeper than others. From my experience of scroll scholarship, I have no doubt that scholars will indulge in furious debate for years to come over the lost words that might have been held by the now desolate 'valleys', rather than on the words still preserved in the 'peaks'.

The closer we came to the inside of the scroll, the better preserved were the leather and the columns (except for the damaged section). The end was extremely well preserved. It was customary to add a

OPPOSITE RIGHT A poorly preserved wad, with words from different columns stuck together.
OPPOSITE LEFT The very end of the scroll as it appeared when the unrolling was completed, showing the remains of moths and other insects that had made their way into the document after its removal from the cave and its storage by the dealer in an unsuitable cache.

BELOW The 'peaks and valleys' edge at the top of the partially unrolled scroll.

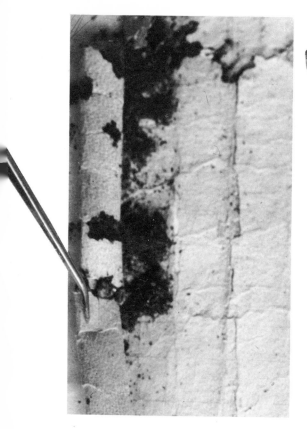

blank closing sheet after the final column of text. In this scroll it was intact. It formed, in fact, the core of the rolled scroll, and when we unrolled it we found the remains of insects that had begun to eat their way through it. We had stopped them just in time.

Some time after the Six Day War, I had been asked by the Israeli Government's Department of Antiquities together with the Shrine of the Book to make a thorough inventory of the scrolls and fragments in the Rockefeller Museum, and to check whether all that had been there before the war was still there. I was ably assisted in this task by Dr Magen Broshi, curator of the Shrine of the Book. In the course of this investigation, I was struck by the similarity of the contents of several fragments with texts in the Temple scroll. It was clear to me, who by then knew the full text almost by heart, that these fragments had belonged to another copy or other copies of our scroll. But they were relatively small fragments, and the text was meagre, so that no

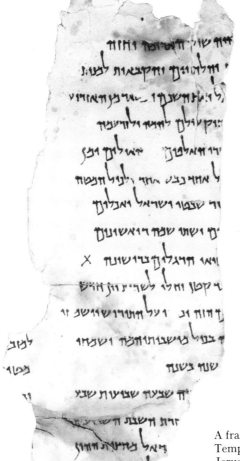

A fragment from another copy of the Temple scroll, also found in Cave 11, now in Jerusalem's Rockefeller Museum.

scholar studying them as isolated writings could possibly have grasped their meaning, the context and their interrelationship. This explains no doubt why the international team of scholars in Jordan engaged in scroll research had failed to identify and publish them. They had marked them with suggested titles which were highly inaccurate.

I called on Father de Vaux, drew his attention to these fragments, and said I would like to use them in restoring the text of certain columns in my scroll. I would also wish to publish photographs of them in my scientific publication, and would, of course, make suitable acknowledgement. I explained that if the scholars responsible for this material published before I was ready with my scroll, I would anyway be free to use it. And if I were first, they, for their publication, would benefit by being able to draw on my studies of the entire scroll, set their work in its accurate context and give it its true significance. Father de Vaux not only granted my request, but even instructed one of his colleagues to provide me with additional photographs.

These fragments of other copies of the Temple scroll were to be of considerable importance in helping me restore missing lines in my scroll where the leather had perished. One tiny fragment was to prove of special value in enabling us to date the original composition of the scroll to not later than the latter half of the second or the very beginning of the first century BC.

PART TWO

ANATOMY OF THE SCROLL

4 The Physical Features

Before proceeding to the content, I have thought it well to follow the scientific practice in scroll studies of describing first the physical features of the leather document. These have often provided helpful clues to its date, a vital element in determining the significance of the text and of the prevailing ideas of a particular historical period.

In those days the scribes engaged in copying what were considered to be timeless sacred works followed a prescribed pattern, with leeway permitted only within a specific framework. There might be slight changes from one generation to the next, and these, too, would be important clues to dating. Furthermore, knowledge of the features of one scroll might be useful in determining or confirming certain aspects of other ancient scrolls.

Thus, for example, I soon discovered when I started examining the Temple scroll that its physical features and workmanship were generally similar to those of the other Qumran scrolls I had studied. Yet I also found certain characteristics unique to this scroll, relating to the 'sheets' of leather, the number of columns and of lines per column, as well as the type of script.

The animal skin on which the text was written is extremely thin, never exceeding one-tenth of a millimetre (1/250th of an inch), one of the thinnest of all the Dead Sea scrolls I know. As with all the scrolls, the scribe, before beginning to write, would rule his guidelines not with ink but with a sharp-pointed instrument. In this scroll, despite its thinness, he did so with such a light touch that nowhere did he cut the skin.

Some of the leather sheets of the scroll are in a poorer state of preservation than others. This is because not all the skins had received the same tanning treatment, and not all had been exposed to the same degree of humidity. The different shades of the sheets are attributable not to the state of preservation but to the variation of treatment. By and large, the original shade was close to ivory, but in

Ruled lines made with a sharp instrument by the highly skilled scribe without cutting through the extremely thin skin – only one-tenth of a millimetre.

several cases it was lemon or dark ivory.

This scroll is made up of nineteen leather sheets which are sewn together with thread. Each sheet contains a few columns, with margins left at the top and bottom and between the columns. The length of the sheets and the number of columns in each vary. Seven sheets have three columns, and ten have four. The first sheet is estimated to have had five columns, and the last sheet, the shortest of all, was left almost completely blank.

The number of columns per sheet is in accordance with the scribal tradition at that time. This we know from the injunction (Tractate Sofrim [Scribes] 2:10): 'No sheet should have less than three columns or more than eight.'

The average length of the three-column sheets is 40 cm, the shortest being 37 cm and the longest 43 cm. The sheets with four columns have an average length of almost 52 cm, the shortest 47 cm and the longest 61 cm. Incidentally, of the ten sheets in the complete Isaiah scroll, which was the longest we had until the discovery of this Temple scroll, three have three columns, five have four, and two have only two columns despite the rules of the mishnaic tradition.

The present total length of the Temple scroll, excluding the first and opening sheet, is 8.148 metres. The length of the first sheet cannot be determined as its columns are fragmented. However, if, as it appears, it had five columns, this would add about 60 cm to the length of the scroll, bringing it up to at least 8.75 metres, roughly one and a half metres longer than the 7.35 metre Isaiah scroll.

Since the scroll was properly rolled from the end, so that the beginning was on the outside, it was mainly the opening columns that suffered damage. It is indeed virtually impossible to establish with certainty how many of the original columns are missing. However, on the basis of the contents of the first well-preserved column, it seems probable that not more than one column was lost. It is possible, too, that, as with some other scrolls, this one had an extra blank column before the beginning of the text, which would give the scroll an original length of 9 metres (about 30 feet).

This exceptional length has a bearing on the script. The scribe was evidently unable to do all the writing with a single quill, and one can tell that he had had to replace it more than once. It is equally evident that at a certain point in his labours, he must have realized that the text would be too long to be carried by the sheets at his disposal – or that using additional sheets would result in a scroll of unwieldy length. He had accordingly, towards the end, increased the number of lines in each column.

The scroll has sixty-six columns, and the lower margin of most of them has been preserved. In none, however, is this the case with the upper margin, so the top lines of the columns were missing. However, I was able to reconstruct some of them with the aid of fragments from other copies of this scroll. They were especially helpful in retrieving the tops of Columns 21, 29 and 41. In this way I was able to establish with certainty that Columns 6 to 48 and 61 to 66 had originally comprised twenty-two lines. In Columns 49 to 60 (on sheets 14, 15 and 16), however, when the scribe felt he was running out of space, he had increased the number of lines per column to twenty-eight. He had done this by adding three lines to both the top and bottom of each column, and narrowing the space between the lines (from 1.1 to 0.8 cm). (Photograph shows transition from 22 to 28 lines per column.)

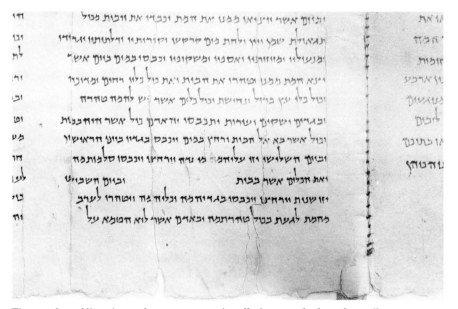

The number of lines in a column was occasionally increased when the scribe perceived that the length of a text would outrun the available 'sheets' of skin.

Assuming that the scribe had allowed a 3 cm (1.17 in.) margin at the top of the columns, in accordance with the contemporary scribal tradition, the original height (or width) of the scroll was between 24 and 26 cm. This is close to the comparable height of the Isaiah scroll – 27 cm – and the 24 cm of the sectarian Manual of Discipline.

The sheets are not uniform in length, no doubt because of variations in the sizes of the skins. But there are also some minor variations in the width of the columns and the margins on each side, though there must have been certain criteria for these dimensions. The Babylonian Talmud (in Tractate Menahot, p. 30a) has the following scribal prescription for copying the Pentateuchal scrolls: 'In the Five books of Moses, the lower margin shall be three fingers' breadth, the upper [margin] two fingers, and between one column and another the space of a thumb breadth.'

The scholarly estimate of a cubit – the ancient measure of length, approximately that of an average forearm – followed by the scribes of the period was 45.72 cm; of a hand-breadth, 7.62 cm; of a thumb, 1.9 cm; and of a finger, 1.5 cm. In all the Dead Sea scrolls I have examined, it is clear that the margin and other measurements accord with this prescription. In the Temple scroll, most margins are indeed the stipulated 1.9 cm thumb-breadth. It is also noteworthy that in three columns where the left margin is the 1.5 cm width of a finger, all occur at the end of a sheet.

Scribal fingerprint: clue to dating

The script of a scroll can frequently offer a clue to its date, the form of lettering, like the style of writing, serving as a scribal fingerprint. The fascinating discipline of paleography, the highly technical study of ancient writings and inscriptions, has made great strides in recent years, with the relative abundance of Dead Sea scrolls from various periods discovered since 1947. One aspect of the advances in this field was to be of special importance to me in determining the date of our copy of the Temple scroll.

We now know, largely as a result of the studies of America's Professor Frank Moore Cross, Jr, and Israel's Professor Nahman Avigad, that the handwriting of the Dead Sea scrolls in general may be divided into two broad categories. The first and oldest is known as Hasmonean or Maccabean, and covers roughly the hundred years between about the middle of the second to the middle of the first century BC. The second is called Herodian, and runs from the middle of the first century BC to about the fall of Jerusalem and destruction of the Temple in AD 70, the time-span of Herod the Great and his dynastic successors. There are of course subdivisions within each of these two groups, some narrowing the periods to Early, Middle and Late Hasmonean and Herodian, and others relating to style – formal and semi-formal, cursive and non-cursive. (The paleographers have a far longer list with more detailed subdivisions, each with its technical term.)

When the scroll had been partially unrolled and the fragments in the wad separated, I had my first opportunity of examining a good portion of the text. I noticed almost immediately that the writing of the opening columns, which were on the wad, was slightly different from that of most columns in the main body of the text. This meant that two scribes had been at work on the scroll. The phenomenon was not uncommon. We had come across several scrolls in which there were two distinctive handwritings, the most notable being the Thanksgiving scroll. Indeed, in that one, after the first scribe had written a considerable part of the text, the second one had taken over in the middle of a column!

What was puzzling in the Temple scroll, however, was that while the writing of both scribes was Herodian, that of the beginning of the text by Scribe A (as I called him) looked to me to be relatively later, or more developed, than the work of Scribe B, who was the main scribe of the scroll, and whose script was very formal, typical of a slightly earlier period. How was it, then, that the beginning of the scroll should have been written after the main text?

Only when the scroll was completely unrolled could I study all the columns, and only then did I find the probable answer. Scribe B had written the text from its very beginning; but after the entire scroll had been completed, his first sheet had been damaged or mutilated in antiquity by prolonged usage, and the later scribe had rewritten and replaced it. Evidence to support my reasoning lay in the fact that the last column in the first sheet – written by Scribe A – duplicates part of the first column in the handwriting of Scribe B. Moreover, from all the photographs we took during the process of unrolling, it is clear that this first sheet, which was added later, was the outer sheet that was rolled round the scroll. While this offers no clue to the *earliest* possible date for the composition of the scroll, it provides the *latest* possible date for this copy, namely, some time during the Herodian script period.

The oldest fragment

Of greater importance for the dating of the composition of the Temple scroll is not our copy but a fragment of another copy which was among the pieces in the Rockefeller Museum. As soon as I saw it and glanced at the script, I placed it somewhere within the Hasmonean

A fragment from Cave 4 of an earlier, 2nd
century BC, copy of parts of the Temple
scroll. This fragment provides important
evidence for fixing the latest
possible date of the composition
of this scroll.

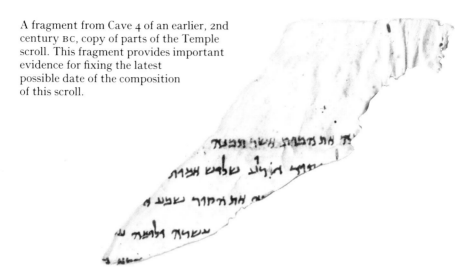

group, at least several decades earlier than either of the two scripts
in our scroll. It was therefore essential that I examine this fragment
with the utmost care to see whether it was Early, Middle or Late
Hasmonean, as this would give me the latest possible date for the
composition of the text. And, indeed, I found it to be typical of the
script known as 'Middle Hasmonean semi-formal style'. It greatly
resembles the script of the complete Isaiah scroll which I had acquired
from Archbishop Samuel. It is also similar to the handwriting in
another document – a copy of Deuteronomy that had been found in
Cave 4.

If I was correct in my classification, it would put the date of this
Temple scroll fragment within the last quarter of the second century
BC or the very beginning of the first century BC. To make sure, I
showed a photograph of it to my colleague, Professor Nahman Avigad, one of the leading authorities on paleography, without giving
him my conclusions, or the information of what it was and where it
came from. To my delight, he gave his written judgement that it
'greatly resembles Isaiah A', and should therefore be dated to the
same period, namely, around 100 BC.

Establishing the latest possible date for the composition of the
Temple scroll was to prove of importance in enabling me to understand the full significance of certain parts of its contents.

Scribal errors

However careful the ancient scribe, and however strict the regulations
governing his work, he occasionally made mistakes in the writing of
a scroll, though it is remarkable how few are the errors, considering

the length of the texts. This was true of the scribes who wrote our copy of the Temple scroll and of those who wrote the other Dead Sea scrolls. When this occurred, how did a scribe deal with the problem? How, for example, did he correct a spelling error, or restore an omitted letter, word or sentence?

There were three ways. One, called dotting, was to put a dot above the wrong letter he wished to cancel – sometimes a dot both above and beneath – with the offending letter remaining in place. The second and more drastic method was erasure. Though permitted by scribal tradition, both these methods were rather primitive, and were used only rarely in the Temple scroll. The third procedure, widely used in several of the Dead Sea scrolls, was to insert the correct or missing letter, word or sentence in the space immediately above the line of writing. This was resorted to particularly where the scribe had inadvertently missed out a letter or even a whole line. It was also used, though rarely, when he was required to amend an already written text. The technique in these cases was rigid. To correct the error of a missing letter, or change the spelling or introduce other textual emendations, the scribe would add the required letter or word above the succeeding letter or word. If, to use an English example, he had intended to write 'Temple' but had omitted the 'p' and written 'Temle', he would insert it above the 'l', thus: 'Tem^ple'. If he were required to insert a phrase, and the space between the lines was narrow, his script would need to be tiny, and one would need good eyesight to read it. This may well have been the origin of the expression 'reading between the lines' for a person of acute perception.

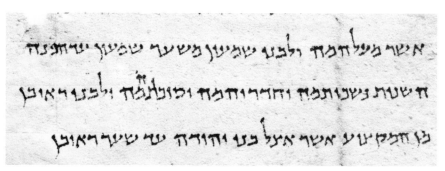

The scribe corrected his mistakes – mainly a missed word or letter – by 'hanging' the insertion above the line in its correct place.

I detected altogether some seventy corrections or emendations in the Temple scroll, and nine apparent errors which were left uncorrected. I say 'apparent' for a few may not have been mistakes but simply alternative forms of spelling. On the whole, it may be said that Scribe B, who wrote the bulk of the scroll, was an excellent scribe – and a good proof-reader.

The language factor

While, as we have seen, the script holds the clue to the *latest* possible date an ancient scroll could have been written, a close study of the language itself, style, syntax and the use of certain words and expressions, can help narrow the time bracket by telling us the *earliest* possible date it could have been composed. This may be readily understood if, to take a hypothetical though comparable case, we imagine an English document being discovered in the year AD 3984, two thousand years from now. A scholar is racking his brains trying to find out, with nothing in the text to guide him, whether it was written in the nineteenth or the twenty-first century, or even earlier or later. He then comes across the word 'television', and this tells him at once that it could not have been written earlier than the specific date in the twentieth century when television was invented and came into universal use.

There was a special problem, however, in the search for such obvious signs in the Temple scroll because of the special nature of the text and the aim of the author. He had clearly set himself the task of composing a work in the very language style of the Hebrew Bible, seeking in his own writing to match the syntax, wording and phraseology of the direct biblical quotations to which he frequently referred. I therefore applied myself to examining each word and sentence to see if he had struck a wrong note somewhere, and had had recourse to an expression or a grammatical form that was current at the time of writing but was not to be found in the biblical texts.

I was intrigued to discover that he had. I came across a number of cases where he used compound verbal forms, technical terms and words characteristic of the language known as 'rabbinic Hebrew' or 'the language of the sages', the Hebrew of the final centuries of the Second Temple period. Among the post-biblical works in which they occur, of course, are also some of the other Dead Sea scrolls, but several of them are most pronounced in the Temple scroll. It seems evident that the author used these contemporary words and linguistic forms inadvertently, not only because they were in such general use at the time, but also, and especially, because they were precisely the terms and expressions he needed, though they were not in the Bible.

Most useful for dating, of course, were those non-biblical words which had been introduced into the Hebrew language during a particular period, known to us from other sources. An example of such a word occurs in a passage in the scroll where the author needed a technical term for a specific distance. The entire column (Column 52) is written in biblical Hebrew style, or very close to it, and suddenly, in verse 18, he uses the term 'thirty ris'. He was dealing with the slaughtering of blemished animals, which, though fit for eating, were unfit for Temple sacrifice. He wrote: 'You shall eat it within your

towns far from my Temple, thirty ris around it. You shall not slaughter near my Temple for it is foul flesh.'

The word 'ris' is used in the Mishnah to denote a measurement unit
of distance, and the very expression 'thirty ris' appears in the Tractate Baba Kama 7:7 regulation on the right to hunt wild pigeons:
'They may not set snares for pigeons unless it be thirty ris distance
from an inhabited place.' 'Ris' is a Persian word that was introduced
later into the Aramaic and Hebrew languages as the equivalent of the
Roman 'stadium', and 30 stadia, or 30 ris, was the equivalent of the
Persian and Greek 'parasang', about 4 miles. 'Ris' became part of the
Hebrew language in Palestine during the Hellenistic period, the third
and second centuries BC. Thus the word 'ris' in the Temple scroll, and
a few other words of a similar character, clearly indicate without any
other supporting evidence that this document could not have been
written before the beginning of the Hellenistic period. Other evidence
shows that it was composed towards the end of that period, during
the latter part of the second century BC, some two hundred years
before the destruction of the Second Temple.

5 The Nature of the Text

The Dead Sea scrolls discovered up to now consist mainly of biblical
Books and sectarian works. The Temple scroll is unique in that, while
it is a sectarian book, it contains direct quotations from biblical texts;
it expounds and expands on these texts without indicating that this
is what it is doing – which it would if it were a commentary; it codifies
many of the biblical injunctions; and, most interesting of all, it adds
a considerable volume of supplementary text as though it were part
of the very words uttered by the Lord on Mount Sinai. It also has
the evident sectarian purpose of establishing that the regulations
governing the religious life of the Essenes are the only ones that truly
followed the Law as revealed by God to Moses. In so doing, it tells us
a great deal about hitherto unknown religious, political and military
patterns in the Holy Land in the second half of the second century BC.

The principal themes, dealt with in fascinating detail, are the
Statutes of the King, including the organization of the army, the
stages of mobilization in face of enemy attack, the rules for distribut-
ing the spoils of battle, the duties of the king to his subjects, the ban
on polygamy and divorce, the judicial council; a unique Temple plan
and Temple ritual; the sect's calendar and its impact on the Israelite
festivals, both those known from the Bible and also 'new' ones; and
the Laws of Purity and Impurity, with a strong emphasis on those
concerning sexual intercourse.

The immediate question that sprang to mind when I deciphered and read it for the first time was whether this scroll had been conceived as part of the Holy Scripture, and accepted as such by the Dead Sea community, or whether it was a biblical commentary, or perhaps a literary work which made free use of the biblical text. (Fragments of works of the latter type were found among the Dead Sea documents.)

The Lord in the first person

One of the most unusual features of the text which struck me immediately and which long puzzled me is that the Lord is presented as speaking in the first person singular. The author does this for the most part even when he quotes passages from the Bible which contain such phrases as 'the Lord said' and 'to the Lord'. He changes them to 'I said' and 'to me'. He does the same in the writings of his own composition where he supplements the biblical text. However, this is not his exclusive practice throughout the scroll. On occasion, he quotes from the Pentateuch without change, so that if the quoted passage happens to contain 'the Lord', instead of substituting 'I', 'me' or 'my', he retains the original form of the name of God. This form consists of four Hebrew letters, known as the tetragrammaton. This lapse, if it can be so called, was to provide an unintentional but vital additional clue to determining the nature of the scroll.

The change to the first person where the biblical text uses the third person may be readily seen in the following examples.

Deuteronomy 12:26 reads:

But ... your votive offerings you shall take ... to the
place which the Lord will choose ....

The scroll reads:

But ... your votive offerings you shall take ... to the
place in which I will put my name ....

The same Deuteronomy injunction continues (12:27):

and offer your burnt offerings ... on the altar
of the Lord your God.

The scroll reads:

and you shall sacrifice there before me ....

Numbers 30:2 reads:

When a man vows a vow to the Lord ....

The comparable sentence in the scroll reads:

And when a man vows a vow to me ....

And 'me' or 'I' is substituted for 'the Lord' in the rest of this passage on vows and pledges.

The clear aim of the author is to dispel any doubt that it is God himself who is uttering not only the known injunctions in the Pentateuch (the Torah), even when they are presented in reported speech, but also the supplementary text that appears in the scroll.

The scroll is rich in such supplementary material, none of which is to be found in our Bible. It may be called 'additional Torah' or 'additional Law', and the following brief extract is sufficient to indicate the author's style and his use of the divine first person. It is taken from the section on the Statutes of the King:

If he walks in my statutes and observes my commandments and does what is right and good in my sight, a man of his sons shall not be cut off from sitting on the throne of the kingdom of Israel forever and I will be with him and deliver him from the hands of those who hate him and from the hands of those who seek to take away his life. And I will give up all his enemies before him and he will rule over them . . . .

These are but a few of the examples which offer incontrovertible evidence of the author's intention to present divine Law directly and at all times through speech by God himself, rather than as declared through the mouth of Moses. To whom, then, does the scroll indicate the Lord is speaking? In most cases he is addressing someone in the second person, and this is especially true in the section where the Lord commands the building of the Temple. The style there is very similar to that in Exodus, where the Lord speaks to Moses directly and instructs him to build the Tabernacle. It may be assumed, therefore, that in the scroll, too, the person addressed is Moses.

Unfortunately, the tops and some other parts of the columns which may have contained the sections where Moses is mentioned are missing, and Moses does not appear in the rest of the text. Nowhere is there a verse such as 'And the Lord said unto Moses'; yet I have little doubt that this may have been written on the missing parts, and no doubt whatsoever that the author had Moses in mind as the person to whom the Lord was speaking.

I published this view in my scientific writings on the scroll, and was challenged by one scholar. He had apparently missed my reference to the definite proof I had found in an unexpected part of the scroll, the part dealing with the allocation of the Temple chambers to the various tribes. Concerning those to be set aside for the priests, the Lord, speaking in the first person, commands someone addressed in the second person, as follows:

And all the right of and the left of the Gate of Levi you shall allot to the sons of Aaron your brother, eight and one hundred chambers.

Who but Moses, brother of Aaron, was the person being addressed?

Holy Scripture?

Was this scroll conceived as Holy Scripture, intended as part of the canon of the Hebrew Bible? The question is fundamental, and will figure also in later discussions. But it is relevant at this stage to consider a point that indicates the area in which the answer is to be found. We have seen that in some cases, quoting from the Pentateuch, the author did not change the name of the Lord, the tetragrammaton, into the first person singular, either for reasons of syntax or for inherent content. As a result, we have instances in which the tetragrammaton, the four Hebrew letters Yod, Heh, Vav, Heh, have been preserved, and the way in which they are written tells us much about the nature of the scroll.

These four Hebrew letters, like the entire contents of the Bible, were written in the old texts without vowels. Thus, we do not know how they were pronounced. It is most probable, however, that they constituted the Hebrew word Yahveh (or Yahweh), the Creator. Because this denoted the sacred name of God, from the Second Temple period onwards it was never uttered by Jews, and the practice is followed to this day. Thus, when the Jews read these four letters in the Bible or the Prayer Book, they use the substitute word 'Adonai', an archaic Hebrew form of 'My Lord'. In the Middle Ages, when the Hebrew biblical text was supplied with vowels, the name YHVH (or YHWH) was vowelled according to the vowelling of Adonai – which incidentally is the origin of the faulty hybrid: Jehovah.

TOP In this text from the Habakkuk Commentary, the tetragrammaton (underlined) is written in the old Paleo-Hebrew script, different from the square-lettered script of the rest of the passage, the common custom of the sect with works considered to be non-canonical.

BOTTOM The tetragrammaton, the Hebrew name of the Lord, YHVH (underlined), is written in the Temple scroll in the same square script as the rest of the text, which follows the scribal custom with biblical books, an indication that the Qumran sect considered this scroll to be Holy Scripture.

What is of special interest is that those Dead Sea scrolls which may definitely be called non-canonical, and were considered as such by the sect, always followed the practice of generally using 'el' (Hebrew for 'a god' or 'god') wherever there is a reference to the Lord. But when quoting from the Bible, the scribe always wrote the four Hebrew letters of the tetragrammaton not in the same square script used uniformly throughout the scroll, but in the old Hebrew script which originated in the First Temple period (tenth to sixth centuries BC). The very writing of these letters in this script was a further indication to the reader not to pronounce the name of God.

On the other hand, in the scrolls of the biblical Books found at Qumran, such as Isaiah or the Books of the Pentateuch, the tetragrammaton is always written in the same square script as the rest of the scroll. And that is how these letters for the name of the Lord are written in the Temple scroll, exactly as in the canonical Books of the Bible! This is one indication – there are others – that this work was considered by the sect as Holy Scripture.

I should add that there is a certain controversy over the question of whether any definite conclusions can be drawn on the nature of the text from the form of the script, square or old Hebrew, in which the tetragrammaton is presented. It is pointed out, for example, that old Hebrew is used for the name of God in the Psalms scroll mentioned in an earlier chapter – Dr Sanders's Psalter of which I had been sent a fragment by Mr Z; and the Book of Psalms, after all, is a biblical Book. However, there are some scholars who believe that this Psalter was not considered canonical by the Dead Sea sect, and was probably used as a Prayer Book and not a biblical Book. They argue that not only is the order of the psalms different from that of the masoretic text, but it also contains many additional psalms not included in the canonical Book of Psalms. Whatever the case with the Psalter, I have no doubt that as a rule the tetragrammaton was written in old Hebrew in non-canonical Books, and in the uniform script of the texts in Books deemed canonical. That the Temple scroll was conceived and accepted by the Essene community as a sacred canonical work is supported by additional evidence that will be discussed later.

The author as editor and codifier

The extraordinary parts of the scroll, of dramatic interest and importance, are those which contain the supplementary text – the 'additional Torah'. These constitute a hitherto unknown composition to which, as we have seen, there is no reference in any version of the Scriptures. However, we shall appreciate more fully the total contents of this manuscript if we bear in mind that the other parts of the scroll

The entrance to Cave 4, the only cave close to the site of the Qumran settlement. (The others are in the nearby cliffs.) Thousands of fragments of several hundred scrolls were found in this cave, including a fragment of the oldest copy of the Temple scroll, belonging to the 2nd century BC.

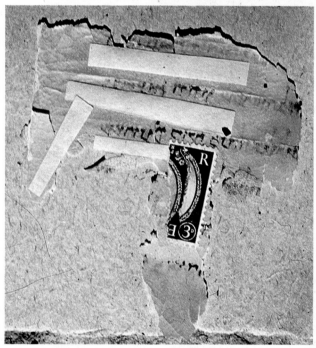

ABOVE The two sides of the first fragment of the Temple scroll seen by the author six years before he acquired the complete scroll. The fragment had been mailed to him by Mr Z, its back reinforced by British postage stamps. Written in Hebrew by a superb scribe, the words 'The High Priest' appear in Line 3.

LEFT A 1984 photograph of Cave 11, the latest cave to yield ancient documents. As in Cave 1, the Bedouin found complete scrolls, among them the Temple scroll (© *David Harris*).

The cliffs of Qumran (© *David Harris*).

are directly concerned with biblical texts, and these show the fine hand of an author who was also a skilful editor and an ingenious codifier.

The fact is, as anyone can gather on even a first reading of the Pentateuch, that many of the various biblical commands are scattered among these Five Books of Moses, often within a single Book and at times within the narrow span of a few chapters, without any apparent order. Thus, those who since early times were engaged in the formulation of Jewish law had to tackle the problem of codifying those injunctions.

What the author of the Temple scroll did was to take commands in the Pentateuch relating to a particular subject and merge them. The overall result was the assembly of the commands into a system of coherent groups classified according to subject. He often quoted almost verbatim the biblical passages he collected together. In some cases he combined them into a single flowing text. Where he found an extraneous command in the midst of a series of injunctions on another subject, he omitted it from the original passage and transferred it to its own subject group. The product was a clear text on each subject.

Curiously enough, the historian Josephus some 200 years later sought to achieve the same aim as the author of our scroll, and in his *Antiquities of the Jews*, in the preface to his catalogue on the Mosaic Law, Josephus describes his intention in words which apply with perfection to our author:

Our one innovation has been to classify the several subjects, for he [Moses] left what he wrote in a scattered condition, just as he received each instruction from God. I have thought it necessary to make this preliminary observation, lest perchance any of my countrymen who read this work should reproach me at all for having gone astray. (*Antiquities* 4:197)

This was without doubt a logical method, and one need not suppose that Josephus was influenced by someone else's work. However, we know from his autobiography that he was familiar with the writings of the Essenes, and there is reason for conjecture that some of the laws he cited are to be found only in the Temple scroll.

This mode of editing according to subject is followed throughout the scroll, both in its general structure and in its arrangement by principal themes. In general, the author presented his main topics in the same order as they appear in the legislative Books of the Pentateuch – Exodus, Leviticus, Numbers and Deuteronomy.

In so doing, he was aspiring in fact to do what was achieved by the great rabbinic sages of the Mishnah, which is the codified 'Halachah' – the religio-legal system of Judaism – based on oral tradition. This was developed in the course of the final centuries of the Second Temple period and the early centuries of the first millennium AD, with all the Pentateuchal injunctions grouped by subject in six major divisions.

Harmonization

The editing we have considered so far, primarily presenting the biblical injunctions according to theme, is straightforward. But the author's originality – and the main significance of this aspect of the scroll – emerges in his unification of similar biblical commands and his harmonization of variant commands. Here, his editing is of a distinctly halachic nature, namely, it lays down the law based on a particular interpretation of the biblical intent.

Our author, like the rabbinic halachists before and after him who were engaged in formulating the laws of Judaism based on the Bible, well knew that there is duplication and even apparent contradiction in the commands of the Pentateuch. Modern scholars attribute this to the various 'sources' from which the Pentateuch was compiled. But the halachists of those days, and our author, too, regarded the Law as having been given to the Children of Israel through Moses on Mount Sinai. They therefore attached significance to all instances of apparent duplication and contradiction, and spent much thought on how they were to be interpreted and dealt with. As the Talmud put it (in Tractate Sotah 3a): 'It was taught in the school of Rabbi Ishmael: whenever a scriptural passage is repeated, it is only because of some new point contained therein.'

The 'seized' and the 'seduced' woman

A good example of how the author of the scroll on his part and the rabbis on theirs tackled such problems – and gave different rulings – are the two biblical commands on the subject of the violation of a virgin. One concerned the 'seized' woman and the other the 'seduced' woman, where the Bible gives different penalties for the violator. Our author unified and harmonized the two commands by holding that they dealt with a single issue – from the standpoint of the woman – even though they seemed to differ from one another from the legal standpoint. The rabbis followed the straightforward meaning of the text, but their reasoning, interesting in itself, is of special relevance to the Temple scroll since, by representing a different school of thought, it throws light on the prevailing views at the time the scroll was written. Incidentally, this example provides a fascinating glimpse into the manner in which Jewish halachah was settled.

Deuteronomy 22:28–29 sets out the case of the 'seized' woman:

If a man meets a virgin who is not betrothed, and seizes her and lies with her, and they are found, then the man who lay with her shall give to the father of the young woman fifty shekels of silver, and she shall be his wife, because he has violated her; he may not put her away all his days.

Exodus 22:16–17 deals with the case of the 'seduced' woman:

If a man seduces a virgin who is not betrothed, and lies with her, he shall give the marriage present for her, and make her his wife. If her father utterly refuses to give her to him, he shall pay money equivalent to the marriage present for virgins.

Accepting the plain meaning of the biblical text, we have here two separate cases on a similar subject, where the behaviour of the 'violator' is different, and so is the penalty. The purpose of both in those days, of course, was to protect the violated woman.

The editing, the unifying, and the ruling given in the Temple scroll are as follows:

If a man seduces a virgin who is not betrothed but is fit for him according to the law, and lies with her and is found, then the man who lay with her shall give to the father of the young woman fifty shekels [of silver] and she shall be his wife because he has violated her. He may not put her away all his life.

A glance at the scroll text quickly shows that the author begins with the 'seduces' of Exodus; drops the 'meets' and 'seizes her' of Deuteronomy; adds his own explanatory or qualifying 'but is fit for him according to the law'; and ends with Deuteronomy. Some of the wording of course is common to both biblical passages, and the author has combined the two into a smooth text, most of it taken from Deuteronomy. But the 'legal situation' is based on Exodus: he rules that the seized (raped) woman and the seduced woman are regarded as identical in circumstance and in law.

Before comparing this judgement with the rabbinic law and the biblical text, it is worth considering the author's addition 'but is fit for him according to the law'. The significant point about the legal terminology used here – and throughout the scroll – is that it is virtually identical with the terminology in the Mishnah. Tractate Ketubot 3:5, for example, reads: 'For it is written "And she shall be to him for a wife". A wife? That is, fit for him [according to the law].'

This shows, since there is clear evidence that our scroll is not copied from the Mishnah nor the Mishnah from the scroll, that both the author and the mishnaic sages used the same general halachic terminology in which all halachists, irrespective of sect, were well versed. In certain instances, as in this one, the language and jurisprudence were similar in a specific detail, but on the issue itself they differed

basically in their views. This was also true of most of the cases dealt
with in the scroll.

To return to the verses in Exodus and Deuteronomy, it is plain
that, whatever their original biblical meaning, the author of the scroll
held that the status of the seduced woman was the same as that of
the seized woman in so far as it was the man's duty to take her to
wife with or without the father's consent. I think the author considered that even in the case of the seduced woman the act was
performed against her will, for if it were with her consent it would
not be seduction.

Interestingly enough, modern scholars like Professors Moshe Wein-
feld and Moshe Greenberg, both great authorities on biblical texts,
who reached their findings before the publication of the Temple scroll,
also hold that the two cases refer to the same situation, though they
reach this conclusion through reasoning diametrically opposed to that
of the author of the scroll. They say that neither was a case of rape
in the accepted sense. The meaning of the Hebrew words which are
given the standard translation of 'seized' and 'violated' refer, as Professor Greenberg puts it, 'not strictly to rape . . . but to other instances
of sexual intercourse which are innocent but which involve an element
of imposition upon the woman. It might then still refer to seduction.'

Their argument thus gives greater flexibility to the two terms and
the two cases: both are the same in that both fall short of rape. The
text of the scroll, on the other hand, considers, to my mind, that both
are the same as far as the woman's status is concerned through a
more rigid interpretation of the biblical terms.

Spoils of battle

A second example is taken from the section of the Temple scroll
dealing with the Statutes of the King, which includes the rule to be
followed in the division of the spoils of battle. Here, however, the
special interest lies in the ingenious way in which the author solved
a puzzling riddle posed by contradictory directions in the Bible.

The Israelite victory over the Midianites is recounted in the Book
of Numbers, which then goes on to give this directive on the division
of the war booty:

[God speaks to Moses]: . . . and divide the booty into two parts, between the
warriors who went out to battle and all the congregation. And levy for the
Lord a tribute from the men of war who went out to battle, one out of five
hundred, of the persons and of the oxen and of the asses and of the flocks;
take it from their half, and give it to Eleazar the priest as an offering to the
Lord. And from the people of Israel's half you shall take one drawn out of

every fifty ... and give them to the Levites who have charge of the tabernacle of the Lord. (Num. 31:27–30)

This division clearly gives the fighting man a larger portion of the
spoils than the rest of the congregation who remained in the rear. The
warriors received one half of the total minus one five-hundredth, while
the rest received one half less one fiftieth.

The Temple scroll gives the following command on how the spoils
are to be divided:

And if they are victorious/over their enemies, and break them, and smite
them with the sword, and carry away their booty, they shall give/from it to
the king his tenth, and to the priests one of a thousand, and to the Levites
one of a hundred/of the total, and they shall halve the remaining between
the warriors who went out to battle and their brothers/whom they stationed
in their cities. (Col. 43:11–15)

Why would the author of the scroll, while using much of the text of
Numbers, appear at first glance to change the shares of the priests
and Levites from 'one out of five hundred' to 'one of a thousand', and
'one drawn out of every fifty' to 'one of a hundred'? And why, after
closer comparison, would he make a real change in the apportionment
between the front-line troops and the rear echelon personnel, giving
them equal shares whereas in Numbers they are unequal?

He did so because, like the other biblical codifiers, he was faced
with the problem of a contrary ruling given by King David after his
victory over the Amalekites. The Book of Samuel gives an account of
the feud that followed between the combatants and the non-combatants over the division of the booty, and David gave this decision:

For as his share is who goes down into the battle, so shall his share be who
stays by the baggage; they shall share alike. And from that day forward he
made it a statute and an ordinance for Israel to this day. (1 Sam. 30:24–25)

To cope with this contradiction, the author of the scroll harmonized
the two biblical texts in such a way as to give the appearance of
bringing the division in Numbers into line with the share-and-share-
alike ruling by David. He used the text of the situation in Numbers,
with its provision for the priests and Levites, but altered the stages
at which those were to be allocated, so that their shares came 'off the
top', as fractions of the *total* booty. Thus, the scroll gave one thou-
sandth of the total to the priests, which is the equivalent of one
five-hundredth of the half as in Numbers, and one hundredth of the
total to the Levites, equalling one fiftieth of the half. Thereafter, the
balance was divided evenly between the warriors and the others, as
prescribed by David in the Book of Samuel.

Thus, aided by an arithmetical sleight of hand, the author presented
a composite law, combining the priestly and levitical shares of

Numbers and the absolute equality of portions for warriors and non-combatants of Samuel. Ingenious indeed.

A word must be said about the scroll's provision of one tenth for the king. This is part of the author's own 'additional Torah', and though this royal portion will be discussed more fully later, it is relevant to note at this stage that in his Statutes of the King, the author prescribes that under no circumstances should the king take with him into battle more than one half of the army and the people. The other half were to remain behind to defend the cities. It was thus important for the author to address himself to this question of the division of the spoils, and to interpret the contradictory biblical injunctions in a manner that would give equal portions to both halves.

6 'Additional Torah'

I have offered, so far, examples from those parts of the Temple scroll that are biblical texts as edited and harmonized by the author. We now come to the main portions of the scroll – or rather those which are of principal interest for our understanding of the Dead Sea sect and of views current at the time which differed from rabbinic Judaism. I have called these portions 'additional Torah', for the author presents them as specific statutes given by God directly on subjects which are not found in this form in our Bible, or using textual expressions on topics that have no biblical parallels.

The section of the scroll dealing with the religious festivals, which contains such additional portions, is of special interest, for it prescribes festivals that do not appear in the Bible, or are mentioned there but given no specific statutes. Above all, the directives on these new festivals show beyond doubt that the calendar used by the author of the scroll was exactly the same esoteric calendar used by the community of Qumran, the Essenes.

A good example of the nature of the author's innovations is a festival he introduces that has its origin in a ceremony referred to in the Pentateuch as the Days of Ordination or Investment. This was the ceremony in the wilderness of the sanctifying of the Tabernacle (the mobile sanctuary), the ordaining of Aaron as high priest and the investiture of his sons with priesthood. The ritual at this important occasion is dealt with twice in the Pentateuch. Chapter 29 of Exodus is prescriptive: 'Now this is what you shall do to them [Aaron and his sons] to consecrate them, that they may serve me as priests.' Later, in Leviticus 8, there is a description of the event at which the instructions in Exodus 29 were carried out.

At that event in the wilderness as narrated in Leviticus, it is Moses who plays the principal role. It is he who directs the proceedings and officiates at the ordination ceremony, since Aaron and his sons, who are to be sanctified and thereafter tend the holy Tabernacle, cannot do so until they are ordained and clearly cannot serve in their own ordination. It was for this reason that the rabbinic ruling, incorporated in normative Judaism, was that this ceremony, enjoined and described in the Pentateuch, was a one-time ceremony, and the ordination of priests ever after was to be carried out in a different manner.

The principal innovation in the Temple scroll associated with this festive ceremony is that it is to be held annually. Each year, new priests are to be ordained in almost the same manner as that described in Leviticus: the one difference is that the role played by Moses at the first ceremony in the wilderness is now to be performed by the high priest; and when he himself is to be ordained, the function of Moses is undertaken by the 'Elders of the Priests'. It may be assumed that this was so important a festival to the Essenes that it was held even in Qumran.

Incidentally, the text containing the author's prescription on the ordaining of a new high priest by the Elders of the Priests was contained in the small fragment that I had received by mail in London from the Virginian clergyman, Mr Z. When I had examined it at the time, I could make out quite clearly the words 'high priest', though of course I had no notion to what they referred. Only after I had acquired the scroll and fitted the fragment in its proper place did I find that it related to this extremely significant, hitherto unknown, festive ceremony described in the hidden Torah of the Essenes.

Though the main change, as we have indicated, was turning what rabbinic Judaism considered a one-time event into an annual ceremony, there are other innovations introduced in the Temple scroll. To understand them fully – and incidentally to bring to light a possible clue to the solution of a New Testament enigma that has baffled scholars to this day – they must be set against the instructions in the Pentateuch on the ritual of consecration and ordination. But it is sufficient to quote the basic elements from the record in Leviticus 8 to show the deviations in the Temple scroll. We may then seek an explanation for such a departure, for none of the author's changes could have been accidental.

Leviticus 8 opens with:

The Lord said to Moses, 'Take Aaron and his sons with him, and the garments, and the anointing oil, and the bull of the sin offering, and the two rams, and the basket of unleavened bread; and assemble all the congregation at the door of the tent of meeting.'

Then followed a special ceremony, 'a wave offering', consisting of parts of the ram:

and out of the basket of unleavened bread which was before the Lord he [Moses] took one unleavened cake, and one cake of bread with oil, and one wafer, and placed them on the fat ... and he put all these in the hands of Aaron and in the hands of his sons, and waved them as a wave offering before the Lord. (8:26, 27)

Aaron and his sons were to remain within 'the tent of meeting for seven days, until the days of your ordination are completed', and 'on the eighth day' there is a ritual that is described in detail in the following chapter (9) of Leviticus.

This brings us to two further changes found in the scroll, in addition to the fundamental change of turning the ordination ceremony into an annual event. One is a departure from the rabbinic ruling; the other deviates from the text as recorded in the Pentateuch.

The first concerns the day of the month when the original ordination ceremony in the wilderness was believed to have been held. The scroll prescribes that the celebration of the Days of Ordination is to begin on the first day of the first month (the Hebrew month of Nissan), so the ritual 'on the eighth day' would take place on the eighth of Nissan; and this would appear to be the plain meaning of the Pentateuchal text. The rabbis, however, discussing when the inaugural ceremony had been held in the time of Moses, took the view that that ritual had taken place on the first of Nissan. That day, they believed, marked the completion, not the start of, the seven days of ordination, which had therefore begun on the twenty-third of the previous month (Adar, the twelfth Hebrew month).

It must be said, however, that the ruling in the Temple scroll was not at variance with some of the rabbinic views at the time. And we know that the celebrated Rabbi Akiva – though admittedly some two centuries later – also held that the eighth day of the ordination fell on the eighth and not the first day of Nissan. So did Ibn Ezra, the eleventh–twelfth-century Spanish Hebrew poet, philosopher and renowned Jewish commentator. 'It would appear', he wrote, 'that "on the eighth day" means the eighth of Nissan, because the tabernacle was erected on the first of the month.'

Clue to the enigma of Mark

The second change by the scroll concerns an item in the Pentateuchal ritual – 'the basket of unleavened bread'. The Temple scroll prescribes not one but seven baskets of bread. It is assumed that the Qumran community held the ceremony annually. Since they could not hold it in the Temple, nor offer sacrifices either there or anywhere else, they were unable to make the sacrifice of a 'ram of ordination'. Thus, their seven baskets of bread may have become a central element of their celebration.

The author, of course, was prescribing for his concept of the Temple:

And for the ordination, one ram for every day and baskets of bread for all the rams of the ordination, one basket for one ram. And they shall divide all the rams and the baskets for the seven days of the ordination . . . .

When I was studying this text in the Temple scroll, and noticing that the author had substituted seven baskets for the single one prescribed in the Pentateuch, I recalled an obscure passage in the New Testament which had never been satisfactorily explained. It follows the narrative (in Mark 8:1–9) of the miracle of the loaves and fishes, when, after the hungry crowd had been satisfied, Jesus and his disciples had got 'into the boat' and 'departed to the other side' of the Sea of Galilee:

Now they had forgotten to bring bread; and they had only one loaf with them in the boat. And he cautioned them, saying, 'Take heed, beware of the leaven of the Pharisees and the leaven of the Herodians.'

(Some manuscripts of Mark have 'the leaven of Herod'. And in the parallel version in Matthew 16:6, the text reads 'Sadducees' instead of 'Herodians', namely, 'beware of the leaven of the Pharisees and Sadducees'.)

The passage continues (Mark 8:14–21):

And they discussed it with one another, saying, 'We have no bread.' And being aware of it, Jesus said to them, 'Why do you discuss the fact that you have no bread? Do you not yet perceive or understand? . . . And do you not remember? When I broke the five loaves for the five thousand, how many baskets full of broken pieces did you take up?' They said to him, 'Twelve'. 'And the seven for the four thousand, how many baskets full of broken pieces did you take up?' And they said to him, 'Seven'. And he said to them, 'Do you not yet understand?'

Mark adds no explanation. And the reader, of course, cannot understand, any more than the disciples themselves understood, what Jesus was talking about. The version in Matthew, on the other hand, does give the explanation. After asking his disciples about 'the seven loaves of the four thousand, and how many baskets you gathered', Jesus says:

'How is it that you fail to perceive that I did not speak about bread? Beware of the leaven of the Pharisees and Sadducees.' Then they understood that he did not tell them to beware of the leaven of bread, but of the teaching of the Pharisees and Sadducees.

This, perhaps, is an explanation which Mark either did not know or did not dare to add.

However, of special interest to us, concerned with the intentions of the author of the Temple scroll, are two basic questions to which the text of Mark gives rise: Who are the 'Herodians'? And what is the significance of the 'twelve' and the 'seven' baskets, and why were the disciples expected to infer that they were an allusion to the bread of the Pharisees and Herodians?

Most New Testament commentators have addressed themselves to the second question alone, their principal concern being to suggest that this chapter in Mark contained the kernel of the Eucharist concept, namely, that the one loaf refers to Jesus. A closer study of the text, however, makes it clear that the two miracles – filling the twelve and filling the seven baskets – symbolized the bread of the Pharisees and the bread of the Herodians. It would seem evident that the twelve alludes to the Pharisees and to the twelve loaves of the Presence eaten weekly by the priests in the Temple. If so, the seven baskets would refer to the Herodians, and this would mean that one of the principal rites practised by the Herodians involved seven baskets, and that this was one of the significant differences between the Herodians and the Pharisees.

It seems to me, therefore, that the prominence of the seven baskets in the Temple scroll's account of the ordination ceremony provides a basis for identifying the 'Herodians' as the sectarian Essenes. If this should prove to be the case, it would solve another historical puzzle that has long baffled scroll scholars, namely, why there is no reference in the New Testament to this Dead Sea sect? If I am right, then there *is* such a reference, except that the Essenes are called the 'Herodians'.

As to why they should be so called, the answer is to be found in Josephus. Indeed, even before my decipherment of the Temple scroll, a few scholars offered the hypothesis that 'the Herodians' might refer to the Essenes; but they had no proof. Their proposal was based particularly on a curious story told by Josephus in his *Antiquities* (15:372–379), in which he relates that King Herod showed special kindness to the Essenes, who were, in fact, under his protection. Here is the relevant passage from that work:

It is but fit to set down here the reasons wherefore Herod had these Essenes in such honour, and thought higher of them than their mortal nature required; nor will this account be unsuitable to the nature of this history, as it will shew the opinion men had of these Essenes.

Now there was one of these Essenes, whose name was Manahem, who had this testimony, that he not only conducted his life after an excellent manner, but had the foreknowledge of future events given him by God also. This man once saw Herod when he was a child, and going to school, and saluted him as king of the Jews; but he, thinking that either he did not know him, or that he was in jest, put him in mind that he was but a private man; but Manahem smiled to himself, and clapped him on his backside with his hand, and said, 'However that be, thou wilt be king, and wilt begin thy reign happily, for God finds thee worthy of it; and do thou remember the blows that Manahem hath given thee, as being a signal of the change of thy fortune; and truly this will be the best reasoning for thee, that thou love justice [towards men] and piety towards God, and clemency towards thy citizens; yet do I know how thy whole conduct will be, that thou wilt not be such a one, for thou wilt excel all men in happiness, and obtain an everlasting reputation, but wilt forget piety and righteousness; and these crimes will not be concealed from God at the conclusion of thy life, when thou wilt find that he will be mindful of them and punish thee for them.' Now at that time Herod did not at all attend to what Manahem said, as having no hopes of such advancement; but a little afterward, when he was so fortunate as to be advanced to the dignity of king, and was in the height of his dominion, he sent for Manahem, and asked him how long he should reign. Manahem did not tell him the full length of his reign; wherefore, upon that silence of his he asked him further, whether he should reign ten years or not? He replied, 'Yes, twenty, nay, thirty years'; but did not assign the just determinate limit of his reign. Herod was satisfied with these replies, and gave Manahem his hand, and dismissed him, and from that time he continued to honour all the Essenes. We have thought it proper to relate these facts to our readers, how strange soever they be and to declare what hath happened among us, because many of these Essenes have, by their excellent virtue, been thought worthy of this knowledge of divine revelations.

If my interpretation of the 'seven baskets' ritual in our scroll is correct, it would provide decisive evidence for what up to now could have been no more than a hypothesis, and that the New Testament's 'Herodians' were in fact a derogatory nickname for the Essenes. It would also clear up the obscurity in chapter 8 of Mark.

Furthermore, the Feast of Ordination according to the Temple scroll was to take place about a week before the Festival of Passover. In the New Testament's John 6:4, we read that the miracle of the bread occurred when Passover 'was at hand'.

PART THREE

NEW FIRST FRUITS FESTIVALS

7 A Unique Calendar

The section in the Temple scroll on the Laws of the Festivals is of profound interest both for what it has to say about those prescribed in the Bible and for its revelation of extra-biblical festivals. Of particular importance is the scroll's account of the Pentecost, also known as the Feast of the First Fruits as well as the Feast of Weeks. In this account we learn for the first time of additional first fruits festivals which have no mention in our Bible. That in itself is startling. Of even greater moment is an element that sparked a fascinating exercise in halachic study over a fundamental issue in Judaism – the specific day of the month on which the Pentecost fell. The rabbinical ruling on this date, based on the interpretation of the biblical texts, was challenged by a different interpretation held by certain Jewish sects, among them the Qumran community. Furthermore, this community used a calendar that differed from the one followed in Jerusalem, and what emerges from this section of the scroll is absolute proof that the author followed the Qumran calendar.

What was this special calendar? And why did the issue of the date of the Pentecost arouse such sharp controversy that the Essenes and other sects cut themselves off from normative Judaism?

It will be helpful in our discussion of the controversy over the date if we first consider the calendar.

The calendar of the Essenes

Without exaggerating the radical implications of different calendar-reckonings by religious sects, and without underrating ideological differences, it is clear that so fundamental a deviation from the norm as the adoption of a different calendar drastically affects not only the religious practice of the sect but the whole pattern of living in a society.

As my colleague, Professor Shmaryahu Talmon, who has devoted much study to the Qumran calendar, has written:

No barrier appears to be more substantial and fraught with heavier consequences than differences in calendar calculation. An alteration of any one of the dates that regulate the course of the year will inevitably produce a break-up of communal life, impairing the co-ordination between the behaviour of man and his fellows, and abolishes that synchronization of habits and activities which is the foundation of a properly functioning social order. Whoever celebrates his own Sabbath, and does not observe the Festival of the Year at the same time as the community in which he lives, removes himself from his fellows and ceases to be a member of the social body to which he had hitherto belonged. One may venture to say that the deviation from the calendar accepted by the normative community was, for the Dead Sea sect – as it was for other ... groups such as the Samaritans and the Karaites – a sign and symbol of their disobedience towards the contemporary public leadership of Judaism, and of their dissidence from the body of politics. Their opponents rightly interpreted this act as a proclamation of a civil revolt.

Talmon was writing, of course, before my decipherment of the Temple scroll. This scroll then revealed that the fundamental differences between the Essene sect and the main Jewish community were far greater than had been previously thought. It was not only the calendar that divided the two – and I agree entirely with Talmon's opinion of the profound impact this had on a whole way of life and worship. The division went much further. It is now seen that the Qumran sect had entirely different concepts of the Temple itself, of the sacrifices, the laws of purity, and the religious festivals.

The calendar of normative Judaism was based on the lunar year – a year of 354 days, approximately ten days shorter than the solar year. The gap was rectified in this calendar – a practice which is followed to this day – by the device of the leap year, adding one lunar month roughly once every three years.

The Essene calendar, on the other hand, was based on the solar year. This was known already from certain pseudepigraphic writings, notably the Book of Jubilees and the Book of Enoch, considered by some scholars to have been composed by circles close to the Dead Sea sect, if not by members of the sect itself. Their calendar is clearly defined in Jubilees 6:32:

And command thou the Children of Israel that they observe the year according to this reckoning, three hundred and sixty-four days, and these will constitute a complete year ....

There is a further obvious reference to the 364 days of the solar year in Jubilees 2:9:

And God appointed the sun to be a great sign on the earth for days and for Sabbaths and for months and for feasts and for years ... and for all seasons of the year.

In this calendar, the year was divided into two halves, with the beginning of each six-month period marked by a special 'new year' ceremony, at the start of the first and of the seventh month. Each of these halves was further halved into two three-month periods. The month had thirty days, but one day was added to the last month of each three-monthly period, so that the third, sixth, ninth and twelfth month of the year each had thirty-one days, giving a total for the year of 364 days. This calendar, as we have seen from the passage in the Book of Jubilees, was followed explicitly by the Qumran sect. And there is a clinching reference in another scroll, known as the Damascus Document, which states: 'and the exact account of the periods ... behold, it is accurately defined in the book of the divisions of times into the jubilees and weeks', namely the Book of Jubilees.

Though the Qumran community based their calendar on the sun, they decided arbitrarily, for purposes of symmetry, that the year would comprise 364 days, which meant the loss of one and a quarter days from the true solar year of $365\frac{1}{4}$. (The 365-day year we use today follows the Julian calendar that was introduced in 47 BC, and the deficiency of a quarter of a day is made up in a leap year once every four years.) There is no mention in the scrolls published so far of how the sect made up for the loss of $1\frac{1}{4}$ days in their calendar, but they may have had a system of adding one month every twenty-four years.

Despite its inaccuracy, the symmetrical 364-day Qumran year had one great advantage over the lunar calendar of normative Judaism: while the dates of the religious festivals were fixed by the Bible according to the day in the month and were common to both calendars, in the Qumran calendar the date always fell on the same day of the week (since 364 is divisible by 7). Thus, if the date of a particular festival were a Sunday, it would be celebrated on a Sunday each year, whereas in the lunar calendar if it were a Sunday one year it would be a different day the next year.

The crucial question then arises: on what day of the week did the Qumran year begin? The answer was simple: the first day of the year was a Wednesday, for was this not written explicitly in the opening chapter of Genesis? Verses 14–19 state:

And God said, 'Let there be lights in the firmament of the heavens to separate the day from the night; and let them be for signs and for seasons and for days and years.... And it was so.... And there was evening and there was morning, a fourth day.

Thus, the calendar reckoning was to begin on the 'fourth day' of the week, the day when there were 'lights in the firmament' separating day from night which were to 'be for signs' marking off the 'days and years'.

With the fixing of the first day of the first month of the year as a Wednesday, all the other festivals were automatically given fixed days in the week when their prescribed dates occurred. Thus, for example, the Day of Atonement, its date ordained in the Bible as the tenth day of the seventh month, was to be observed by the Qumran community each year on a Friday.

I have been dealing so far with the calendar used by the Qumran sect. But in deciphering and trying to understand the text of the Temple scroll, it was not enough to assume that the author of the scroll followed the Qumran calendar. I had to determine categorically whether he did, or whether he used the calendar of normative Judaism. Proof that he based himself on the 364-day solar year would offer additional evidence that the Temple scroll was not only part of the library of the Qumran sect, like the scrolls of biblical Books, but was an original work by a member of the sect. And there might also be sufficient proof, as we shall see, that the author may have been the very founder of the sect, the Teacher of Righteousness himself.

8 The Pentecost Controversy

With all the grave implications of different calendars, the prime issue, irrespective of which calendar was followed, was over the day of the month on which the Pentecost was to be celebrated. This was the subject of controversy within Judaism from time immemorial, and became, as we have seen, a source of bitter division between Jewish sects and normative Judaism in the latter part of the Second Temple period (and continues to this day with the Samaritans and the Karaites).

The problem was occasioned by ambiguous dating in the Bible. Indeed, this festival, and the preceding Feast of Waving the Sheaf, are the only ones prescribed in the Pentateuch without the usual dating formula specifying the day and the month. In Leviticus 23, God tells Moses to announce to the people: 'These are the appointed feasts of the Lord ... which you shall proclaim at the time appointed for them.' And the list begins with Passover: 'In the first month, on the fourteenth day of the month in the evening, is the Lord's passover. And on the fifteenth day of the same month is the feast of unleavened bread to the Lord; seven days you shall eat unleavened bread.' (Lev. 23:4–6) Similarly, other feasts are given a specific day and month – except for the Sheaf-waving and Pentecost feasts.

The Leviticus text prescribing these two feasts immediately follows the commands of the Passover ritual and the seven days of unleavened bread: 'When you come into the land which I give you and reap its harvest, you shall bring the sheaf of the first fruits of your harvest to the priest, and he shall wave the sheaf before the Lord ... on the morrow after the sabbath' (23:10, 11). No day, no month, simply 'on the morrow after the sabbath'.

The Pentecost is dated in the same way:

And you shall count from the morrow after the sabbath, from the day that you brought the sheaf of the wave offering; seven full weeks shall they be, counting fifty days to the morrow after the seventh sabbath; then you shall present a cereal offering of new grain to the Lord. (Lev. 23:15, 16)

'Pentecost' is the shortened form of the Greek for 'the fiftieth day'. And 'seven full weeks' is the basis for the Hebrew name of this festival, the 'Feast of Weeks'.

Thus, with no mention of a day or month, the only certainty being the fifty-day link between Pentecost and the Waving of the Sheaf, all depended, for accurate dating, on the interpretation of 'the morrow after the sabbath'. Which sabbath of the month? And what was the meaning of the word 'sabbath' in this context? It was the different answers to these questions that contributed to the basic rifts between the several Jewish sects in antiquity. The rabbis, upon whose decisions rests normative Judaism, held that 'sabbath' in this context meant 'Passover', the day following the evening ritual, namely, the fifteenth of the first month. The 'morrow' would therefore be the sixteenth of the first month, and that should be the date of the Sheaf-waving Feast, with the celebration of the Pentecost fifty days later. The Sadducees, the Samaritans and several additional Jewish sects, on the other hand, gave the Pentateuchal words their plain and literal meaning, with 'sabbath' signifying simply 'the sabbath day', namely, the sabbath after Passover.

The Essenes, and others who followed the Qumran calendar, went one step further. It has been pointed out by scholars that they interpreted 'sabbath' in this context to be the first sabbath after the entire seven-day Festival of Unleavened Bread. Thus, since this festival, beginning on the 15th of the 1st month, always fell on a Wednesday – as their calendar year began on a Wednesday – the date of the first sabbath following the seven days of Passover was the 25th of the 1st month. Accordingly, Sunday the 26th was the date of the Sheaf-waving Feast; and the date of the Pentecost Festival fifty days later, on 'the morrow of the seventh sabbath', was Sunday, the 15th of the 3rd month.

There remains, of course, the question of how they coped with the problem of matching the 'seven full weeks' – forty-nine days – with the qualifying 'counting of fifty days' in the same Leviticus sentence prescribing the time of the Pentecost. We shall deal with this problem when we come to consider how the author of the Temple scroll, while basing himself on the Pentateuch, determined the dating of a host of new first fruits festivals – additional Pentecosts – which are not prescribed in the Bible, and which are the most novel feature of this section of the scroll.

The Waving of the Sheaf

While wheat is specifically mentioned in the Bible in connection with the Pentecost – 'And you shall observe the feast of weeks, the first fruits of wheat harvest' (Exodus 34:22) – there is no biblical passage explicitly linking the day of the Waving of the Sheaf, fifty days earlier, with any particular produce of the field. However, the biblical injunction on the 'waving' ceremony was unanimously interpreted both in theory and practice by all sects of Judaism as referring to the first fruit of barley. And there is no question that this interpretation is also implicit in the Temple scroll. The columns in the scroll dealing with this subject are unfortunately damaged; but enough remained to give me my first surprise, one of the many that were to follow.

The controversy between the Essenes and normative Judaism was thus not over the cereal at the waving ceremony – all agreed it was a sheaf of barley – but over the sect's celebration of the Day of the Waving as a fully-fledged feast of first fruits, on a par with the normative First Fruits Festival, the Pentecost, or Feast of Weeks, celebrated seven weeks later.

That the Temple scroll elevated the ritual ceremony of the waving to a major festival became clear from the text in the undamaged columns concerning the nature of the sacrifices that were to be offered on the day of the waving of the sheaf.

The biblical injunction on the sacrifices for that day (in Leviticus 23:12) states that 'on the day when you wave the sheaf, you shall offer a male lamb a year old without blemish as a burnt offering to the Lord'. A single lamb was a very meagre offering compared to the numerous animals offered at the major feasts, and so the rabbis who set down the laws governing normative Judaism did not give the Waving of the Sheaf the importance of a fully-fledged festival. The author of the Temple scroll, on the other hand, prescribed a scale of sacrifices for the sheaf-waving commensurate with that of a major feast. Since he never introduced any new ritual arbitrarily, but always based himself on his own interpretation of the Pentateuchal text, what was the biblical source for his radical departure from normative Judaism?

Well, there is another passage in the Pentateuch, apart from Leviticus 23, which also enumerates the sacrifices in verses which, as in Leviticus, immediately follow the prescription for Passover and the Feast of Unleavened Bread. It appears in Numbers 28:26–30:

On the day of the first fruits, when you offer a cereal offering of new grain to the Lord at your feast of weeks, you shall have a holy convocation; you shall do no laborious work, but offer a burnt offering, a pleasing odour to the Lord: two young bulls, one ram, seven male lambs a year old; also their cereal offering . . . with one male goat, to make atonement for you.

It will be noted that there is no mention here of the waving of the sheaf, nor is the type of grain specified.

The Mishnah ascribes these injunctions in Numbers on the offerings of bulls, ram, lambs, and goat to the standard, traditional major Feast of First Fruits, namely, the First Fruits of Wheat for the Pentecost, or the Feast of Weeks, one of three biblical pilgrim festivals. The author of the Temple scroll, however, interprets these verses in Numbers as applying also to the Day of the Waving of the Sheaf, regarding it, after all, as being equally a Feast of First Fruits – the 'fruits' here being barley. The scroll text shows that he combined the sacrifices specified in Numbers 28 with the injunctions in Leviticus 23, with appropriate deletions, additions and emendations to underpin his introduction of a new major festival.

It was not the only one.

The first fruits of wheat: mathematical harmony

A novel feature of the scroll's treatment of the traditional Pentecost is the author's harmonization of the biblical 'seven full weeks' with 'fifty days' – the period following the Waving of the Sheaf which gives the date of the Feast of First Fruits. The text on this festival immediately follows the scroll's commands on the Day of the Waving. This was to be expected, for it follows the sequence in which the two are dealt with in the Bible; and the order is also chronological. (Incidentally, the text on this theme appears on the scroll fragments that were retrieved from their hiding-place behind the family photographs in the home of antique dealer X's brother.)

This major festival is given its full importance in the scroll, the author taking pains to make the special point that this Feast of First Fruits of wheat, unlike the one of barley, is, in addition, the Feast of Weeks, the Pentecost. The scroll indeed emphasizes that 'It is the Feast of Weeks, a Feast of First Fruits'. Of particular interest is the fact that this phrase has its precise counterpart in the Book of Jubilees: 'For it is the feast of weeks and the feast of first fruits; this feast is twofold and of a double nature: according to what is written and engraven concerning it, celebrate it' (6:21). This passage is undoubtedly based on Exodus 34:22: 'And you shall observe the feast of weeks, the first fruits of wheat harvest', and on a similar verse in Numbers 28:26.

As to the date of the Pentecost, this of course is determined by the day of the bringing in of the sheaf seven weeks earlier, and the author of the scroll bases himself largely on the injunctions in Leviticus 23:15, 16. But he reconciles the mathematical discrepancy of forty-nine days (seven weeks) with the 'counting fifty days' in the biblical verses with his usual ingenuity, and gives stark clarity to his own prescription by his characteristic skill in modifying and recasting the Leviticus text, and, in one case, deleting a phrase.

For easier comparison between the biblical and scroll texts, it is worth recalling the earlier quoted verses of Leviticus 23:15, 16:

And you shall count from the morrow after the sabbath, from the day that you brought the sheaf of the wave offering; seven full weeks shall they be, counting fifty days to the morrow after the seventh sabbath . . . .

This somewhat cumbersome masoretic or traditional text is transformed in the scroll to the following succinct opening:

And you shall count seven full sabbaths from the day you brought the sheaf of the wave offering; you shall count to the morrow after the seventh sabbath, counting fifty days.

Surprise feasts

After deciphering these verses on the Pentecost and turning my eyes to the next column of the scroll, I was astonished to find myself reading what at first sight appeared to be a repetition of what I had just read. Yet this had to be a new subject, as indicated by the space of a full blank line marking it off from the previous subject. Only after deciphering some forty familiar words did I come across a phrase which revealed that I was reading the details of a new feast of first fruits, hitherto unknown. Here is the opening:

And you shall count from the day that you brought the new cereal offering to the Lord, the bread of new fruits, seven weeks, seven full sabbaths shall they be, counting fifty days to the morrow of the seventh sabbath, and you shall bring *new wine for drink offering*, four hins ['hin' was a measure of volume] from all the tribes of Israel. . . . And they shall offer with the wine that day to the Lord twelve rams . . . .

Then follows a detailed account of the sacrifices to be offered that day.

Here, then, was the scroll's prescription for an additional first fruits feast, a third – the Feast of First Fruits of Wine. It was to be celebrated fifty days after the first wheat (Pentecost), which in turn was celebrated fifty days after the first barley. This gave it a date that coincided with the ripening of the grapes in the Holy Land. An interesting point about the scroll's fifty-day counting pattern is that the wheat festival is counted twice: it is the last day of the fifty days from the barley festival, and the first of the fifty days towards the wine festival.

The scroll accords this wine festival the status of a major feast,

The revelation in the scroll of an
important new festival: the First
Fruits of Wine.

with a commensurate abundance of animal offerings. Following the
sacrifices, there is to be rejoicing:

The priests shall drink first and the Levites second and then all the chiefs of
the standards ... and after them all the people both great and small shall
begin to drink a new wine ... for on this day they shall purify [literally,
atone] the wine and the Children of Israel shall rejoice before the Lord.

This was to be not a one-time event, but, like the other major
feasts, celebrated annually by the people 'throughout the generations', as the scroll puts it, 'in all their dwellings, and they shall
rejoice this day, for they began to pour out strong drink offering, a
new wine on the altar of the Lord year by year'. Later in the scroll
the festival is referred to as the Feast of New Wine.

A Bacchanalia?

It is not to be supposed that the rejoicing on that day as decreed by the author of our scroll or indulged in by the Essenes was to take the form of a Dionysian drunken revelry or a Bacchanalia, common in various parts of the Greek and Roman world at the time in honour of the gods of wine.

The Qumran celebration of the First Fruits of Wine festival was nothing like that, as is shown by the account in our scroll. This account may shed light on other Qumran ceremonies, also involving the eating of bread and drinking of wine, that were known to us hitherto only from another Dead Sea scroll, the Manual of Discipline. The description in the Manual interested scholars because it seemed to contradict what historian Josephus had to say about the customs and manners of the Essenes. One ceremony in the Manual is set forth as follows:

And when the table has been laid for eating, or for the wine for drinking, the priest shall be the first to stretch out his hand to bless the first of the bread or the wine for drink.

And this is what the Manual says about another ceremony:

And when they shall gather for the common table to drink the wine, when the [community] table shall be set for eating and the wine for drinking, let no man extend his hand over the first bread and wine before the priest . . . .

What first intrigued scholars about the details of these rituals was their apparent similarity to the subsequent Agape ceremony of the early Christians – the earliest of whom were contemporaries of the Qumran community in its final decades. If it could be shown that there were ceremonials common to the two communities – even though the purposes might have been poles apart, and the dates different – it would indicate that early Christianity was influenced in some way by Qumran, and that influence might have been even more far-reaching.

However, scholars were troubled by the fact that Josephus, in his account of the Essene ceremonies, excluded wine when describing their meals, and elsewhere in his works he noted that the Essenes were sober at all times.

It seems to me now that the Temple scroll may clear up this difficulty. Josephus may have been describing the day-to-day customs of the Essenes, with their simple sober meals. The Temple scroll was giving the injunctions for the full ritual of the annual first fruits festivals in Temple times. But since they had cut themselves off from the Temple and the religious establishment in Jerusalem, their Manual of Discipline had set out ceremonies to be performed once a year on the first day of the wheat and wine festivals respectively, with the priest being the first to stretch out his hand and bless the first fruits.

Yet another festival

Two columns after I had deciphered the surprising revelation of the new wine festival, and following a blank line which indicated that the scroll was beginning a new subject, I had a further surprise: another first fruits feast:

And you shall count from that day on [i.e. from the First Fruits of Wine] seven weeks seven times, nine and forty days, seven full sabbaths there shall be until the morrow of the seventh sabbath you shall count fifty days. Then you shall offer new oil from the dwellings of the tribes of Israel, half a hin from each tribe, new beaten oil, and they shall offer of this oil the first of the oil on the altar of the burnt offering, first fruits before the Lord.

Thus, the Temple scroll introduces a festival unknown to us – the Feast of First Fruits of Oil, like the new Feast of First Fruits of Wine, and though it is not called that in the opening paragraph, it is given that name in a later column. The main feature of this feast is the offering of the oil on the altar, in addition of course to the numerous animal offerings commensurate with a major feast.

It will be quickly noted that here, as against the texts of the previous first fruits festivals, the formula for the counting of fifty days is presented in more specific detail. What the author has done is combine elements and phrasing of the injunctions on other festivals in Leviticus and Deuteronomy, applied them to this new festival, and produced a unified, clear and unambiguous text.

A Josephus comparison

The scroll prescribes that after the offerings on the altar of the Temple and certain other ceremonies in the Outer Court, the feast is to proceed the following way:

they shall anoint themselves with the new oil and eat the olives, for on that day they shall atone on [purify] all the oil of the land before the Lord, year by year, and they shall rejoice all the children of Israel, in all their dwellings, before the Lord, a statute forever throughout their generations.

Thus this oil feast with its ceremonial offerings to the Lord, symbolizing the 'purification' of all the oil produce of the land for the year, ends with an activity which parallels that outlined at the end of the scroll section on the Feast of First Fruits of Wine. There, they drink the new wine and eat the new grapes; here they rub themselves with oil and eat the olives.

This, then, was the prescription of the scroll for the celebration of the Feast of First Fruits of Oil in the Temple. Since the Qumran community were cut off from the Temple, it is possible that they may have held a substitute ceremony on the appointed day once a year, or perhaps not. At all events, it is evident from the scroll's meticulous rules about the observance of this annual oil feast, like the wine feast, that the Qumran community would have refrained from using the oil unless it had been 'purified' through the prescribed ceremonies.

This, in my opinion, provides the clue to – and the correct explanation for – an odd custom of the Essenes which Josephus witnessed in his day and upon which he comments in his *The Jewish Wars* (2:123). He says there that the Essenes avoided rubbing oil on their bodies because

Oil they considered defiling, and anyone who accidentally comes in contact with it scours his person; for they make a point of keeping a dry skin and of always being dressed in white.

We do not know whether or not Josephus was aware of the true reason for this Essene attitude towards the oil; but even if he were, he may have used this explanation so as to make it more understandable to his non-Jewish readers. However, because of this Josephus passage, a few modern scholars have contended that the Essenes spurned oil on their bodies for aesthetic and hygienic reasons. I can find no substance in this contention. In the light of the Temple scroll, it seems to me that the Josephus report can now be set in its proper context and correctly understood. The Essenes considered the oil impure and 'defiling' because they were unable to observe the first fruits ritual of 'purification', complete with the sacrifice of the new oil on the altar of the Temple, as prescribed for the sect.

The clinching clue

We have now seen that what the author of the Temple scroll did was take all the data in various Books of the Pentateuch relating to the first fruits festival – which normative Judaism interprets as the single major festival for wheat known as the Feast of First Fruits, the Feast of Weeks, or the Pentecost – and created three additional major festivals, for the new barley, wine and oil. This, of course, is the prime importance of this section of the scroll. However, lurking among the details of these new festivals was a clue to another area of significance which could add to our understanding of the scroll, the author and the Essenes. This was whether the calendar used by the author was the same as that followed by the Qumran community.

Based on the scroll's special calendar system, on its formula for reckoning the periods between the four first fruits festivals, and on the fact that they always fell on a Sunday, I reasoned that their dates were as follows:

The Feast of Waving the Sheaf (the First Fruits of Barley) – Sunday, the 26th of the 1st month (Nissan);

The First Fruits of Wheat – Sunday, the 15th of the 3rd month (Sivan);

The First Fruits of Wine – Sunday, the 3rd of the 5th month (Av);

The First Fruits of Oil – Sunday, the 22nd of the 6th month (Elul).

I thought my conclusions were reasonable, but there was no certainty, as the scroll gave no specific dates for these festivals but simply prescribed the measure of the periods between them. I set the problem aside for a while, but there was nothing helpful on this point in the rest of the text. As is usual in scroll research, I went through all the published documents from the Dead Sea caves, hoping for a word, a phrase, some hint that might have a bearing on the problem, either confirming or disproving my assumption; but I drew a blank.

And then I remembered an article that had made mention of a tiny scroll fragment from Qumran Cave 4. Its text had not yet been published, but I recalled a comment on it in the article that prompted me to look it up. The article had been written in 1957 by the noted scroll researcher, the former Abbé J.T. Milik, and it gave a survey of the unpublished documents from Cave 4. What Milik said about the fragment was that it contained a list of the Qumran community's festivals together with their dates, and he quoted a single line from it which stated that 'the feast of oil' fell on the twenty-second day of the sixth month.

Milik of course had not been able to identify the festival at that time, and he had had to content himself with the simple observation that this was no doubt a feast 'of an agricultural character'.

We now know from the Temple scroll that this 'feast of oil' celebrated by the Qumran sect was a first fruits festival, and it was celebrated after the counting of two consecutive seven-week periods starting from the date of the regular Feast of First Fruits according to the Qumran calendar. This confirms the assumptions of scholars who have long wrestled with the problem of the sect's calendar. It also confirms that the calendar used by the author of the Temple scroll was identical with the one followed by the Qumran community, for it is precisely according to the calendar prescribed in the scroll that the new feast of First Fruits of Oil falls on the 22nd of the 6th month.

9 The Enigmatic Alexandrian

Various systems of calendars and feasts were current at various times in the ancient Near East, including Judea. One alone was almost the same as that in the Temple scroll. Its source, however, was obscure, and has long posed a problem for scholars. It was particularly intriguing for me, because if we could discover the date and character of its originator, this might shed unexpected light on certain aspects of the Temple scroll and its author.

Knowledge of this system – together with the designation of its originator simply as 'Judah the Alexandrian' – came to light in a random quotation found in a fragment of a book written at the beginning of the tenth century AD by Sa'adiah Gaon, the greatest biblical and talmudic scholar of his age (882–942), who was head of the renowned Jewish religious academy in Sura, Babylonia. One of the scholarly controversies in which he had engaged was with the Jerusalem Academy on questions relating to the calendar. But he was also concerned with rebutting the practices of breakaway Jewish sects, notably the Karaites. Thus, when he came to write a polemical work against the Karaites, he also referred to the calendar differences, and part of this reference was in the fragment of that book which was discovered in the Genizah – the storage place in a synagogue for disused sacred books – of the ancient Ezra Synagogue of Old Cairo which had been founded in 882. The Genizah archives were retrieved by Solomon Schechter of Cambridge University in the 1890s, and were tendered as a gift to that university by the Jewish community of Cairo. The Sa'adiah Gaon fragment was published in 1904, and it contained the following passage:

As for Judah the Alexandrian, he says that, just as there are fifty days between the first fruits of barley and the first fruits of wheat, so there are fifty days between the first fruits of wheat and the first fruits of wine; and it [the first fruits of wine] falls at the end of the month of Tammuz [the 4th month of the calendar year]; and between the first fruits of wine and the first fruits of oil there are fifty days; the oil offering falls on the twentieth of Elul [the 6th month], and he has a proof for that.

Thus, the number, order, terminology, and the fifty-day periods between the four feasts of first fruits are identical with those in the Temple scroll. Moreover, the last feast is given the very designation by which it is first mentioned in the scroll – 'oil offering'. The only difference between the scroll text and the one attributed to Judah the Alexandrian lies in the dates. The wine feast, as we have seen, falls on the 3rd of the 5th month in the reckoning of the scroll, and at the end of the 4th month in the Sa'adiah Gaon fragment – a difference of a few days. And there is a two-day difference between the scroll date of the oil feast – the 22nd of the 6th month – and that of the fragment, the 20th of the same month. We cannot know whether the dates are from the original text of Judah the Alexandrian, or whether they were intercalated, as they may have been, by Sa'adiah on the basis of data taken from another calendar.

Who was Judah the Alexandrian? It would clearly be of considerable importance to our study of the Temple scroll if we were to discover the identity of the person who could show knowledge of a calendric system and an order of festivals so startlingly similar in so many details to those in the scroll. Who, then, was this writer, and what had been his source?

Fortunately, there is an even more intriguing reference to 'the Alexandrian' in the works of a celebrated scholar in the late ninth century, roughly of the time of Sa'adiah Gaon, who was an outstanding member of the very Karaite sect of which Sa'adiah was so critical. He was Jacob al-Kirkisani, most noted for his *Book of Lights*, which has a chapter on the history of old Jewish sects, and another on the Feast of Weeks (Feast of First Fruits). In the first he mentions a certain sect which he calls 'the Sect of the Cave, because their books were found in a cave'. He notes that this sect was different from other sects in that it followed a separate calendar, and that among its archives were books on biblical exegesis and commentary. These two features are indeed characteristic of the scrolls that came to light in our generation – as is the fact that they, too, 'were found in a cave'. It is generally accepted by modern scholars that Kirkisani was referring to the Essenes, the Qumran sect of the Dead Sea scrolls.

Of key importance for us is what Kirkisani says when commenting on the writings of this sect. He singles out the work of

the Alexandrian, whose book is widely renowned and numbers among the superior writings of the sect of the caves.

These 'writings' were scrolls retrieved from Dead Sea caves in an astonishing discovery made several decades before the time of Kirkisani and Sa'adiah Gaon – in much the same way as the chance find of Dead Sea scrolls by the Bedouin in our own day, the ones who brought them to the antique dealer in Bethlehem in 1947. This we know from a description in the only existing document which makes mention of the discovery. The document is a letter written in the Syriac language by Timotheus I, Christian Patriarch of Seleucia, to Sergius, Christian Metropolitan of Elam, at about the end of the eighth century. (This is the most likely date, as Sergius died in AD 805 and Timotheus in 819.) The letter was first brought to the notice of scholars some fifty years ago by the German Lutheran Bible scholar Professor Otto Eissfeldt, and is here quoted from Professor G.R. Driver's book *The Hebrew Scrolls* (Oxford, 1951).

Timotheus writes:

We have learnt from trustworthy Jews who were then being instructed as catechumens [Christian converts under instruction before baptism] in the Christian religion that *some books were found ten years ago in a rock dwelling near Jericho.* The story was that a dog of an Arab out hunting, while in pursuit of game, went into a cave and did not come out again; its owner went in after it and found a chamber, in which there were many books, in the rock. The hunter went off to Jerusalem and told his story to the Jews, who came out in great numbers and found books of the Old Testament and others in Hebrew script; and since there was a scholar well-read in literature among them, I asked him about many passages which are quoted in our New Testament [as] from the Old Testament but are not found anywhere in it, neither [in copies found] amongst the Jews nor [in those found] amongst Christians. He said that they are there and can be found in the books discovered there. When I heard this from the catechumen and had also interrogated the others without him and heard the same story without variations, I wrote about it to the eminent Gabriel and also to Subhalmaran, Metropolitan of Damascus, [asking them] to search those books and see whether the passage [saying] 'He shall be called a Nazarene ...' and other passages quoted in the New Testament as from the Old Testament but not found in the text which we have could be discovered anywhere in the Prophets. I also asked him if the following words, namely, 'Have pity upon me, God, according to Thy mercy ... sprinkle me with the hyssop of the blood of Thy cross and cleanse me', should be found in those books, without fail translate them for me. This expression does not appear in the Septuagint nor in those other [translations] nor in the Hebrew [text]. But that Hebrew said to me: 'We have found more than two hundred Psalms of David among our books.' I wrote to them about this. I thought nevertheless that these books had been deposited [in the cave] by the prophet Jeremiah or Baruch or by some other of those who had heard the word of God and been moved by it; when indeed the prophet learnt by divine revelation of the conquest, plundering and burning, that was to come upon the people for their sins, they then hid and secreted the scriptures [in holes] in rocks and caves, being firmly convinced that nothing of the word of God falls to the ground, in order that they might not be burnt in the fire nor carried off by plunderers; those, however, who hid them died in the course of seventy years or before that and, when the people returned from Babylon, there was no one left of those who had deposited the books [in the cave].... If these passages occur in the books named, they are clearly more trustworthy than those [in use] amongst the Hebrews and amongst us. I have received, however, no answer to my letter from them on these points, and I have no suitable person whom I can send. This is as fire in my heart, burning and blazing in my bones.

The most significant part of this letter for us, of course, is Timotheus's news that many of these manuscripts reached the Jews of that period, and must have had some bearing on the writings, during the decades that followed in the ninth and early tenth centuries, of such scholars as Jacob al-Kirkisani and Sa'adiah Gaon.

For years some researchers tended to consider that Kirkisani's 'Alexandrian' was none other than the Jewish philosopher Philo Judaeus (*c.* 20 BC to AD 50), commonly known as Philo of Alexandria. If this were true, however, it would mean either that Philo's works figured in the library of the Dead Sea sect, or that writings of the sect had been attributed to Philo in medieval times. At all events, Professor Isidore Levy, an expert on the ancient history of religion, challenged this view and demonstrated convincingly that it has no basis in the known facts about Qumran and about Philo. But if not Philo, who?

It is surely feasible to propose that if, by 'the Alexandrian', Kirkisani was referring to 'Judah the Alexandrian' quoted in Sa'adiah Gaon's book, it would make 'the Alexandrian' a prominent scholar and ideologist of the Qumran community, and one who, in his treatise, had written a text on the feast of first fruits that, as summarized by Sa'adiah in the earlier quoted passage, was almost exactly the same both in language style and in calendric calculation as the text of the Temple scroll. This could be a startling though unlikely coincidence; or it may have been simply a medieval view or interpretation of the original writings.

There is a third possibility, which I offer with great circumspection: that the 'widely renowned' book by 'the Alexandrian', so highly esteemed by Kirkisani as among 'the superior writings' of the Dead Sea sect, may be none other than the Temple scroll itself. And is it then beyond the realm of possibility that, whatever his true name, the man referred to by both medieval scholars Sa'adiah and Kirkisani as 'the Alexandrian' may have been the author of the scroll?

We may conclude this section on the scroll's system of first fruits feasts with an interesting sidelight offered by the rites of the Nestorian Church. This is an Eastern Syriac Church that broke away from the Eastern Christian establishment in the fifth century. The Nestorians celebrate five 'fifty-day festivals: from the seventh Sunday before Easter to Easter; from Easter to Pentecost; from Pentecost to the Feast of the Twelve Apostles; from that feast to the Feast of Summer; and from Summer to the Feast of Elijah. Sunday, the last day of each cycle, is also the first day of the new seven-week period to the next feast.

This was but one of several calendar and festival systems with a pattern and structure similar to those in the Temple scroll, though unlike it in name, number and in the elements they comprise. One, for example, had a festival calendar based on seven fifty-day periods, of which five are known – the first fruits 'of the Land', 'the figs', 'the fuel' [wood], 'the vines', and 'the fresh herbs'.

Thus it is evident that the Temple scroll's fundamental approach to the festivals, particularly those of the first fruits, was not original, and must have been influenced by the long calendric history of the ancient Near East. Nevertheless, the text of the scroll on these feasts remains unique in its details, terminology and purpose. And, as we have seen, the system closest to it is the one mentioned in Sa'adiah Gaon's book and attributed to 'Judah the Alexandrian'.

10 The Feast of Feasts

Towards the end of this section on the first fruits festivals, and immediately following the account of the oil feast, is a long text, covering almost two columns, on yet another new feast. To judge by the rites of its celebration, it was undoubtedly the most important of all. While the others were to be observed for only one day, this was to last six days; and throughout this six-day feast, each of the twelve tribes, two per day, was to bring a burnt offering to the Lord. The scroll lays down the exact order in which they are to appear at the Temple with their offering, and gives precise details of the ritual to be performed.

The author was at great pains to emphasize that the Levites were to be the first with their sacrifice, followed by the tribe of Judah: 'And the high priest shall offer the burnt offering of the Levites first, and after it he shall offer the burnt offering of the tribe of Judah'. The author then gives a detailed account of how the offering is to be made, and returns to stress the priority of the tribe of Levi over Judah by this double repetition: 'And after this burnt offering [of Levi] he shall offer the burnt offering of the tribe of Judah by itself. As he did to the burnt offering of the Levites he shall do to the burnt offering of the sons of Judah after the Levites.'

This insistence on the precedence of Levi over Judah is of considerable significance, for it relegates the king to second place in relation to the priest. The theme of Levite primacy recurs elsewhere in the Temple scroll, and it also appears in other Qumran writings as well as in works of the Apocrypha.

The text continues with the order of sacrifice by the other tribes. On the second day they were Benjamin followed by the sons of Joseph together, Ephraim and Manasseh (who counted as one); on the third day, Reuben and Simeon, in that order; on the fourth, Issachar and Zebulun. 'And on the fifth day', the scroll continues, 'he shall offer the burnt offering of Gad by itself, and the burnt offering of Asher by itself. And on the sixth day he shall offer the burnt offering of Dan by itself.'

At this point in the text the scroll is damaged, but presumably the line went on to name the remaining tribe, Naphtali. And, indeed, in a fragment of a parallel copy preserved in the Rockefeller Museum, there is a similar enumeration of the tribes and their days of sacrifice during this festival. In the line prescribing the sacrifices on the sixth day, after the mention of Dan come the words 'and Naphtali'.

It was with the help of this and another fragmentary Rockefeller Museum copy, as well as several allusions in other parts of our own Temple scroll, and also of biblical and mishnaic references, that I was able to ascertain that this six-day festival was called the Feast of the Wood Offering, and that it followed the Feast of the First Fruits of Oil. We find a reference to this feast, for example, in these lines from another section of the Temple scroll: 'and on the feast of the first fruits of oil and on the six days of . . .', indicating that the celebration of a festival of six days came after the oil feast. Yet another column in our scroll reads as follows (after the restoration of the damaged parts, which appear in square brackets): 'and on the days of the first fruits of the grain, of the wi[ne and of the oil]/[and on the feast of the] wood [offering]', leading us to infer that a festival involving wood is spoken of after the Feasts of First Fruits.

The fragments from the Rockefeller Museum are even more definite about a festival involving wood, and about its occurrence immediately after the oil feast. One, giving the order of sacrifices for the tribes during the six days, ends the passage with the words: 'the wood a burnt offering to'. The second, enumerating the feasts and sacrifices, states:

[. . . and after (?) the fea]st of oil, they shall offer the wood, the twe[lve tribes of the people of Israel . . . two each day; and thos]e who shall offer the first day (are) Levi and [Judah . . .].

The date

The scroll's prescription of this festival poses three principal questions. What could have been the biblical sources which the author interpreted as calling for a festival important enough to be celebrated for six days? What guided him in his order of priorities for the sacrifice of each tribe? And what was the exact day of the month on which the festival was to begin?

As to that day, there is nothing specific in the preserved parts of the scroll – beyond its occurrence immediately after the feast of oil – though it may possibly have appeared in the parts that are missing. However, there is enough data to offer a reasonable deduction. The columns dealing with this festival at considerable length fall between the passages on the oil feast and the one on the Day of Memorial, the modern Rosh Hashanah, or the Festival of the New Year. Since the

date of the oil feast, as we have seen, was Sunday, the 22nd of the
6th month (Elul), and the date of Rosh Hashanah is the 1st of the
7th month (Tishri), it is evident that the wood festival was celebrated
at some time between the 23rd and the 31st of the 6th month. (The
6th month, it will be recalled, was one of the four months in the year
which had thirty-one days.) Where precisely did the six days of this
festival fit in between those two dates?

There are several possibilities. Theoretically, it could have begun
on Thursday, the 26th of Elul; but this is hardly likely, for the festival
would then end on Tuesday, the 31st, with no break between that
day and the Day of Memorial which was celebrated the next day.
Moreover, it would mean the inclusion of a Sabbath, the 28th, as the
third day of the festival sacrifices, and we have enough data for
presuming that the Essenes held there were to be no festival sacrifices
on the Sabbath. This also rules out Wednesday the 25th as the beginning, for if the Sabbath is skipped, the end of the festival would again
merge with the beginning of Rosh Hashanah. There would be no such
obstacle if the feast began on Tuesday the 24th, but I am inclined to
believe it most likely that it began on Monday the 23rd of Elul, and
that this six-day feast of wood offering was joined by the sect to their
feast of the first fruits of oil, thereby creating a holiday that lasted
seven days, like the Festival of the Unleavened Bread (today's Passover) and the Feast of Booths (Succoth). By skipping the Sabbath,
this feast would thus begin on a Sunday and end on a Sunday, like
the other feasts of first fruits.

However, no matter on which day it began, it was assuredly celebrated between the 23rd and the 31st of the 6th month, namely, at
the end of the summer. This was the most appropriate time to collect
and bring dry wood to the Temple and stock its stores with sufficient
quantities for the sacrifices on the festivals in the following winter,
spring and summer.

The sources

The author unquestionably derived his ruling on the wood offering
from Nehemiah, giving his own interpretation of two verses in that
biblical Book to introduce a new major festival, and to determine its
'appointed times'. The first verse reads:

We have likewise cast lots, the priests, the Levites, and the people, for the
wood offering, to bring it into the house of our God, according to our fathers'
houses, at times appointed, year by year.... (Neh. 10:34)

The dependence on Nehemiah is evident not only from the similarity
of the phrasing, but also from the prescription in both texts that the

wood offering is to be brought not only by the priests but also by 'the Levites, and the people'. And Nehemiah's 'according to our fathers' houses' is the counterpart to the scroll's order of the tribes. Furthermore, another verse in Nehemiah shows that there, too, the wood offering is associated with the feasts of first fruits:

and I provided for the wood offering, at appointed times, and for the first fruits. (Neh. 13:31)

The original Hebrew term that is translated into English as 'times appointed' or 'appointed times' was subject to divergent interpretations. Our author clearly understood it to mean fixed times. In so doing, he broke with the interpretation by normative Judaism, at least according to the Mishnah, which held the meaning to be 'at various times throughout the year'.

As to its link with first fruits, it may be said that the wood offering was indeed a celebration of new fruits of sorts, since, according to the scroll, only *new* wood was to be offered and used on the altar. An interesting reason for this appears in the Book of Jubilees:

and do not lay thereon [on the altar] old wood, (for its fragrance is gone), for there is no longer fragrance in it as before. Besides these kinds of wood there is none other that thou shalt place [on the altar], for the fragrance is dispersed and the smell of its fragrance goes not up to heaven. (21:13–14)

Also of interest is a brief passage on the wood offering by Maimonides in his *Code* 'Laws Concerning the Vessels of the Temple':

What was the Wood Offering? There was a set time when certain families would go out to the forests to bring wood for the array [upon the altar]. When the day would arrive for the members of a particular family to bring in the wood, they offered freewill burnt offerings, and this was the wood offering. That day was like a holy day for them, and they were forbidden on that day to mourn, to fast, and to toil. This was a matter of custom. (6:9)

According to Josephus, it appears that at one time there was a single holiday or festival called the Wood Offering, when, he says, 'it was customary for all to bring wood for the altar' (*Jewish War*, 2:425).

However, the detailed instructions in the Mishnah show quite clearly that in normative tradition there was no single festival for the wood offering, let alone a major one like that described in the Temple scroll. Thus, in the Supplement to the Mishnah, Bikkurium (2:9), we read:

The wood offering of the priests and the people was brought nine times [in the year].

The most detailed description in the Mishnah of the way in which the 'appointed times' for this offering were divided among the tribes appears in Tractate Ta'anit (4:5):

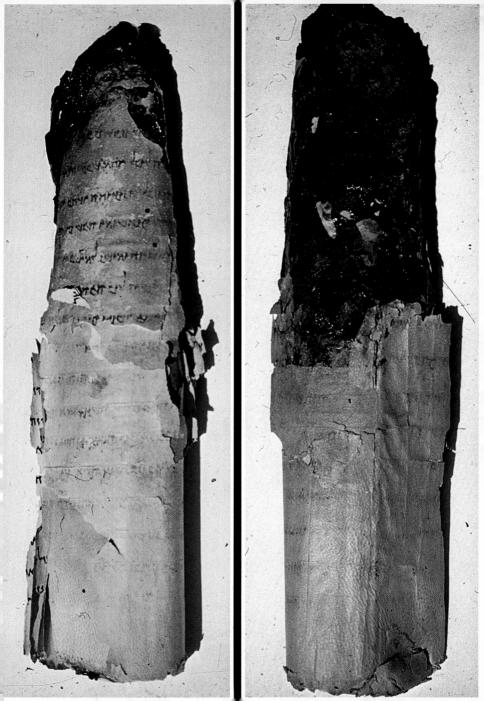

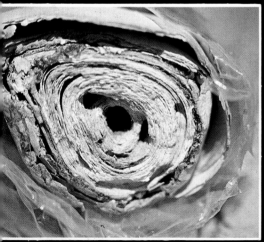

...ps of the numerous 'turns' of the tightly rolled
... a clue to its unusual length. Also discernible are
...d fragments inside the scroll

עשרים שנה ושר כי שלושים שנה עד לחמש לוד
ברו ודשיו שרי אלפים ושרי מאות וש
ושרי עש רות בכול עדהכה ובור לו מדבא
בן בפטו להיות עמו שנט עשר שנה אלף א
אשר לא ישוכוחו לכרו ותמצש בור חא
חבורים אשר ובור וחו אנשי אעתגי
יונש בעע ואבורו חיל למלחמה וש
ועפ ולהלה ישור וחיו שוברים אותו גב
וסו ראו נגפ אושך לא ותגש ומפלה וש
נשו שבי עך ומן חוטוד עם שאטו עשר
שנט עשר שך ערב וודי וויכאש עמו וחו
ולתורי ולויושחיו לכבו פה תוד ולו עע
לכול ע יה חון עהמה ואמה לי
כו תחזורים תאם מבו מבוע אבוש וחח
בעשפחת אבות ה י א וחח עלאש אשד
וראה לכסה ה חוד ח עמו כל ופו חווד ו
לו ורת בבאוה אבורה ופ שגחת מלו לו
ולה ורה שוחור לרסות פשענט ערק
שרוד ורח ולו לחון ובות ובול חמור כ

The Wood Offering of the priests and the people was brought nine times [in the year]: on the 1st of Nissan, by the family of Arah of the tribe of Judah; on the 5th of Av, by the family ... of the tribe of Judah; on the 7th of the selfsame month ...; on the 10th, by ... Senaah of the tribe of Benjamin; on the 15th, by the family of Zattu of the tribe of Judah together with the priests and Levites and *all whose tribal descent was in doubt.*

The last phrase in italics shows that the distribution of the offerings was based on tribal lineage. The Mishnah mentions only three tribes, Levi, Judah and Benjamin, for those were the known tribes living in the Palestine of mishnaic times. The author of the Temple scroll, in line with his general approach, makes these offerings incumbent on *all* the tribes. Thus, the fundamental difference between the two is that, according to the Mishnah, there are to be nine appointed times for the wood offering of 'the priests and the people' which extend over several months, while the author of the scroll groups them all together into six fixed days of festival at the end of the sixth month – which is also the end of summer and the ideal time for collecting wood for the ensuing seasons.

The tribal order

The order in which the tribes were to bring their wood offerings to the Temple, as prescribed in the scroll, may seem odd at first sight to the reader who is more familiar with the Genesis account of the order in which the sons of Jacob were born, Reuben first and Benjamin last.

However, closer inspection reveals a distinct pattern to the scroll's order: the author has clearly grouped the tribes according to the maternal lineage of the twelve sons, giving priority to the sons of Leah and Rachel, Jacob's wives, over the sons of Zilpah and Bilhah, the respective maids of Leah and Rachel. Thus, the author begins with the sons of Leah, with precedence given to Levi and Judah – priesthood and royalty. He then proceeds to the two sons of Rachel, Joseph (through his sons Ephraim and Manasseh) and Benjamin. But the author puts Benjamin ahead of Joseph's sons. The reason, I believe – and in this I agree with certain other scholars – is that the Dead Sea sect, who bore a deep animosity towards the Sadducees and the Pharisees, identified them symbolically with the tribal descendants of Ephraim and Manasseh, the sons of Joseph. This animosity is apparent in other Qumran scrolls, particularly the commentaries. The author completes the daily pairing of the tribes for the wood offering with the remaining sons of Leah – Reuben and Simeon, Issachar and Zebulun; goes on to the sons of Zilpah – Gad and Asher; and ends on the sixth day with the sons of Bilhah – Dan and Naphtali.

The other festivals

This section of the scroll ends with the remaining festivals prescribed in the Pentateuch: the Day of Remembrance, the Day of Atonement and the Feast of Booths (Succoth). These of course are major religious occasions, and the first two are the most important. There are no radical departures in the scroll text from normative Judaism on the way in which these festivals and fast-days are to be solemnized, although they differ in many details.

In the scroll's two and a half columns devoted to the laws and order of activities on the Day of Atonement, the author fashions the main instructions scattered throughout the Pentateuch into a unified whole, as he does with the other festivals, adding or deleting to clarify the basic laws whose apparent lack of clarity led to conflicting interpretations. In so doing, he clashes with the rabbinic decisions on two issues which were considered fundamental at the time. They were the number and nature of the rams to be offered on that day, and the order of the offering. On the main elements of the ritual to be followed, however, there is absolute conformity with traditional normative Judaism, based on the unequivocal injunctions in the Torah.

Similarly with the Feast of Booths, Succoth, also known as the Feast of Tabernacles, there is no basic difference in the scroll from the normative manner of its celebration. Starting on the fifteenth of the seventh month, as prescribed in the Pentateuch, it is to last seven days, followed by a day of 'Solemn Assembly', eight days altogether. The only novelty in the scroll's prescription is that booths were to be erected also in the Temple courts, and the significance of that will be discussed in a later chapter.

Sacrifices on the Sabbath

The final subject to be considered in this section of the scroll dealing with the calendar and the feasts concerned a serious issue at the time in Judaism: should additional sacrifices be offered on a Sabbath day that fell during a festival, over and above those prescribed in the Bible for the Sabbath?

The preserved columns of the Temple scroll make no mention of this. However, in the Damascus Document, one of the important scrolls laying down the decisions of the Dead Sea sect, and closely related to both the Manual of Discipline and our Temple scroll, we read: 'No man on the Sabbath shall offer anything on the altar except Sabbath Burnt Offerings; for it is written thus, "except your Sabbath Offerings".'

It seems that the sectarians interpreted the biblical injunctions as precluding other than the daily offerings and the Sabbath sacrifices on the Sabbath. And, according to their calendar, this applied not only to the biblical Feast of Booths and Passover, but to their own Feast of the Wood Offering as well, which must also have included a Sabbath day.

Further support for this comes from the earlier mentioned book of Jacob al-Kirkisani. Describing another Jewish sect which he called the 'Zadokites' – very similar to, if not the same as, our own sect – he observed that they excluded the Sabbath from the seven days of the Feast of Unleavened Bread and the Feast of Booths.

It is a reasonable assumption that this was also the view of the author of our scroll.

PART FOUR

CONCEPT OF THE TEMPLE

11 Now or Hereafter?

The most fascinating part of the scroll is perhaps the section devoted to the design and construction of the Temple, its rituals and procedures, and the sundry ordinances to safeguard the purity of the structure, the compound, and even the entire city in which it stood. This section takes up almost half the document, and because of its length and importance I have called the entire composition the Temple scroll. The true name, given it by the author and with which the sectarians must have been familiar, is not known, though there are several intriguing possibilities.

Of immediate interest to us, however, before exploring the intricate byways of the author's composition, are the answers to two fundamental questions. What kind of Temple was he talking about, prescribing such elaborately detailed ordinances? And on what biblical sources did he draw, sources that could justify his putting into the mouth of God, speaking in the first person singular both as master-architect and law-giver, a revolutionary 'Torah' on the Temple?

Here and now, or eschatological?

As to the first question, was the Temple of the scroll conceived as the real, earthly Temple recorded in the Bible as the House of God that the Children of Israel were to construct when they reached the Promised Land? Or was it the plan for an eschatological Temple, the Temple for the 'End of Days' when the world of iniquity would cease to exist and be created anew as a world of righteousness and goodness, rather like the Temple in the vision of Ezekiel? Or could it be, perhaps, that the scroll reflected the author's conception of a heavenly Temple? So basic a question might well have become the subject of interminable controversy among scholars. Fortunately, the answer

Despite damage to this portion of the scroll, enough text is preserved to provide the crucial information that the Temple discussed in the scroll is to be built by man, as opposed to the Temple in the 'New Creation' at the 'End of Days' that is to be made by God himself.

was to be found in the scroll itself, as I discovered from the circumstantial evidence, and later, on closer study of the text, directly, from the phrasing of certain commands.

The ordinances are conveyed by God to Moses exactly as are the laws of the Tabernacle in the Book of Exodus, where God tells Moses to command the Children of Israel to 'make me a sanctuary, that I may dwell in their midst. According to all that I show you concerning the pattern of the tabernacle, and all of its furniture, so you shall make it' (Exodus 25:8, 9).

Moreover, as though to dispel any doubt, the author has a crucial transitional sentence (Col. 29:8-10) in which God, still speaking in the first person, makes the meaning explicit. These words appear in the scroll at the end of the ordinances on the festivals and before this section on the Temple plan. This part of the document, incidentally, was very difficult to decipher, as three columns were stuck together, and it was impossible at first to determine which lines belonged to which column. Only after careful treatment and separation were we able to read the text in the order in which it had been written. In the crucial sentence, God says:

And I will consecrate my Temple by my glory, [the Temple] on which I will settle my glory, until the day of the blessing [or, the day of creation] on which I will create my Temple and establish it for myself for all times, according to the covenant which I have made with Jacob at Bethel.

Here, then, is the answer. The author was definitely writing about the earthly man-made Temple that God commanded the Israelites to construct in the Promised Land. It was on this structure that God would settle his glory until the day of the new creation when God himself would 'create my Temple . . . for all times' in accordance with his covenant 'with Jacob at Bethel'.

Our author believed in the heavenly Temple, as well as in the future Temple that God would eventually bring into being. In the scroll, however, he is concerned with God's law on the Temple, which refers to the earthly Temple of the present, the only one of the three that was to be man-made.

The idea of a Temple made not by man but by God at the End of Days was common among several Jewish sects at the time. The Book of Jubilees, for example, has a passage in which God says: 'And after this they will turn to me from amongst the Gentiles ... *and I will build my sanctuary in their midst, and I will dwell with them....*' Another passage in Jubilees elaborates on this Temple that God himself will build:

And he said to the angel of the presence: 'Write for Moses from the beginning of creation till my sanctuary has been built among them for all eternity....' And the angel ... took the tables of the division of the years from the time of the creation of the law ... *until the sanctuary of the Lord shall be made in Jerusalem* on Mount Zion, and all the luminaries be *renewed* for healing and for peace and for blessing for all the elect of Israel.

A more explicit expression of the divine Temple idea of those times appears in the pseudepigraphal Book of Enoch, that has certain affinities with the Dead Sea scrolls and Jubilees. In it, Enoch speaks of the ultimate replacement of the 'old House' – the man-made Temple – by the God-made Temple, a 'new house greater and loftier than the first', which would be set 'up in place of the first'.

The brief reference to an eschatological Temple in our scroll contains the puzzling mention of 'the covenant which I have made with Jacob at Bethel' – God's promise to build a Temple with his own hands at the End of Days. There is no such direct mention in the biblical narrative of Jacob at Bethel. From where, then, did our author pluck this notion?

Certain texts from other writings of the period can help clear up this problem, just as our scroll can illuminate obscurities in other books. It is evident from such writings, particularly from the Book of Jubilees and the pseudepigraphal Testament of Levi, and indeed from the source itself, the Book of Genesis, that Bethel played an extremely important part in the whole cycle of stories concerning Jacob and his dream. This was climaxed by Jacob's ladder reaching to heaven, with angels going up and down. 'And behold, the Lord stood above it' (Gen. 28:13). According to the Testament of Levi, which enlarges upon the Genesis narrative, it was at Bethel that the Lord revealed to Jacob and to Levi that Levi would be Priest in the Temple of the Lord God.

The Book of Jubilees holds that Jacob arrived in Bethel on the first day of the first month, and that day is linked with the building of the Tabernacle, providing, perhaps, a link with the Temple. Jubilees also tells us that God warned Jacob not to build the House of the Lord at Bethel: 'And he said unto him, "Do not build this place, and do not make it an eternal sanctuary"' (ch. 32). Despite this statement, the same book records earlier that 'the House of God ... the Gate of Heaven' (ch. 27) was revealed to Jacob at Bethel.

Curiously enough, though there is a great deal in these two books on the eschatological Temple as well as on Jacob and Bethel, whereas these subjects receive scant treatment in our Temple scroll, our scroll alone, and neither of the other two, contains the forthright statement that the creation of the future Temple would be the fulfilment of the Lord's pledge in his covenant with Jacob at Bethel.

The source

We now return from the End of Days to the 'earthly' reality of the second fundamental question concerning the author's sources for his new 'Torah' of a Temple. What prompted him to write such a 'Torah' in the first place? And what biblical text could he have used as his authority?

Strange though it be, the fact is that although one of the principal obligations of the Children of Israel was to build the Temple once they were established in the Holy Land, there is no Torah, no divine law recorded in the Bible, governing the plan for its construction. Already in ancient times Jews were perplexed by the absence of such biblical directions. True, there are descriptions of the Temple of Solomon. But there is no divine law presented by God to Moses as to how the Temple was to be built, as there is on how the Tabernacle was to be fashioned.

What deepened the mystery were certain verses in chapter 28 of 1 Chronicles. Verses 2 and 3 set the stage:

Then King David rose to his feet and said: 'Hear me, my brethren and my people. I had it in my heart to build a house of rest for the ark of the covenant of the Lord, and for the footstool of our God; and I made preparations for building. But God said to me, "You may not build a house for my name, for you are a warrior and have shed blood."'

David then announces that his son Solomon has been chosen both to succeed him on the throne and to build the Temple. And now comes the following surprising news – surprising in the absence of any pre-scriptive ordinances on the construction of the Temple:

Then David gave Solomon his son the plan of the vestibule of the temple, and of its houses, its treasuries, its upper rooms, and its inner chambers, and of the room for the mercy seat; and the plan of all that he had in mind for the courts of the house of the Lord, all the surrounding chambers, the treasuries of the house of God, and the treasuries for dedicated gifts; for the divisions of the priests and of the Levites, and all the work of the service in the house of the Lord; for all the vessels for the service in the house of the Lord, the weight of gold for all golden vessels for each service, the weight of silver vessels for each service, the weight of the golden lampstands and their lamps. . . .

And the list continues with details of the remaining appurtenances of the Temple, from bowls and cups and basins to the altar and the golden chariot of the cherubim, ending with the crucial sentence:

All this he made clear by the writing from the hand of the Lord concerning it, all the work to be done according to the plan. (1 Chr. 28: 11–19)

So there *had* been a plan, and there *had* been a law written by 'the hand of the Lord', a Torah prescribing all the details of the construction and furnishing of the Temple 'according to the plan'. But where was this plan, this law, this Torah? Beyond this mention in Chronicles, there is nothing of it anywhere else in the Bible.

The sages of old had long pondered the conundrum of there being no law on the Temple in the Bible, yet there was the biblical affirmation that such a law, and a plan, in writing, had been handed by David to Solomon. There was a tradition, which they record, that a Temple scroll had indeed been given to David. In Midrash Samuel, for example, we read the following:

The Temple scroll which the Holy One, Blessed be he, committed to Moses while standing . . . Moses stood and transmitted it to Joshua while standing . . . and Joshua to the Elders, and the Elders to the Prophets, and the Prophets to David, and David to Solomon.

(The stress on 'while standing' was to emphasize the solemnity of the occasion.)

It is of no mean interest that this Midrash speaks specifically of 'the Temple scroll', originally given by the Lord to Moses and handed down from one generation to the next until it reached David and Solomon.

Another passage from a rabbinical source is worth quoting. It is taken from a work called Agadat Bereshit – the Legend of Genesis:

And David said before him: Master of the Universe, make me arise for the sake of the temple scroll that Samuel the Prophet transmitted to me; I pray you: Make it possible for me . . . that I may rise from this bed and transmit to them the scroll for building the temple.

Not for a moment, of course, do I seek to hint that our Temple scroll, the scroll I handled and deciphered, is the scroll, or a copy thereof, that Samuel gave to David, and David to Solomon. Nor is it at all likely that our scroll is the one to which the rabbis were referring. Indeed, if they had seen it at all, it would have been anathema to them, for all its prescriptions contradict in their severity those of normative Judaism.

However, I am convinced that it was the very passage in chapter 28 of 1 Chronicles that prompted our author to write his Temple scroll. Believing, no doubt, that he was divinely inspired, and basing himself on an older tradition, he had produced this missing Torah of the Temple – or, as he may have believed, this 'hidden' Torah. What is noteworthy is that the author gave special emphasis to the very items detailed in Chronicles – the vestibule, the courts, the chambers, their division among the priests and Levites, and the rest.

Whatever the origin and the prompting, the fact remains that we have here in the scroll an extraordinary Temple Torah in which God the law-giver speaks as a master-architect, providing precise instructions on the design of each unit and article.

12 The Inner Court

The author of the scroll dealt somewhat briefly with the main Temple structure, but dwelt at length on the Temple courts, prescribing for them laws and plans in great detail. This may have been due to the paucity of the material in the sources he used relating to the Temple proper, the House. But I think a more important reason is that it was in the Temple courts that the main worship was held, there that the ritual sacrifices were offered, and only there that the populace was allowed to gather. Indeed, because of their central role, the courts, with their chambers and installations, and the activities for which they were designed, form the main subject of our narrative on the Temple scroll, and they reflect the scroll's most novel and revolutionary features – as well as the prime objective of the author.

What comes first?

However, what the scroll has to say about the Temple and its furnishings – and how it says it – is not without interest. The odd feature of the sequence in which the commands are given is that certain prescriptions on the furnishings are interpolated in the overall prescriptions on the structure, and are then resumed in greater detail upon completion of the text on the structure. First comes the specific command to build a House and its furnishings, followed by instructions on the materials to be used for both. Then come brief orders on the manner in which the Temple is to be built, together with its dimensions. Following this are the itemized commands on the Temple vessels and furnishings.

It is clear that the author well knew the obvious answer to the question of what comes first, a building or its contents. Why, then, would he not have adopted the logical course – and his own general practice – of dealing wholly with the structure, and gone on to do the same with the furnishings? Why did he find it necessary to give a few commands on the structure, then a few on the furnishings, then back to complete the text on the structure, and follow it with the main text on the furnishings?

The explanation for this strange procedure no doubt lies in the general editorial method of the author. One of his purposes, as we have noted, was to unify duplicate commands and reconcile seemingly contradictory ones in those parts of the Bible which served as the basis for his own prescriptions. In the particular case of his commands for the Temple building, I believe he used as his biblical model, both for content and style (including God's speaking directly to Moses), the chapters in Exodus which deal with the Tabernacle. He must therefore have been aware of the difference between the sequence of the commands that are given in chapters 25–27, and the sequence in which the commands were executed as recorded in chapters 36–38. The commands deal first, in chapter 25, with the ark and vessels and furnishing of the Tabernacle, and only in the next chapter comes the command to 'make the tabernacle'. In the subsequent record of how the work was accomplished, chapter 36 begins with an account of how they 'made the tabernacle', and only thereafter is there a description of how the furnishings were crafted.

The rabbis sought to resolve this contradiction by homiletics, and there is a charming treatment in the Babylonian Talmud in the form of a dialogue between Moses and the artist Bezalel, who designed the Tabernacle:

Bezalel was called on account of his wisdom. At the time when the Holy One, blessed be he, said to Moses: Go and tell Bezalel to make me a tabernacle, an ark and vessels, Moses went and *reversed* the order, saying, Make an ark and vessels and a tabernacle. Bezalel said to him: Moses, our teacher, as a rule a man first builds a house and then brings vessels into it; but you say, Make me an ark and vessels and a tabernacle. Where shall I put the vessels that I am to make? Can it be that the Holy One, blessed be he, said to you, Make a tabernacle, an ark and vessels? Moses replied: Perhaps you were in the shadow of God, and knew! (BT Berakhoth 55a)

(Bezalel, with a slight difference in one vowel, is Hebrew for 'in the shadow of God'.)

Unlike the rabbis, who went in for exegesis and homiletics and would hardly tamper with a biblical text, our author resorted to editorial devices to resolve a textual difficulty. In this case, I believe he combined the Exodus chapters, with appropriate deletions, into a unified whole. It was clear to him that the edifice had to be built first, and so he started his commands with the main Temple building, using the sequence as in Exodus 36–38, but broke off to insert certain prescriptions for the furnishing as in the sequence in Exodus 25–27. Returning to complete the text on the structure, he followed it with the rest of the commands on the furnishings by drawing very fully on the details, but not the sequence, of Exodus 25–27. He ended with the Temple courts, in the order in which they are dealt with in both sources of Exodus. A neat solution, if I have understood his reasoning correctly.

Of what little remained from the passages on the ordinances for the construction of the building, there was enough to reveal that the main elements were the vestibule, the measurements of the structure, the exterior and some details on the interior, particularly the Holy of Holies. These will be discussed later when we consider the sources on which the author had drawn, sources in the Bible, and others which describe the Temple of Solomon (built in the tenth century BC), the Second Temple (built in the sixth century BC), the Herodian renovation (first century BC), as well as the vision of the future Temple in Ezekiel. We need only mention at this stage that from the measurements in the scroll it is evident that our author relied mainly on the account of Solomon's Temple in 1 Kings 6, and on some of the data on the Second Temple given in the Book of Ezra. He did not resort, as does the Mishnah, to the measurements recorded in the Book of Ezekiel which describes the eschatological Temple, the future Temple for the End of Days.

The inner court

The most interesting of the innovations in the Temple scroll is the plan of the Temple courts. There were to be three square concentric courts, the inner, the middle and the outer court, and the system of ordinances adopted by the author is to proceed from the centre and move outwards. Thus, the prescriptions begin with the Temple structure, the House itself, and the various small structures adjoining it used for various cultic purposes, all within the inner court, and continue with details of the wall, gates and dimensions of that court. Then come the commands for the middle court. This is then followed by the outer court, arrangements for purity round this court, the purity of the city of the Temple, and finally the purity of the other cities in the land.

It is the installations in the inner court and the activities therein which are of principal interest, but their layout may best be followed if we first present the dimensions and structure of that court. This was the holiest of all three courts surrounding the Temple building, for that building was sited within its confines. Unfortunately, while the scroll columns on the installations are relatively well preserved, the text on the gates and walls was fragmentary. However, from what remained, and with the aid of the author's method in describing the other two courts, it was possible to reconstruct its main features.

Jigsaw puzzle

This reconstruction was rather like tackling a jigsaw puzzle – with missing pieces! Finding the pieces required a certain amount of detective work, and only then could one try to fit each of them into its proper place.

I came across three hints of a clue during my early examination of this fragmented text. One was a line which read: 'And from the corner of the gate to the second angle of the court twenty and one hundred cubits.'

(The author used the term 'corner' to denote the outer corner, namely the meeting of the exterior faces of two thick walls. 'Angle' was his term for the inside corner formed by the meeting of the interior faces. The cubit, as we have seen earlier, is believed to be roughly $1\frac{1}{2}$ feet.)

The second hint of a clue was a broken line which could be reconstructed as: 'From the angle [. . . to the corn]er of the gate [twenty and one hundred cubits].'

The third was an explicit reference in the better preserved portion of this section of the scroll to 'the west gate'. This implied that there was only one gate in the western wall of the square inner court.

It was possible to deduce from the measurements and phrasing of the first two quotations that this west gate was located in the centre of the wall: one gave the distance from one angle of the court to one corner of the gate, and the other from the second corner of the gate to the second angle of the court; and each was 120 cubits. Put more simply, and excluding for the moment the width of the gate, one could imagine a wall 240 cubits long, 120 cubits from one end to one side of the gate, and 120 cubits from the other side of the gate to the other end of the wall. It was very evident that the author had gone out of his way to emphasize the measurement of 120 cubits, specifying that this was arrived at by taking it from the inside (angle) and not the outside corner of the court.

Since I could make little more of this damaged text, I went on to decipher the parts that dealt with the middle and outer courts. There I found the clear prescription for both those courts that each of the four walls were to have three gates, twelve in all. If, unlike them, the inner court had only one gate in the west wall ('the west gate'), it seemed logical that each of the three other walls would also have only one gate. I also noticed that the dimensions of the walls of those two courts were taken from their 'corners', while those of the inner court, as we have seen, were taken from their 'angles' so as to produce the measurement from angle to gate of 120 cubits. That figure must therefore have been important to the author, possibly because of its relationship to the multiple 360, the days of the Dead Sea sect's calendar year (excluding the three-monthly additional day).

From a fragmentary line, it appears that the exterior width of the gates was 40 cubits. These gates, it must be remembered, were not the simple entrances with which we are familiar today but really gate-houses, formidable structures of stone, with walls of immense thickness containing chambers on either side of the passage-way. If, as we have reason to believe, the thickness of the walls was 7 cubits, the entrance-way and its flanking chambers would be 26 cubits.

We can now calculate from this data that the external length of each wall of the inner court was 294 cubits: 2 × 120 (angle of court to nearest gate wall) + 40 (overall width of gate-house) + 2 × 7 (thickness of two court-walls) = 294. Deducting the thickness of the walls therefore gave the interior face of each wall a length of 280 cubits. Without the width of the gate it would be 240 cubits, and I do not think it circumstantial that this figure is half the 480-cubit length of a wall of the middle court, as recorded later in the scroll. This may provide an additional explanation for the author's measurement of the inner court's walls from the angles and not the outer corners, because only their interior sides were properly considered part of the inner court, the court of extreme holiness and purity. Their exterior sides were in fact the interior sides of the walls of the middle court, and rightly belonged to that court.

Thus, with the retrieval of the 'pieces', we can complete the jigsaw puzzle of this fragmented opening section of the scroll's prescriptions on the inner court. It appears to be a square, 280 × 280 cubits, with a gate in each of its walls, and the main Temple building standing within it.

There are descriptions of the Temple of Solomon, the visionary temple of Ezekiel and the Second Temple in certain ancient sources, which record the existence of an inner court. But some offer no details of its plan, while others describe a court that is different from the one in the Temple scroll.

However, there is an intriguing account of Solomon's Temple by Josephus, in which he writes that built around the Temple was a sacred quadrangular precinct that had wide covered colonnades (stoas), and these were entered 'by high gates, each of which faced one of the four quarters and was closed by golden doors' (*Antiquities*

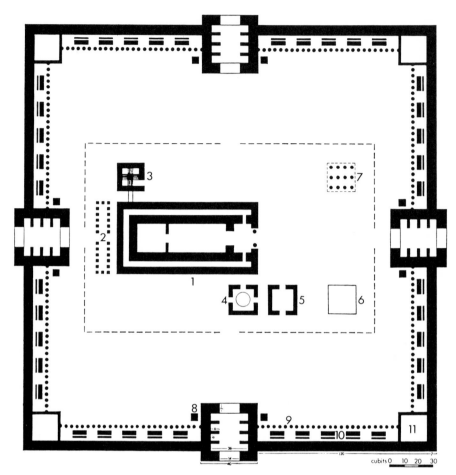

The plan of the inner court drawn to scale, the measurement figures representing
cubits, according to the injunctions in the Temple scroll: (1) the Temple; (2) the
Stoa of Columns; (3) the Stairhouse; (4) the House of the Laver; (5) the House of
Utensils; (6) the Altar; (7) the slaughter-place (the 'Ceiling over the Twelve
Pillars'); (8) the 'cooking places'; (9) the inner court Stoa; (10) the sitting places
and tables; (11) the 'places for the stoves'.

8:96). This is almost identical with the description in our scroll.
Josephus, of course, was writing more than a thousand years after
its construction and some six centuries after it was destroyed. But
he may well have based himself on written documents describing
the Solomonic Temple, and this will be the subject of closer examination in a later chapter.

Incidentally, the Mishnah, in its rabbinical discussions on the
Temple, never uses the term 'inner court'. It does, however, describe
a structure very similar to the Temple scroll's inner court – a quadrangle with four gates – though it calls this the 'Women's Court'; it
was the outermost court, and the only one that women were allowed
to enter. And the overall plan of the Herodian Temple, which was the

one the rabbis were talking about, was entirely different from the plan in the scroll. The Herodian courts adjoined one another. In the scroll, the courts are concentric.

13 The 'Houses'

We can now proceed with the better preserved columns of writing that deal with the installations within the inner court. These are, among others, the Altar, the House of the Laver, the House of Utensils, the Stairhouse and the Stoa, for all of which there are detailed prescriptions. In deciphering this scroll, even when working on the commands set forth about such mundane installations as the Temple kitchens, one had always to be alert to the possibility that among the prescriptions lay buried a clue to items not recorded elsewhere in the text.

I came across such a clue in a passage dealing with the cooking and dining arrangements within the inner court. It was a phrase giving a certain location as being 'in the inner stoa by the outer wall of the court' (Col. 37:9). If there was an 'outer wall', this court must also have had an inner wall. From certain references in the scroll, which would have remained vague, as well as from other sources, it seems reasonably certain that this inner wall, probably not as high or as thick as the walls of the court itself, enclosed the main Temple building and its immediately adjacent structures. There is a hint of this in an earlier column (35:8, 9): 'And you shall sanctify the surroundings of the altar and the Temple and the laver and the stoa, and it shall be holy of holies for ever and ever.'

This wall apparently was to serve as a further protective barrier against unauthorized entrants to the holiest core of the Temple complex. This may also be deduced from a passage in Josephus (*Antiquities* 13:373) in which he writes about Alexander Jannaeus, the Hasmonean king who ruled at the beginning of the first century BC. Jannaeus, he says, built 'a wooden barrier around the altar and the Temple as far as the coping, which the priests alone were permitted to enter'. Such a barrier was there also in the Temple as reconstructed by Herod towards the end of that century, for in describing that one Josephus writes (in his *War* 5:226): 'Surrounding both the sanctuary and the altar was a low stone parapet, fair and graceful, about a cubit high, which separated the laity outside from the priests.'

The 'stoa' referred to in the quotation above from the scroll's Column 35 shows that there was a roofed colonnaded area within the inner wall. (I determined later that it lay to the immediate west of the Temple building.) From a subsequent badly damaged passage in the scroll I was able to glean that there was a more extensive stoa, outside the sacred enclosure but inside the inner court, which was a colonnaded porch in front of all four walls of the court itself. It was when the author was prescribing the table and seating arrangements for the priests in the inner court that he wrote the sentence, quoted earlier, which held the clue to an inner wall.

Three more fragmentary passages enable us to complete the puzzle posed by the poorly preserved parts of this section of the scroll. They deal with subjects which may appear trivial but which were highly important to the Temple ritual – the places for the cooking appurtenances and the priestly seating. Column 37 in our scroll gives the location of the 'cooking places near [entrances? or corners? of the] gates, on both [sides of] the gate'. We may take it, therefore, that there were 'cooking places' or kitchens for various purposes at both sides of each of the four gates of the inner court.

The immediate lines that follow in the same Column 37 mention 'sitting places for the priests, and tables in front of the sitting places in the inner stoa'. These tables were designed for the priestly offerings, the first fruits and the tithes, so that 'there shall be no mixing of the sacrifices of the peace offerings of the children of Israel with the sacrifices of the priests'.

The House of the Winding Stair

We are on firmer ground in dealing with the structures of the inner court, as this section of the scroll is relatively well preserved. The text is intriguing because it has no parallel in any of the sources.

The structures, to be grouped round the main Temple building, comprise the Stairhouse, the House of the Laver, the House of Utensils, the contrivances for slaughtering the sacrificial animals, and a group of columns, the Stoa, to the immediate west of the sacred House.

The opening command calls for 'a house for the stairs in the House which you shall build'. Later in the text this stairhouse is specifically designated the House of the Winding Stair.

The scroll first gives its location as 'north of the Hekhal' – the Temple building, or the House – follows with its description and measurements, and ends with the more precise siting: 'on its north-west side'. Another verse records that 'its distance from the wall of the Hekhal seven cubits'. This unremarkable fact was to enable us more accurately to conceive the overall plan of this Temple court.

The architectural function of this structure was to offer access to the roof of the main Temple building 7 cubits ($10\frac{1}{2}$ feet) away. There was probably a bridge from the upper part of the stairhouse to the

Temple roof, though there is no description of this in the preserved parts of the scroll; and the text on the upper chamber of the stair building is largely missing. Enough, however, can be salvaged to support the assumption that there was indeed a bridge:

And in the upper chamber of this house [stairhouse] you shall make a gate, opening unto the roof of the Hekhal [the Temple building], and a way made through the gate on to the entrance to the roof of the Hekhal, through which one may enter unto the upper chamber of the Hekhal.

Thus, the 'way', or bridge, would span the seven cubits, and run from the upper chamber of the stairhouse to the upper chamber of the Temple building.

The plan of this structure is different from the one in the Mishnah, which was largely a description of the Herodian Temple. Nevertheless, there are certain similarities in terminology and function. Thus, the winding stairhouse in the Mishnah is also called *mesibah*. Its location is also much the same as that in the scroll: 'And a *mesibah* went up from the north-eastern corner to the north-western corner' (Tractate Middoth 4:5). But the architectural design is different.

The scroll prescribes that the stairhouse is to be 'a square house, from one corner to another twenty cubits, according to its four corners'. To leave no doubt that these are the exterior dimensions, and that his 'corners' are outer corners, he gives the thickness of the walls – 'the width of its wall four cubits' – so that its interior dimensions would be 12 × 12 cubits. To make doubly sure, he confirms this: 'its inside from angle to angle twelve cubits'. The stairs wind round a square column inside this square building: 'and in its midst, in the centre, shall be a square column, its width four cubits on all its sides'. Thus, the space this would leave for the stairs would also be four cubits wide.

From the mention in a fragmented part of the text of 'and its gates', it is evident that there was more than one. And the description that follows (on the function of the stairhouse) says that access to the roof of the Temple building shall be through a gate to be built in a wall of the upper chamber of the stairhouse. The stairhouse, therefore, no doubt also had an entry gate at the bottom. And it is reasonable to assume, since the stairhouse lay on the north-western side of the Temple building, that this top gate was in the southern wall of the upper chamber. The bottom gate was either in the northern or more probably in the eastern wall of the stairhouse.

The scroll contains the injunction to 'overlay with gold all this stairhouse, its walls and its gates and its roof inside and outside, its columns and its stairs'. Because of its proximity to the Temple's Holy of Holies, and also by reason of its function, this building, like the other structures adjacent to the Temple, was to have this special ornamentation of gold plate (see colour reconstruction on page 144).

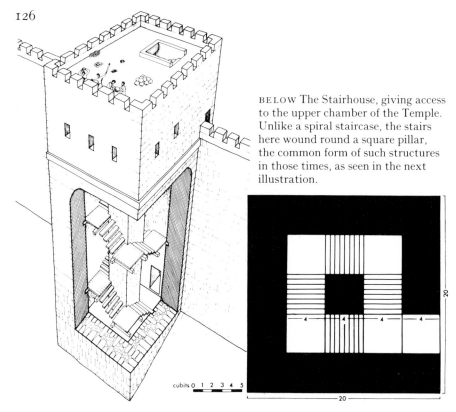

BELOW The Stairhouse, giving access to the upper chamber of the Temple. Unlike a spiral staircase, the stairs here wound round a square pillar, the common form of such structures in those times, as seen in the next illustration.

ABOVE A reconstructed stairhouse in the Hellenestic (3rd–2nd century BC) city wall discovered at the recent archaeological excavation of the city of Dor in Israel, just north of Caesarea (© L. Ritmeyer).

As for its ritual function, this was apparently recorded on a fragment that is badly mutilated. But from the few decipherable words, two are definitely 'deputy priest' and two others seem to be 'high priest'. The reference may be to a certain ritual function of the priests to inspect the upper structure of the Temple, which would be reached through the top gate of the stairhouse. But I cannot be certain of this.

Exactly the same plan of this stairhouse is given for a winding stairway in the scroll's description of the three-storeyed covered colonnades (stoas) of the outer court: 'And you shall make a stairhouse by the walls of the gates, inside the stoas, in which spiral stairs shall go up to the second and the third storey.'

From archaeological evidence we know that this type of stairhouse was common at least from the time of Solomon. A similar one was found in a palatial Solomonic building at Megiddo – a square stairhouse with stairs spiralling round a square column from one storey to another. Such staircases were also discovered at Dor from the fourth–third century BC period; in Masada, leading from one to another of the three terraces of the hanging palace-villa; and at a number of Nabatean and other buildings in the Dead Sea area, the Negev and elsewhere. Thus, the concept was no fantasy of the author's, nor was it new. What was different from the Herodian Temple, as described in the Mishnah, were its plan and location and its gold plating.

The House of the Laver

The second structure within the inner court prescribed by the scroll is the House of the Laver. No less than three columns of text are devoted to it, which is understandable, for this was the place where the priests were to lave and purify themselves before and after the sacrifices.

The instruction was to build it to the south-east of the Temple building, diagonally opposite the stairhouse, which was in the north-west. It was not possible from the preserved parts of the scroll to determine its precise distance from the Temple building, but the text places it 'at a distance of fifty cubits from the altar'. While this 'fifty cubits' differs from the distance given in the Mishnah's description of the Temple of Herod's time, which states that 'between the vestibule and the altar were twenty-two cubits' (Tractate Middoth 3:6), the same mishnaic passage records that 'the laver stood between the vestibule and the altar towards the south'. And this 'twenty-two cubits', which in the Mishnah is the distance between vestibule and altar, is the very figure given in the scroll as the distance between the altar and another building, the House of Utensils.

While we cannot determine the precise location of the Laver from the incomplete data, I think there is enough information to do so by deduction. It was to be built 'south-east' of the Temple building, which may be interpreted in three different ways: facing the southern part of the east side, the Temple façade; directly opposite its south-eastern corner; or opposite the eastern part of the south side of the Temple.

The first two possibilities are ruled out in the face of the dimensions of the inner court; the fact that there was an inner wall enclosing the principal structures; that the House of Utensils, as we shall see, lay to the east of the House of the Laver; and that beyond the House of Utensils, at some distance, stood the altar.

If it were on the east side, it would put the altar so close to the east gate of the court as to leave virtually no space for the inner wall. Moreover, if that had been the author's intention, he would have written 'in the east and its south-eastern part', the method he used in describing the location of the stairhouse.

As to the second possibility, had the author wished to locate it opposite the south-eastern corner, he would have said so specifically, either using the word 'corner', or resorting to the mishnaic terminology, 'the south-eastern horn' of the Temple.

It seems to me that the third interpretation is the only acceptable one, namely, on the south side of the Temple at its eastern end. This would also fit the scroll's requirement of symmetry, with its prescription of 'south-east' for the House of the Laver, balancing the 'north-west' for the stairhouse.

It is evident that by placing the House of the Laver in this location, the author was attempting to relate – and bridge the gap between – the reference in Exodus 30:18 on the Tabernacle: 'You shall also make a laver of bronze. . . . And you shall put it between the tent of meeting and the altar', with the phrase on Solomon's Temple in 1 Kings 7:39: 'and he set the sea [laver] in the south-east corner of the house'. Indeed, the rabbis tried to do the same, relating the biblical text on the Tabernacle to the one on Solomon's Temple, which produced the result in the Mishnah: 'The laver stood between the vestibule [the porch] and the altar, towards the south' (Tractate Middoth 3:6). That, however, was interpreted in a way that gave a location different from the one prescribed by the author of our scroll.

The plan

One of the fascinating elements in deciphering and trying to understand the full meaning of an ancient text is probing the mind of the writer, attempting to recapture the thought, purpose and reasoning behind each carefully crafted phrase, and analysing the contemporary literature known to us today which may have influenced him.

Thus, when I examine the plan and dimensions set out in this scroll for a particular Temple structure – in this case the purification chamber called the House of the Laver – what interests me is not only the architectural design but also why the author chose it, how he conceived it, what were his sources, and why he felt it essential to go into such detail. The product of such an approach can often tell us more than we already know of the life and times of an era that gave birth to our civilization. And occasionally a chance phrase can shed light on obscurities in the Scriptures that have puzzled scholars for some two thousand years. This is what happened with the text on the House of the Laver.

The Laver was the place where the priests had to cleanse themselves after, and probably before, performing the ritual sacrifices. In addition to bathing facilities, it had to provide the technical means for such services as maintaining the purity and separation of the various priestly garments. The author was clearly much concerned to match the instructions in certain biblical sources, and in this he showed his usual ingenuity.

The plan and dimensions of this building are defined in the scroll's

Column 31. It reads, after the fairly easy reconstruction of several words which had missing letters, that the House of the Laver should be

square on all its sides one and twenty cubits, at a distance of fifty cubits from the altar; and the width of the wall shall be three cubits, and the height twenty cubits [...] and gates shall be made for it on the east and on the north and on the west; and the width of the gates shall be four cubits, and their height, seven.

Subtracting the thickness of the walls gives us the interior dimensions of the ground plan as 15 × 15 cubits. The author seems to have gone out of his way to reach these figures by making the external length of the sides of the square 21 cubits, as against the 20 of the stairhouse, and reducing the thickness of the walls to 3 cubits, where in the stairhouse it was 4. What, then, was special about the size 15 × 15?

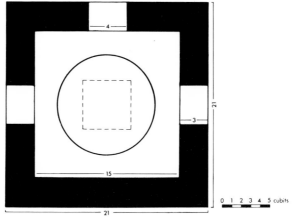

Plan of the House of the Laver, drawn to scale in cubits. It is suggested that the circular laver rested on a square base (broken line).

There is no doubt that the author had carefully contrived to reach these internal measurements in order to fit the mathematical data provided by two biblical sources which, it appears, he tried to interconnect. While no measurements are given in the description of the laver in Exodus, details appear in the accounts on the building of Solomon's Temple in Kings and Chronicles, and it was on these that the author apparently based himself.

In 1 Kings 7:23, we read:

Then he made the molten sea; it was round, ten cubits from brim to brim, and five cubits high, and a line of thirty cubits measured its circumference.

The identical information is also given in 2 Chronicles 4:2. But further data appears in 2 Chronicles 6:13:

Solomon had made a bronze platform five cubits long, five cubits wide, and three cubits high, and had set it in the court....

The consonants that make up the Hebrew word for 'platform' in this
biblical sentence are exactly the same as those used in the scroll for
'laver'. It was commonly regarded as meaning a platform, a dais or
a pillar, and not necessarily an actual laver. But if the author of the
scroll interpreted the data in the two sources literally, he might have
envisaged a square plinth of 5 × 5 cubits – as in the 'bronze platform'
of 2 Chronicles 6:13 – and upon this plinth stood a round laver of 10
cubits in diameter – as in the 'molten sea' of 1 Kings 7:23. His 15 ×
15 interior dimensions of the House of the Laver would thus meet the
requirements of the dimensions in the biblical sources, affording 5
cubits of space on either side of the plinth for passage around it
(equals 10), plus the 5 cubits of the plinth itself, totalling 15 cubits
from wall to wall of the laver house. There is no absolute certainty,
of course, in view of the lack of further details in the scroll, but it
seems to me to follow the most probable line of the author's reasoning.

In support of this hypothesis is a brief text in the Babylonian
Talmud which expresses a traditional interpretation of the biblical
verses we have quoted on Solomon's Temple. We have seen in 1 Kings
7:23 that the round 'molten sea' was 'five cubits high', and we have
proposed that this rested on the square 'bronze platform' mentioned
in 2 Chronicles 6:13, which adds that this platform or plinth was
'three cubits high'. Here, now, is the relevant observation in the
Babylonian Talmud (Tractate Eruvin 14b): 'Rami ben Ezekiel
learned that the sea that Solomon made was square in its lower three
cubits and round in its upper two.' (Incidentally, in the 1 Kings 7
account, the 'sea' rested on twelve oxen, three on each side of the
square plinth.)

The scroll's three gates in the House of the Laver, on the eastern,
western and northern sides, were 4 cubits wide and 7 cubits high.
These very measurements appear in an interesting Dead Sea document, fragments of which were found in Qumran Cave 4, known as
The New Jerusalem. Describing certain houses in Jerusalem, this
document states that their length was 'three cannes', that is,
'twenty-one cubits'; and as for their gates, 'their width four cubits
and their height seven cubits', exactly as in our House of the Laver.
This shows an undoubted connection between this Cave 4 document
and our own scroll from Cave 11.

The interior

The scroll's description of the interior arrangements of the House of
the Laver makes important mention of 'niches' in the interior wall.
The text was fragmentary, but I was able to decipher the phrase: 'in
the wall of this house niches in its inner face'. Then came an almost

illegible Hebrew word meaning 'and inside them', followed unfortunately by words that had not been preserved. This space was followed
in turn by a partly preserved text which may be reconstructed as
'wide one cubit'. It would seem that this sentence refers to additional
recesses within the niches. The scroll prescribes that these niches were
to be 'overlaid with gold'. And they were to be set at eye level: 'from
the ground four cubits high'. They were designed as receptacles for
the garments of those using the laver.

Though several details are missing, it is possible to gain a general
impression of these clothing niches (see illustration of the reconstruction); and they are very similar to those described in several known
sources, though the plan in the scroll may have been different. In the
Mishnah (Tamid 5:3) there is a description of the procedure in the
'dressing-room' where 'the ministers of the Temple' stripped the
priests 'of their raiment and left them with their drawers only'. Then
comes this sentence: 'There were wall niches there whereon were written the names of the several articles of raiment.'

Elsewhere in the rabbinic sources (Tosefta to Sukkah 4:27) we read
that 'There were twenty-four niches [blocked windows] there, corresponding to the twenty-four courses of the Levites.'

Maimonides, in his *Code*, 'Laws Concerning Temple Vessels' (8:9),
basing himself on these two mishnaic quotations as well as other
sources to describe the installations in the Second Temple of Herod's
day, says there were actually ninety-six 'windows', 'four for each
course' (of the Levites), so that the different types of clothing would
not be mixed. Commenting on the end of Tractate Sukkah quoted
above, he adds that there was one large 'window' with three small
ones inside it, which would correspond to those of the scroll's niches
which had additional recesses within them.

The arrangement described in the scroll, together with the parallels
in the Mishnah and Maimonides, are reminiscent of bath-houses in
general during that period. Writing of a case in which an ordinary
ritual bath-house is mentioned, the Mishnah's Tohoroth (Purities) 7:7
begins a text with: 'If a man left his vessels in a wall-niche of the
bath-house attendants. . . .' During my own excavation at Masada, we
discovered an installation very similar to the one we have been describing, though of much simpler construction. Alongside the bath
itself stood a square building with rows of small niches in its interior
walls.

The niches in the House of the Laver were plated with gold because
they held holy garments. The author attaches great importance to
the whole subject of purity and impurity – a later section of the scroll
goes into great detail – and he therefore gives careful prescriptions to
ensure the purity of the priestly garments. His prime concern is with
the clothes to be donned by the priests before they come 'to minister
in the holy place'; they were not to approach the altar unless 'clothed

Niches in the walls of the House of the Laver held the clothes of the priests during the ritual bathing. Similar niches were found in a changing room close to a *mikveh* (ritual bath) discovered at Masada.

with the holy garments'. But he also issues careful orders about the reverse procedure of clothes-changing, when the priests, after officiating and sacrificing at the altar, change from sacred to ordinary garments. These orders end with the ban on priests when leaving the inner court and going out to the people to do so while still dressed in their holy robes: 'and they shall not communicate holiness to my people with their holy garments in which they minister'.

The terminology and style of these commands are clearly influenced to a considerable extent by the language in chapters 42 and 44 of Ezekiel – particularly the ban on priests from wearing their official garments when mixing with the people. They are warned that 'when they go out into the outer court to the people, they shall put off the garments in which they have been ministering, and lay them in the holy chambers; and they shall put on other garments . . .'.

It should be borne in mind, however, that while the terminology is similar, there are variations because of the fundamental difference between Ezekiel and our scroll: the prophet mentions only two courts, while our author prescribes three.

The conduit and the cavern

Immediately following this text on the garments are the author's prescriptions for the disposal of the unclean water after the priests had finished bathing. This water was not to be used or even 'touched by anyone, for it is mixed with the blood of the burnt offerings'. The command, therefore, was to 'make a conduit around the laver, near its house. And the conduit shall lead from the house of the laver into a pit, extending downwards into the land [ground], [so that] the water ... flowing into it ... will be lost in the land.' Thus, the water mixed with the blood washed off from the priests after their sacrificing was to flow from the House of the Laver directly into the ground. This method was similar to the one governing the disposal of the blood that dripped from the altar.

The phraseology of this text in the scroll betrays a divergence from prevailing views. I found throughout the document that whenever the author is at issue with other views, he takes great pains to be explicit in his ordinances. The bone of contention here is over the question of whether the water, after the priests have laved themselves, is to be unused and untouched, just as is the blood from the altar. In principle, there is no difference in view between the author of the scroll and the rabbis, as far as we can judge from the sources at our disposal, namely, the Mishnah. For example, in Tractate Me'ilah (3:3), which deals with the laws of sacrilege, we read that 'Rabbi Ishmael says: In what concerns the blood ... after it has flowed away to the brook of Kidron [east of the Temple and below it] the law of Sacrilege applies to it.'

However, this was one of many ordinances where the Torah forgives offenders if their transgression was inadvertent: they could bring a guilt offering and reimburse the Temple treasury. We have evidence that the rabbis, in the case of the blood and the water flowing from the Temple to the Kidron valley, were rather lenient – even though the blood of the burnt offerings was sacred – just as they were with many other laws, giving them a liberal interpretation which people could live with. In fact, the water mixed with blood was much coveted by the farmers and gardeners at the time who grew vegetables in the Kidron valley. (To this day, there are flourishing vegetable allotments in this valley.)

We have seen from the mishnaic prescription in Tractate Me'ilah that the law of sacrilege applied to the blood and water. But in another tractate, Yoma, which deals with the Day of Atonement, we read: 'Both [kinds of blood] mingled together in the channel and flowed into the brook Kidron.' But then comes the following very interesting addition: 'And it was sold to gardeners as manure, and the law of Sacrilege applied to it' (5:6). This meant that the mixed blood and water was sold for the benefit of the Temple.

Thus, where the rabbis were lenient, deciding that people could use the mixture to fertilize their gardens and pay the Temple treasury, the author of the scroll was strict and rigid, decreeing that the blood and water should be lost in the ground, and no one should either touch or use it.

Light on a New Testament enigma

While deciphering and studying these passages in the scroll, and setting them in the context of the disputes, rulings and traditions prevailing at the time – which was also close to the time of Jesus – it occurred to me that they may well hold the clue to the simple explanation of a strange story that appears in the New Testament in two variations. The story concerns the fate of Judas Iscariot, and the name given to his burial place.

Acts 1:18, 19 tells how Judas 'bought a field with the reward of his wickedness' – the thirty pieces of silver – 'and falling headlong he burst open in the middle and all his bowels gushed out. And it became known to all the inhabitants of Jerusalem, so that the field was called in their language Aceldama, that is, Field of Blood.'

The version related in Matthew 27:3ff. is different, both as to the manner of Judas's death and the explanation for naming the burial area 'field of blood'. Here we are told that Judas 'repented and brought back the thirty pieces of silver to the chief priests', and he then

went and hanged himself. But the chief priests, taking the pieces of silver, said, 'It is not lawful to put them into the treasury, since they are blood money.' So they took counsel, and bought with them the potter's field, to bury strangers in. Therefore that field has been called the Field of Blood to this day.

Aceldama, which the field was called, according to Acts, in the language of 'all the inhabitants of Jerusalem', is simply the Greek transliteration of two Aramaic words which mean 'field of blood'. It seems to me that that was the traditional name of the area of the field of the potter in the Kidron valley because it was fertilized by the mixture of water and blood from the Temple sacrifices. The 'blood money' explanation in Matthew seems to have been added in order to tie the name of the place to the act of Judas. And this explanation was given greater force by the sophisticated recognition that the Hebrew word for 'blood' in the plural is also one of the words for 'money'.

To return to our scroll, its detailed description of the House of the Laver, which I believe was also based on an existing building in the Second Temple, or even on an older tradition, provides a clear idea of a structure that was of special importance to the Essenes because of their very strict adherence to the laws of cleanliness and uncleanliness.

The House of the Altar Utensils

Following the texts on the Stairhouse and the House of the Laver come the prescriptions for the third building in the inner court close to the main Temple structure. This is the House of the Altar Utensils, and it was to stand 7 cubits to the east of the House of the Laver – between it and the altar – in accordance with the opening command:

You shall make a house east of the house of the laver, the same size as the house of the laver, and its wall shall be a distance of seven cubits from its wall. (Col. 33:8, 9)

Thus, its general plan and dimensions are the same as for the House of the Laver – a square building of 21 × 21 cubits on the outside, with walls 3 cubits thick, giving it an interior area of 15 × 15 cubits. However, unlike the laver house which has three gates, the House of Utensils 'shall have two gates, one in the north and one in the south, one opposite the other, of the same size as the gates of the House of the Laver', namely, 4 cubits wide and 7 cubits high.

The description of this building is mainly concerned with the interior arrangements, for therein lies its distinctiveness, in conformity with its purpose. Thus, its principal clause prescribes that

all the walls of this house shall have niches [or, blocked windows] in their interior faces, two cubits wide by two cubits, and their height four cubits, and they shall have doors, for the utensils of the altar, that is, the basins and the flagons and the firepans and the silver bowls [or, ladles] with which one brings up the entrails and the legs on the altar.

Our scroll does not specify the number of niches, but since there are exact measurements for each of these recesses – 2 cubits wide, 2 cubits deep (cut into the 3-cubit thickness of the wall) and 4 cubits high – and assuming they take up the entire wall space, as well as allowing for the space between one 'window' and the next, there would be a total of twenty: six each in the eastern and western walls, and four each in the northern and southern walls which have gates 4 cubits wide.

It is doubtful whether the author attached importance to the number of these recesses. If he had, knowing his style and approach, I am sure he would have specified it. However, his insistence that all four walls were to have them, including the two with the gates, may indicate that the recesses were designed to hold the four categories of altar utensils recorded in his opening prescription – basins, flagons, firepans and silver bowls. The fact that they were to 'have doors' shows that these recesses were what we would call today built-in cupboards. Incidentally, in prescribing doors, the author coined a new Hebrew term, turning the Hebrew noun for door, '*delet*', into a passive verb, the literal translation of which is 'They shall be doored'.

There are references to similar houses for storing sacred vessels both in the Mishnah and in Josephus. In the mishnaic Tractate Tamid (3:4) we read: 'They went into the Chamber of Utensils and brought forth ninety-three vessels of silver and vessels of gold; and they gave [the lamb that was to be] the Daily Whole-offering to drink from a cup of gold.' However, in another tractate, Shekalim 5:6, the same term denotes a structure with an entirely different purpose – a repository of gifts to the Temple: 'The Chamber of Utensils: whosoever made a gift of any article used to cast it therein, and every thirty days the treasurers opened it; and any article which they found of use for the Temple fund they left there.'

Josephus, on the other hand, in *Antiquities* 3:150, says that altar utensils were kept in the Tabernacle 'opposite the altar'. He is not more specific; but, transferred to the context of the Temple, his location could fit, or at least not conflict with, that of the House of Utensils as specified in our scroll. There will be more in a later chapter on the similarity between much in the accounts by Josephus on the Temple of Solomon and the concept of the Temple in the scroll.

14 The Slaughterhouse and the Altar

The text on the House of the Altar Utensils is immediately followed by the ordinances on the structure and installations of the slaughterhouse. Curiously enough, it is precisely these passages that provided a crucial clue to the date of composition of this document.

The ordinances, alas, are very fragmentary; but there is sufficient to make possible a feasible reconstruction. The surviving fifteen lines of Column 34, with square brackets to indicate the gaps and the reconstructions, read as follows:

1 [   ] ... in a bron[ze] tablet [   ]
2 [   ] ... and between one pillar and ano[ther   ]
3 [   ] which is between the pillars [   ]
4 [   ] ... (perhaps, the bulls) between the whee[ls   ]
5 [and] they [shall open(?)] and close the wheels, and th[en(?)   ]
6 and tie the heads (perhaps, the horns) of the bulls to the rings and [   ] in the rings.
7 Then they shall slaughter them, and they shall gather th[e blood] in the basons
8 and throw it around against the base of the altar. And (then they shall) open
9 the wheels, and flay(?) the skins of the bulls off their flesh, and cut

10   them up into their pieces, and salt the pieces with salt, and wash the
11   entrails and the legs, and salt them with salt, and burn them on
12   the fire which is upon the altar, each bull and its pieces by it, and its
        cereal offering of fine flour upon it,
13   and the wine of its drink offering by it, of which will be poured upon it.
        And the priests, the sons of Aaron, shall offer everything
14   upon the altar, an offering by fire, a pleasing odour before the Lord.
15   And you shall make chains hanging from the ceiling of the twelve pillars.

Here, then, are a building and contrivances that comprise the following elements: a ceiling supported by twelve columns; chains dangling from the ceiling; rings to which the animals' heads are tied; wheels to regulate the shackling and release of the beasts; and another object connected in some way 'between the pillars' and 'a bronze tablet'. Each was clearly designed for its special role in enabling the entire process of the ritual sacrifice to be performed in accordance with the prescriptions, ranging from the slaughter and the sprinkling of the blood round the base of the altar, to the flaying, cutting, salting and washing of the parts, and arranging them for the actual sacrifice upon the altar. The parts of the animal were to be grouped in one place and not mixed together with the accompanying cereal and drink offerings.

This detailed information in the scroll would alone have been of importance, for there is no description in the Bible of the slaughter-house in the Temple of Solomon. There are some references to the slaughtering of the sacrifices in the vision of Ezekiel (ch. 40:38–43) of an 'end of days' temple, in which the prophet talks of the place 'where the burnt offering was to be washed', the 'tables, on which the sacrifices were to be slaughtered' and other tables where 'the flesh of the offering was to be laid'; and there are some interesting additions to the masoretic text in the Septuagint. But there is nothing in any of the other biblical books.

There is, however, a good deal in the Talmud. The prime passage in the Mishnah which is worth comparing with the text in our scroll is the one relating to the structure with pillars, and such installations as the rings in the slaughterhouse, that were a feature of the Second Temple as reconstructed by Herod. It appears in Tractate Middoth 3:5:

To the north of the Altar were rings, six rows of four each (and some say four rows of six each) at which they slaughtered the animal-offerings. The shambles lay north of the Altar, and there stood there eight short pillars; upon these were 'four-sided blocks' [literally, square objects] of cedar-wood into which were fixed iron hooks, three rows of each, whereon they used to hang the slaughtered beasts. They used to flay them on marble tables be-tween the pillars.

There is thus a similarity between the two descriptions, though there are differences in detail. Both have rings at which the animals are slaughtered. Both have pillars, though the Mishnah records eight, while the scroll prescribes twelve. And in both, apparently, there are tables between the pillars for the flaying. The Mishnah also reports that there were iron hooks, and these may possibly have been prescribed in our scroll, in the missing part of the very fragmentary passage that mentions 'a bronze tablet'.

The rings

This similarity of the two descriptions would appear, at a quick glance, to be of sole importance. A close study, however, brought out a more important revelation which points to the probable date of the composition of the Temple scroll. The clue was provided by the mention of 'rings' in both texts.

There is a repeated statement in the talmudic sources that it was 'Johanan the High Priest' who introduced rings into the slaughterhouse of the Temple, and there is general agreement that 'Johanan' was John Hyrcanus I, who reigned from 135 to 104 BC. Thus, in Ma'aser Sheni (5:15) and Sotah (9:10) we read that 'Johanan the High Priest ... made an end also of the Awakeners and the Stunners. Until his days the hammer used to smite in Jerusalem.' And the Tosefta to Sotah (9:10) explains that 'The Stunners are those who strike the calf between its horns, as they do in [the practice of] idol worship. Johanan the High Priest said to them: How long will you feed the altar with blemished animals?'

Accordingly, what Johanan did is related in the two tractates of the Palestinian Talmud mentioned above: 'Thereupon he made rings for them ... wide at the bottom and narrow at the top.'

Before returning to John Hyrcanus, a few words may be added about the way in which these rings were used. The exact technique cannot be gathered with certainty from the data in the Talmud, and thus there were different interpretations both by the Sages and by such great later commentators as Rashi and Maimonides. Maimonides, for example, held that these rings were 'fixed in the ground, so as to shackle the legs of the animal at the moment of slaughter'. Rashi, for his part, asserts that it was the head of the animal that was placed in the ring. According to the fragment in our scroll – 'and tie the heads of the bulls to the rings' – it would appear that Rashi's is the correct interpretation. This is also supported by a later halachic book called *Arugat Ha'Bosem* (*The Garden of Spices*), which tells of one of the twenty-four priestly courses 'who had no rings in which to place the neck of the animal and could not slaughter as they wished, since the animal would turn its neck in all directions ...'.

Our scroll provides the additional information that there were 'chains hanging from the ceiling of the twelve pillars', and these were linked to cog-wheels – 'and they shall open and close the wheels'. This made it possible to lift and fasten the bull while it was tied or its head inserted in the ring, and lower and release the carcass when the operation was completed.

There are no exact details of the structure of the slaughterhouse in the mishnaic descriptions, though it seems evident from these texts that it must have been an open pavilion – a structure with no walls, consisting simply of a roof resting on pillars. Curiously enough, the Greek translation of the Bible, the Septuagint, has the following addition to Ezekiel 40:43: 'above [the installations] are ceilings to protect them against rain and drought'.

King John Hyrcanus I

As against the paucity of detail in the Mishnah, the author of the Temple scroll devotes an entire column to the structure and installations of the slaughterhouse. As he tended to be brief when dealing with non-controversial subjects and lengthy when he was at odds with the prevailing views, it is clear that the subject of the slaughtering arrangements must have been controversial in his time. This brings us back to John Hyrcanus – and to the dating clue in the scroll.

Since the author included rings in his list of shambles' gadgets – 'and tie the heads [or horns] of the bull to the rings' – and since talmudic tradition holds that these were first introduced by John Hyrcanus I, the question arises as to whether the author was writing before or after Hyrcanus's action. Was he describing an existing practice, with the rings already in use in the Temple? If he was, then the information we have from the Talmud would support the proposition that the scroll was composed after Hyrcanus had introduced the rings. This is indeed possible, and I imagine it will be so claimed by some scholars.

If, on the other hand, and as I believe, the rings had not yet been installed, and our author was demanding that they should be, it would date his composition before the decision given by Hyrcanus. I consider this to be the case not only for other reasons, as we shall see later, which point to an earlier date, but also for the reason, explained above, that the author was clearly prescribing something that was contrary to contemporary practice. Installing rings was one of them, and it is feasible to deduce that John Hyrcanus introduced these rings into the Temple under the influence of the teachings of this very

Temple scroll, or of the Essenes, or of circles who believed, with the Essenes, that rings were essential to the sacrificial ritual.

An exciting factor reinforcing this thesis is the knowledge that John Hyrcanus, who had been an ardent follower of the Pharisees, later changed his views and sided with the rulings of the priestly Sadducean party. Here is what Josephus says about this in his *Antiquities*: Hyrcanus

joined the Sadducean party and deserted the Pharisees, and ... abrogated the regulations which they had established for the people.

Thus the practices which Hyrcanus had abrogated were those which in his time were championed by the Pharisees. The changes – including the rings which were mentioned so specifically in the Talmud – must therefore have been introduced through the influence of the Sadducees. If this assumption is correct, then we must conclude that the Temple scroll, or its doctrine, was already known during the latter part of the reign of Hyrcanus, which puts the date of composition of this section of the scroll at not later than the final decades of the second century BC.

The Stoa

The text on the structures in the inner court ends at Column 35, with the command to construct in a 'separate place' west of the main Temple building a roofed colonnade: 'a stoa of standing columns for the sin offering and the guilt offering'.

The animals for sacrifice – he-goats for sin offerings, rams for guilt offerings – had to be brought into this inner court, and great care had to be taken to keep those offered for the priests separate from the ones to be offered for the people. According to the scroll, mixing the one with the other was an awesome transgression, and so appropriate facilities had to be provided to ensure that this did not occur. The place where the separate groups were kept, with some indication of which animal belonged to whom and for which offering, was the 'stoa of standing columns'. The columns were for tethering the animals, and they were to be 'separated from one another': certain columns to which the animals of the priests were to be tethered – 'for the sin offering of the priests and for the male goats' – and other columns 'for the sin offerings of the people and for their guilt offerings'. To emphasize the purpose of this command, the text continues: 'and all of them shall not be mixed one with another, for their places shall be separated from one another so that the priests may not err with the sin offering of the people', or, one could add, with the guilt offering. Since all sin offerings were of male goats and guilt offerings of rams,

A reconstruction in perspective of the three storeys of the outer court, with the
booths on the roof of the third storey (© *L. Ritmeyer*).

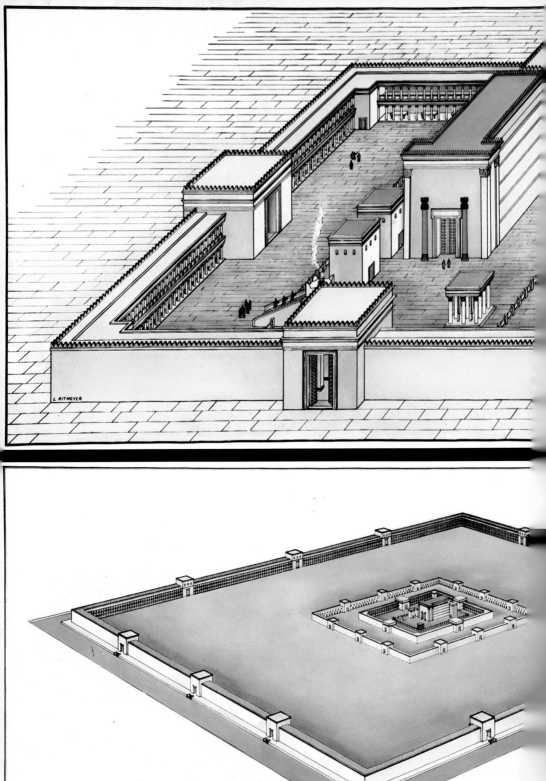

The author's proposed reconstruction as prescribed in the Temple scroll (© *L. Ritmeyer*).

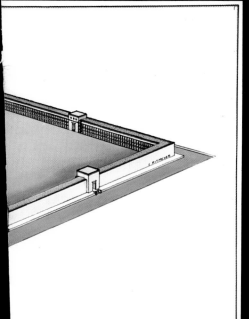

THE TEMPLE AND ITS COURTS

A reconstruction showing the view from the north-east. As specified in the scroll, the House, in the centre, is surrounded by three concentric square courts (© *L. Ritmeyer*).

there was little danger of mistake or confusion. The prime danger was mixing the priestly offerings with those of the people.

As for the scroll's location of the 'stoa of standing columns' to be west of the Temple building, we can gather from the Bible and the Mishnah that there was an old tradition reserving an area west of the Temple for classifying the animals for the various offerings before they were brought to the slaughterhouse and altar. The earliest reference to this location seems to be in Ezekiel's vision, in which he 'saw a place at the extreme western end of them. And he said to me, "This is the place where the priests shall boil the guilt offering and the sin offering, and where they shall bake the cereal offering ..."' (Ezek. 46:19, 20). (Incidentally, the Hebrew word for 'place' in this quotation is translated in the Septuagint as 'a separate place', exactly as in our scroll.)

Another relevant source, this one related by terminology to our scroll, is 1 Chronicles 26:18, which contains the phrases 'and for the parbar on the west ... and two at the parbar'. Now 'parbar' is similar linguistically and textually to the very word 'parwar' generally used in the scroll for the Stoa in the inner court. As spelt in Chronicles, this word was the subject of homiletic interpretation in the Talmud, and based on it is a vague talmudic tradition that this parbar was located 'behind the place of the Mercy Seat', namely, behind the Holy of Holies. It is described in the course of a discussion of the Chronicles term that appears in Tractate Zevahim 55b:

There was a small passage way behind the place of the Mercy Seat, its height eight cubits, in order to make the whole Temple court fit for the consumption of most holy sacrifices and the slaughtering of minor sacrifices and there were two such, and thus it is written, and two at the parbar.

It is evident by now that in this section of the scroll devoted to the inner court, the author went into prodigious detail on those structures, and their installations, which were directly involved with the sacrificial offerings – the House of the Laver, the House of Utensils, the shambles and the roofed tethering columns. These were clearly the main concern of the author in his description of the inner court, for the good reason that the sacrifices were the central feature of the Temple ritual. And the central element in that ritual was the great altar of burnt offering.

The Altar

The ordinances on the construction of the Altar appear earlier, in Column 12, in a part of the scroll that was in a very poor state of preservation. A few surviving decipherable words offered an opening suggestion for a possible reconstruction of the plan of this altar, such as 'its horns and its corners ... all built of [unhewn ?] stones', or 'twenty [cubits from cor]ner to corner'. These were only enough to indicate that it was to be a stone altar, or an altar of stones, at least 20 × 20 cubits. Without further data, we would have known nothing more about this most important object in the Temple complex, and little more about the mind of the author and the reasoning behind his prescriptions.

Fortunately, it was possible to glean additional data from the references to the Altar in the description in other parts of the scroll of the sacrificial ritual at the different festivals, and these yielded fruitful results. In the text on the offering at the Feast of the Wood, for example, in Column 23, we read:

and put some of its blood with his finger on the four horns of the altar of the burnt offering and on the four corners of the ledge of the altar, and pour its blood on the base of the ledge of the altar all around.

The phrase 'the four corners of the ledge of the altar' is found only in the description of the Altar in Ezekiel's vision:

And you shall take some of its blood, and put it on its four horns [Septuagint: 'on the four horns of the altar'], and on the four corners of the ledge, and upon the rim round about. (Ezek. 43:20)

The resemblance of these two quotations is so close that the author of our scroll must have based himself – at least on these points – on Ezekiel. However, the dimensions of Ezekiel's altar are different from those in our scroll – 20 × 20 cubits, if my restoration of the fragmented prescription is correct. Yet the 20 × 20 dimensions do appear elsewhere in the Bible, in 2 Chronicles 4:1, which states that Solomon built 'an altar of bronze, twenty cubits long, and twenty cubits wide, and ten cubits high'.

It is possible, therefore, that our author was trying to harmonize the two different biblical sources, as he did in many other instances, this time using parts of both Ezekiel and Chronicles. My reconstruction is based on this assumption.

An interesting footnote on the dimensions of the Altar and the nature of its construction is provided by another source. A certain Hecataeus of Abdera, speaking of the old pre-Herodian altar of the Second Temple, is quoted by Josephus as saying that it was 'a square altar, built of heaped-up stones, unhewn and unwrought; each side is twenty cubits long and the height ten cubits' (Contra Apion 1:198).

This concludes the long section in the scroll on the sanctuary and its auxiliary structures within the inner court, the most important of the three courts, where the central Temple ritual was conducted. The author proceeds directly to prescribe the ordinances for the middle and outer courts – which hold some surprises.

15 The Middle and Outer Courts

The columns in the scroll on the 'second' or 'middle' court are not too well preserved, though there is enough to show that there were only thirty-seven lines in the original text, of which twenty-six have survived. This is far shorter than the texts on either the inner or the outer courts, mainly because this middle court, reserved for male Israelites from the age of twenty, played a less significant role in the Temple ritual than the other two courts. Though there were sacrificial offerings only in the inner court, certain ritual parts of the feasts were held in the outer court, which was open to all Israelites, including women and children.

The command to 'make a second court around the inner court' is followed by structural prescriptions which give details of the dimensions of its walls and gates. The most astonishing of these ordinances concern the gates: there were to be twelve, three in each of the four walls, named after the sons of Jacob. The commands end with the severe prohibition against entry into this court by the priests while still dressed in their holy garments. They were to wash and change before leaving the inner court for the less holy middle court.

Mathematical ingenuity

The author has been quite generous with his information on the measurements of the architectural components of the middle court. But these still require certain mathematical calculations before we can penetrate his design and reconstruct his plan.

We are told at one point that this court is to be built 'around' and at a distance of 'one hundred cubits' from the inner court. Further along, the scroll prescribes that each side of the middle court is to be 'eighty and four hundred cubits'. This, as the author puts it, is to be 'the length of the east side' as well as the 'length of all its sides: the south, the west and the north'. These are the measurements of the external side of the wall (which includes the 4-cubit thickness of the wall). It will be recalled from our description of the inner court that the overall length of the *interior* face of each of its walls, including the 40-cubit width of the gate, was 280 cubits. It is clear, therefore, that in prescribing the distance from one court to the other of 100 cubits, the author meant the measurement to be taken from the *interior* face of the inner court wall to the *exterior* face of the middle court wall. (A simple geometrical exercise shows that a 280 × 280

cubit square planted dead centre of a 480 × 480 cubit square leaves
a space of 100 cubits between the two. Simple arithmetic gets there
quicker: $\dfrac{480-280}{2} = 100$.)

It is probable that the author took the measurement from the *inner*
face of the inner court in prescribing the 100-cubit distance, because
that face was part of that court, whereas its *outer* face was already
part of the less holy and pure middle court. But from other measurements in the detailed commands it is evident that the author sought
to ensure that the middle court should be a 480-cubit square, neither
smaller nor larger – which it would have been if the 100-cubit distance
had been measured from the outer face of the inner court walls.

We are given the width of the twelve gates, three in each wall,
named after the sons of Jacob – 'eight and twenty cubits' – and the
intervals between the middle and its two flanking gates in each wall,

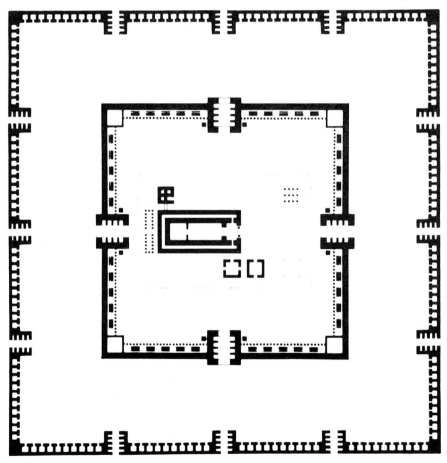

Plan of the middle court, with its twelve gates named after the sons of Jacob. The
arrangement is identical with that of the outer court (see detailed caption to the
illustration on page 151).

and between the flanking gate and its nearest corner – all were to be 'nine and ninety cubits'. Here, the author shows mathematical ingenuity and verbal skill in suggesting a uniform 99-cubit measurement for all the intervals, when some are in fact shorter, in order to achieve a 480-cubit length for each of the four walls of the court. Let us take his text on the eastern wall as an example.

Here, the gate of Levi is in the middle, Simeon to its north close to the north-eastern corner of the court, and Judah to its south, closest to the south-eastern corner. The scroll prescribes that the length of the section 'from this gate [of Simeon] to the gate of Levi, nine and ninety cubits'; and 'from the north-eastern corner to the gate of Simeon, nine and ninety cubits'. The intervals thus appear to be the same. But the author is careful to use the word north-eastern '*corner*', and we have seen in an earlier chapter that he uses this term to denote an *exterior* corner, and the word 'angle' to signify the *interior* corner of a court or chamber. Thus, if we take into account the 4-cubit thickness of the wall, we see that while the sections between the gates of Simeon and Levi, and Levi and Judah, were each 99 cubits, those between Simeon and the north-eastern corner and between Judah and the south-eastern corner were each 95 cubits. If, therefore, the intervals were really to be uniform, the overall 480-cubit length of the wall would need to have been extended by another 8 cubits. As it is, the author has achieved his aim with exquisite skill: width of gate, 28 cubits; 3 gates in each wall: $3 \times 28 = 84$. Distance between gates, and between gates and angles, 99 cubits: $4 \times 99 = 396$; $396 + 84 = 480$.

Why had he gone to such pains to prescribe this figure of 480? We cannot know for certain, but it is assuredly no coincidence that it should be a multiple of 120; and we have seen in the text on the inner court that the author specifically ordained that in the 280-cubit length of each wall, the gate was to be 40 cubits wide, and the sections between the two angles and the gate were therefore each 120 cubits. (We shall see in the chapter on the outer court that the distance between the gates was 360 cubits, also a multiple of 120.)

The figure of 120, as we have indicated earlier, may have some bearing on the calendric reckoning of the sect. In the case of this middle court, however, the 480 may also suggest a link with the number of years that elapsed between the exodus from Egypt and the commencement of the building of Solomon's Temple: 'In the four hundred and eightieth year after the people of Israel came out of the land of Egypt, in the fourth year of Solomon's reign ... he began to build the house of the Lord.'

There is an indication in a fragmentary passage that the walls of this middle court had cells: 'And cells shall be made in the wall on the outside, and the distance between each cell shall be three cubits and a half. ...' But this is the only information we have about them, and although several assumptions come to mind, there is no way of verifying them in the absence of further text with specifications on these cells.

There is much to be said about the surprising command in the scroll that the middle court was to have twelve gates, and named after the sons of Jacob and not the tribes of Israel: Simeon, Levi and Judah in the eastern wall; Reuben, Joseph and Benjamin in the south; Issachar, Zebulun and Gad in the west; and Dan, Naphtali and Asher in the north. But these points are best considered when we discuss the next section of the scroll, which deals with the outer court, for that court had the same number of gates, with the same names, and the text there also contains additional interesting details of the allotment of chambers according to tribes, priests and Levites.

What little remains of the ordinances on who was permitted and who forbidden to enter the middle court indicates that adult male Israelites alone were allowed in. The prohibition for others included 'foreigners', and this ban is similar to the one in the Temple of Herod's day, which forbade foreigners from entering the inner part of the Temple compound. A fragment of such a warning, in Greek, was discovered in the debris outside the Lions' Gate in Jerusalem's Old City wall.

The outer court

The third court in the scroll's Temple complex, the outer court, receives considerable attention from the author, so much so that his ordinances cover no less than seven columns (40 to 46 inclusive). Many of them deal with the plan and location of the court, and include architectural directives on the construction of its walls, gates, chambers, cells, stoas and terraces. Though these ordinances are inspired by the author's interpretation of the meagre biblical sources, they are unique.

There are also specific commands on the rites to be performed in this court at various festivals. Moreover, since this was to be the outermost court, closest to less sacred ground, the author takes the opportunity of issuing sundry prescriptions, touching on intimate details of human behaviour, aimed at ensuring the purity of the Temple and protecting even the perimeter of the entire compound from defilement.

I propose to consider only the salient elements in this section, and some of the problems that render a complete interpretation rather difficult. Though the text on this court is better preserved than that on the inner and middle courts, certain gaps still remain, though fortunately most can be filled with the help of fragments from other copies of this scroll.

The commands open with: 'And you shall make a third court ... around the middle court.' Women and children are permitted in this court together with the men. Then come instructions on the dimensions of the walls – and with it our first puzzle. We are given the overall length of each of the four walls of the court in the following curious terms: 'about one thousand and six hundred cubits from corner to corner. Every side shall be according to this measure.' Why 'about', when the author is usually so specific? The reason seems evident when we examine the additional data on the width of the three gates in each wall – 50 cubits – and the intervals between the central and the flanking gates, and the latter and the corners – 360 cubits. If we add these together – 4 intervals of 360 cubits = 1,440, + 3 gates 50 cubits wide = 150 – we reach a total not of 1,600 cubits but

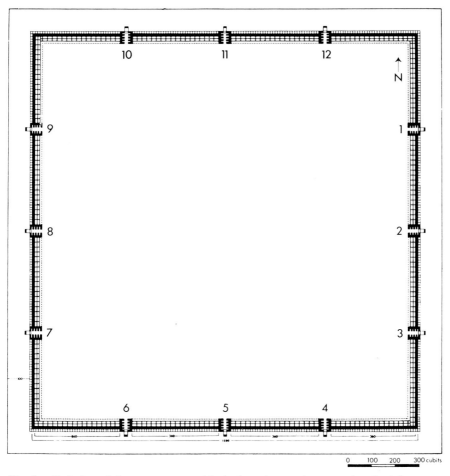

The detailed plan of the outer court, with the locations and names of each of the twelve gates. In the eastern wall: (1) Simeon; (2) Levi; (3) Judah. Southern wall: (4) Reuben; (5) Joseph; (6) Benjamin. Western wall: (7) Issachar; (8) Zebulun; (9) Gad. Northern wall: (10) Dan; (11) Naphtali; (12) Asher. Between the gates are the chambers, rooms and stoas.

of 1,590 cubits. However, the total becomes 1,604 cubits if we add the fact that the gates and the cells connected with them extend outwards from the court wall 7 cubits on either side. (The prescription on these cells which protrude from the exterior face of the wall states: 'And cells shall be made between its gates, on the outside against the foundation up to its crenellations.')

Thus the author used the word 'about' the round number of 1,600 cubits when prescribing the length of the wall (instead of 1,590 or 1,604) because he was clearly intent on ensuring that the intervals between the gates should be 360 cubits (just as he was resourceful in arriving at 120 cubits for those intervals in the walls of the inner court). Again, I believe the 360 had something to do with the sect's calendric concept of 360 days in the year plus the additional day every three months.

The thickness and height of the wall are precisely specified: 'And the width of the wall shall be seven cubits, and the height, nine and forty cubits.' The thickness of the wall in this court, too, is included in the overall measurements, for in the prescriptions on the gates the scroll states: 'From the corner [namely, the outer corner] to the gate of Simeon, sixty and three hundred cubits.' Thus, as with the middle court, the section between the flanking gate and the angle of the court is really 7 cubits less, without the author's saying so directly, since by giving this measurement from the outer corner he is able to retain the uniform 360 cubits.

The gates

The most important prescriptions on this outer court is the one that deals with the gates. As with the middle court, there were to be twelve, three on each side: 'It shall have three gates in the east and three in the south and three to the west and three to the north', 50 cubits wide and 70 cubits high, thus towering above the wall of the court. Then come further details of this formidable gate structure. It was to be 50 cubits deep, and it 'shall protrude from the wall of the court outwards seven cubits, and shall penetrate from the wall of the court inwards six and thirty cubits'. Thus, entering the gate from the outside, one would cross the first 7 cubits in the section outside the court, the next 7 cubits through the thickness of the wall of the court, and the final 36 cubits in the section of the gate that extended into the court itself – a total depth of 50 cubits. I should add that the 50-cubit width of the gate referred to the entire gate-house. Actual entry, however, was through 'gate-openings', as the scroll's Hebrew puts it, the passage with double doors 14 cubits wide and 28 cubits high 'up to the lintel'.

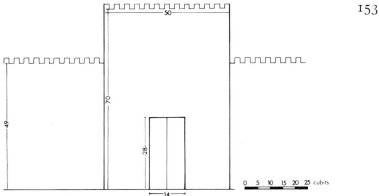

Plan of one of the gates in the outer court (in cubits). The structure was almost entirely within the court, with only 7 cubits protruding beyond the outer wall.

These gates, as in the middle court, were named after the sons of Jacob. In phraseology and form, though not in dimensions, the scroll's prescription is very similar to the description of the city of Jerusalem in the vision of Ezekiel, which appears in the final chapter of the prophetic work:

These shall be the exits of the city: On the north side ... three gates, the gate of Reuben, the gate of Judah, and the gate of Levi, the gates of the city being named after the tribes of Israel. On the east side ... three gates, the gate of Joseph, the gate of Benjamin, and the gate of Dan. On the south side ... three gates, the gate of Simeon, the gate of Issachar, and the gate of Zebulun. On the west side ... three gates, the gate of Gad, the gate of Asher, and the gate of Naphtali. (Ezek. 48:30–34)

Each side of Ezekiel's city was to be the same length – 'four thousand five hundred cubits' – so that, too, was a square, like the concept of the Temple in our scroll.

Very similar to the gates of the middle and outer courts of the scroll, as well as to the city gates of Ezekiel, are the gates in the description of the city of Jerusalem 'coming down out of heaven' in the New Testament's Revelation:

It had a great, high wall, with twelve gates, and at the gates twelve angels, and on the gates the names of the twelve tribes of the sons of Israel were inscribed; on the east three gates, on the north three gates, on the south three gates, and on the west three gates.... The city lies foursquare, its length the same as its breadth. (Rev. 21:12, 13, 16)

The tribal order

To return to the gates of the scroll, their arrangement, by name, in the outer court is exactly like that in the middle court. Running clockwise, the order is: in the east, Simeon, Levi and Judah; in the south, Reuben, Joseph and Benjamin; in the west, Issachar, Zebulun and Gad; and in the north, Dan, Naphtali and Asher. This order is different from the ones in the two biblical sources which arrange the tribes according to the four points of the compass: Ezekiel (48:31–34) describing the gates of Jerusalem, and Numbers (2:3–31) recording the positioning of the camps of the tribes round the Tent of Meeting. Nor, indeed, does the order in Ezekiel match the one in Numbers. What, then, lay behind the arrangement prescribed by the author of our scroll?

I think the principle by which he was guided is easily discernible when we examine the salient features of his plan. He places Levi, the most important of the tribes, in the centre of the most important side, the east. Flanking the gate of Levi are the gates of Simeon and Judah – and he finds the biblical source for that in Deuteronomy 27:12 on the placement of the tribes 'upon Mount Gerizim to bless the people: Simeon, Levi, Judah …'. He omits the tribes of Ephraim and Manasseh and has instead their father Joseph, the son of Jacob (for the reasons given earlier in our discussion of the Wood festival offerings). Issachar, Zebulun and Gad are placed in the west, exactly as in another Ezekiel source (48:26–28) which gives the tribal territories. And the gates in the north, Dan, Naphtali and Asher, are the same as those in Numbers 2:25–29 and Ezekiel 48:1–3 (on the tribal boundaries) though the internal order is different.

Thus, the evident purpose of the author in determining the location of each named gate was to secure the central place in the eastern side for Levi, and to omit Ephraim and Manasseh. This necessitated his deviation from his principal source, Numbers, which gives the disposition of the twelve tribes of Israel. He did this despite his very close adherence to the description in Numbers, particularly the general arrangement of the Levites and the other tribes round the Tabernacle. After all, his main objective, as I understand it, was to translate that arrangement into architectural terms and this served as the basis for his concept of the Temple plan. It finds emphatic expression, as we shall see, in his allocation of the chambers in this court to the Levitical families.

The chambers and stoas

The remarkable features of the outer court are the structures that were to line its inner walls. As the command puts it: 'And between one gate and another, inward, you shall make chambers and rooms and stoas.' 'Inward' indicates that they are to be constructed inside the court, against the inner walls, in contrast to the cells, mentioned elsewhere, that are also to be 'made between its gates', but 'on the outside'.

Though the text uses the specific words 'chambers and rooms', there is no indication of what was the distinction between the two. It is conceivable, perhaps, that one was used for official transactions of Temple business, while the other may have been a dwelling. But this, as I say, is no more than a possible hypothesis, with nothing in the text to substantiate it.

The chambers and rooms were the same size, and their dimensions are clearly defined: 'The width of the chamber shall be ten cubits; and its length twenty cubits; and the width [thickness] of its wall shall be two cubits; and its height, fourteen cubits up to the lintel. And its entrance shall be three cubits wide.' The prescription for the rooms is the same. The stoa, the covered colonnade skirting the structure, was to be 10 cubits wide and 14 cubits high.

It was to be a three-storey structure, and the measurements given of the ground floor were to be repeated for the two upper storeys. On each floor, along the section between the gates, there were to be eighteen chambers, eighteen rooms, and an undivided stoa. As the command puts it: 'And between one gate and another you shall make eighteen chambers, and their rooms, eighteen.' This figure of 18 is reached by dividing the length of the section between the gates, 360 cubits, by the length of each room or chamber, 20 cubits. But those 20 cubits include the thickness of the partition walls between the chambers or the rooms, so that their interior length would be less than 20. Moreover, although the author does not say so specifically, he is also certainly aware of the fact that this is true only of the chambers and rooms in the sections between the gates, and that those between the gate and the *angle* of the court would be shorter by at least 7 cubits – the thickness of the court wall.

With the chamber, room and skirting stoa each 10 cubits wide, the entire structure projected 30 cubits from the wall into the court. There is a certain correspondence between this measurement and the overall width of the stoas in the outer court according to Josephus: 'The porticos [stoas] were thirty cubits broad' (*War* 5:192).

The upper storeys

The command that the two upper storeys be patterned on the plan and measurements of the ground floor reads as follows: 'And you shall make built-up chambers; and their rooms and their stoas shall be like the lower ones, second and third ones, measuring like the lower ones.' Thus, with eighteen chambers, eighteen rooms and one stoa on each of the three floors, the structure in each section between the gates held altogether fifty-four chambers, fifty-four rooms and three stoas. (This of course was not true of the sections between the gates and the angle of the court – and we shall see later that the author was conscious of this difficulty but was unable to solve it in harmony with his overall design.)

The author, still speaking as divine architect, does not neglect the important detail of how the upper storeys are to be reached: 'And you shall make a stairhouse by the walls of the gates, inside the stoa, in which spiral stairs shall go up to the second and third stoas and unto the roof.' Access to the roof was necessary – and here came the surprise – as booths were to be set up on 'the roof of the third' storey in celebration of the Feast of Booths. There is no record of booths being erected for this festival in either the Solomonic or the Herodian Temple. The only reference to booths within the Temple compound relates to the early part of the Second Temple period in the time of Nehemiah, when 'the people ... made booths for themselves ... and in the courts of the house of God' (Neh. 8:16). No details are given.

A novelty: booths

The booths in the scroll were to be 8 cubits high. If we add this to the 14-cubit height of each of the three storeys, we reach a total of 50 cubits. Since the wall of the court was 49 cubits high, the booths would extend one cubit above it. It may be that the crenellations added this one cubit to the height of the wall, though their size is not given in the scroll.

Incidentally, the very language in the command to build three storeys is reminiscent of the description in Genesis 6:16 of Noah's ark: 'make it with lower, second, and third decks'. The most revealing comparison, however, is with chapters 40 and 42 of Ezekiel – though not as we have it in the Hebrew masoretic text but in the Septuagint. It is evident that those responsible for this Greek translation of the Bible must have been working from a different Hebrew text – and it may have been that text which influenced our author in his description of these structures.

Solution to an Ezekiel riddle

The English translation of the Hebrew masoretic text in the common Bible on Ezekiel's Temple states that in 'the outer court ... there were chambers and a pavement, round about the court; thirty chambers fronted on the pavement. And the pavement ran along the side of the gates, corresponding to the length of the gates; this was the lower pavement' (Ezek. 40:17, 18). The exact meaning of this 'lower pavement' has long eluded the scholars. The Hebrew word translated as 'pavement' can indeed be used to mean that; but etymologically its meaning is akin to a running series, one thing after another, and was in fact employed in post-biblical literature to mean a succession of trees. That is precisely the way in which this Hebrew word in Ezekiel is given its Greek translation in the Septuagint: it is called a peristyle in one verse and a stoa in the second: 'and behold, there were chambers and peristyles around the court; thirty chambers within the peristyles' (Ezek. 40:17). 'And the stoas were behind the gates; according to the length of the gates was the lower peristyle' (Ezek. 40:18). Thus, according to the text used for the Septuagint translation, the court had not only chambers but also peristyles, rows of columns round the inside of the court – the very element that is presented in the Temple scroll! This is also apparent from Ezekiel 42:5, 6, even though the original Hebrew text is only partially preserved: 'Now the upper chambers ... from the lower and middle chambers.... For they were in three storeys....' The numbers and measurements are not the same, but the concept of the structure is similar to that in our scroll.

Apportionment of the chambers

There is special ingenuity behind the pattern designed by the author in allotting chambers, rooms, stoas and booths to the priests, the tribes, and particularly to the Levitical families of Kohath, Gershon and Merari, the sons of Levi. He did not simply take the total number of rooms and chambers in the four three-storey sections in each of the four walls and divide them equally between the twelve tribes. He gave more to Levi – the priests and the 'families of the sons of Levi' – than to each of the other tribes. How, and why, had he done this?

He assigned the two entire sections between the gates of the eastern side, chambers, rooms, stoas and booths, to the 'sons of Aaron', the priests. These, it will be recalled, were the sections between the central gate of Levi and the gates of Simeon to its north and Judah to its south. As the scroll puts it: 'From the gate of Simeon to the gate of Judah, shall be for the priests.' They thus received 108 chambers and 108 rooms (fifty-four each on either side of the Levi gate), six stoas, undivided, and two booths, also undivided. Since this differed from the allotment pattern for the other tribes, the author was at pains to emphasize this prescription with an explanatory repetition: 'And the entire right side and left side of the gate of Levi you shall allot to the sons of Aaron, your brother: eight and one hundred chambers and their rooms and their two booths, that are above the roof.' Incidentally, it was this prescription, with its 'allot to the sons of Aaron, your brother', which provided the clear-cut proof, as mentioned earlier, that the author, writing as God speaking in the first person, was portrayed as addressing Moses, brother of Aaron. The entire scroll was designed to appear as an original text of God's instructions to Moses.

The author deals next with the apportionment to Judah, the most important tribe after Levi: 'And to the sons of Judah, from the gate of Judah to the corner, four and fifty chambers and their rooms and the booth that is above them.' His stress on 'to the corner', namely to the outer corner of the court, evades, of course, as we have seen earlier, the fact that 7 cubits must be subtracted for the thickness of the wall. But his specific mention of fifty-four chambers and rooms shows that included in Judah's allotment are the corner rooms and chambers in all three storeys. The author completes the eastern side with the allocation to the tribe of Simeon, located 'from the gate of Simeon to the second corner' of that side.

Thereafter, he proceeds clockwise with the allotments to the re-maining tribes along the southern, western and northern sides, start-ing with the south-eastern angle. And here he encounters his major mathematical difficulty. Occupying the easternmost section of the southern side is the tribe of Reuben, and this section lies between the gate of Reuben and the corner. But the corner rooms have already been allotted to Judah, so Reuben's section can hold not eighteen rooms and chambers on each of the three floors but only seventeen, giving a total of fifty-one. The formulation of the prescription for Reuben shows that the author is well aware of the problem: 'And to the sons of Reuben, from the angle that is by the sons of Judah to the gate of Reuben: two and fifty chambers and their rooms and their booth.' He specially uses the term 'angle' and not 'corner', and the angle is not that of the court but of the meeting point with the structural part occupied 'by the sons of Judah'. But why the fifty-two chambers and rooms and not fifty-one? This figure of fifty-two does not recur, as the number of chambers and rooms for the other tribes is not specified. For example, Benjamin and Issachar, whose meeting-point is the south-western corner, are dealt with in this way: 'And from the gate of Benjamin to the western corner [of the southern side], to the sons of Benjamin. From this corner to the gate of Issa-char [on the western side], to the sons of Issachar.' This problem of the fifty-two or fifty-four arose four times, with the four corners – and only four sets of corner rooms – being the meeting points of eight tribes. The scroll tells us about one of the corners, the one between Judah and Reuben, with Judah getting the corner rooms with a total of fifty-four, and Reuben getting only fifty-two. From the pattern of the author's formulation, it may be conjectured that, with the other three corners, the tribes of Issachar, Dan and Asher were the ones who were allotted fifty-two. But this figure is incomprehensible, as it is not divisible by three (storeys). One can only conclude that the author, no mean mathematician, abandoned his quest for a mathe-matical solution because fifty-two was the figure he wanted. It was important to him, I surmise, as it was the number of the 'fathers of the congregation' recorded in another Dead Sea scroll, the War scroll, as corresponding to the number of weeks in the sectarian calendar.

After apportioning the chambers to the sons of Aaron and to the tribes, the author now addresses himself with special emphasis to the Levitical families who were to minister to the priestly sons of Aaron, Kohath, Gershon and Merari. The text here is very fragmentary, and what is preserved is only the allocation to 'the sons of Kohath, of the Levites', whose chambers are to be 'from the gate of Joseph to the gate of Benjamin', on the south side of the court. The apportionment for Gershon and Merari was without doubt specified in the missing passage that immediately followed. However, it can be reconstructed with relative certainty by examining the positioning of the tribes and the Levitical families round the Tabernacle as described in chapter 3 of Numbers, on which the author assuredly drew. There we read that 'The families of the sons of Kohath were to encamp on the south side of the tabernacle ... the Gershonites were to encamp behind the tabernacle on the west'; and the 'families of Merari ... were to encamp on the north side' (Num. 3: 23, 29, 35). Thus, the 'sons of Gershon' were no doubt located between the gates of Zebulun and Gad, and the 'sons of Merari' between the gates of Naphtali and Asher.

All told, therefore, 270 chambers were reserved for the whole tribe of Levi – the priests and the Levitical families (priests, 108, Levites $3 \times 54 = 162$); and 586 for all the remaining tribes ($7 \times 54 + 4 \times 52$). To sum it up another way, by sections between the gates and between gates and corners, there are 16 sections. Levi gets 5 (priests 2, Levitical families 3). The remaining 11 go to the other sons of Jacob, including Joseph (lumping together Ephraim and Manasseh). The author's ingenious plan, as mentioned, is designed as far as possible to adapt the disposition of the tribes and the Levites round the Tabernacle, as described in Numbers, to his concept of the Temple.

The purification

The text on the construction and allotment of the chambers ends with the important command concerning their purification at the weekly change of the Temple courses or 'shifts', when one ministering group was replaced by another. The passage is fragmentary, but there is enough to reveal the procedure: 'the second shall enter to the left, and ... the first shall go out from the right. And let them not mix with each other and with their vessels. [....] course to its place, and they shall encamp. One enters and the other goes out towards the eighth day; and they shall purify the chambers one after another, when the first one goes out; and let there be no mingling.'

The point of this procedure is clearly to ensure that the new, pure, incoming shift has no contact with the course it replaces. The incoming course enters the Temple court and turns to the left. The outgoing one leaves to the right. They shall 'not mix'. The chambers, too, are to be purified, and there is to be 'no mingling' there of the two shifts or of their vessels. Each is to 'encamp' in its prescribed place, one to the left, the other to the right, and only thereafter can the incoming course begin its systematic cleansing of the chambers, 'one after another'.

The system of keeping apart the pure from the impure by separate entry and exit is also to be found in the mishnaic sources on other Temple practices. It is worth comparing the scroll text with the more general one in Tractate Middoth 2:2:

Whosoever it was that entered the Temple Mount came in on the right and went round and came out on the left, save any whom aught befell, for he went round to the left. 'What aileth thee that thou goest to the left?' 'Because I am a mourner' (says one). 'Because I am under a ban' (says another).

The scroll, however, would appear to prescribe the reverse directions, with those whom nothing 'aileth' entering from the left, whereas in the Mishnah the left entry is for those 'whom aught befell'.

The scarecrow

Wholly concerned in this section with safeguarding the purity of the Temple, the author next tackles the problem posed by the possible overflight of birds who might befoul the holy compound. Though the text is poorly preserved, it could be reconstructed with the aid of fragments from a parallel copy of the scroll to read as follows: 'Let not fly any unclean bird over my temple ... and over the roofs of the gates of the outer court. And an unclean bird shall not be within my temple for ever and ever, all the days that I dwell among them' (Col. 46:1–4). This reconstruction still leaves gaps, and I think it may be inferred that the author included a description of the devices that were to be installed along the top of the gates and walls to keep birds away from the Temple compound. Such devices were known in the Mishnah as 'scarecrows', the Hebrew term used in its literal sense. Middoth 4:6, for example, giving the dimension of the Temple structure, states: 'And the parapet three cubits and the scarecrow one cubit. Rabbi Judah says: The scarecrow was not taken into account; but the parapet was four cubits.'

The noted talmudic scholar Professor Saul Lieberman, who has made a special study of this subject, cites parallels from other sources that mention the existence of scarecrows in Herod's Temple. One is from Josephus: 'From its summit protruded sharp golden spikes to prevent birds from settling upon and polluting the roof' (*War* 5:224). Another source, describing the Temple of Solomon, is quoted by Eusebius, one of the Fathers of the Church: 'And he made the netting strong in order that the bells ring and frighten the birds so that they do not perch on the Temple or nest on the rims of the gates and stoas or dirty the Temple with their secretion.' In a talmudic Midrash (Avoth de Rabbi Nathan) dealing with the slaughterhouse, in language similar to that in the scroll, we read: 'And no fly was found in the slaughterhouse . . . and no fowl passed over it.'

In the light of these sources, and on the basis of the surviving letters in this part of the scroll, it is possible, perhaps, to fill the gaps and expand my earlier reconstruction of the text to read as follows: 'Let not fly any unclean bird over my temple, and you shall make spikes on the wall of the court and over the roofs of the gates of the outer court. And an unclean bird shall not be within my temple for ever and ever, all the days that I dwell among them.'

The terrace and moat

The final commands associated with the outer court are designed to provide a protective belt round the outermost boundary of the Temple compound as an added safeguard to its purity. The first prescription is to construct a terrace: 'And you shall make a terrace around, outside the outer court, fourteen cubits wide, according to the entrances of all the gates. And you shall make twelve steps to it, for the children of Israel to ascend to it to enter into my temple.'

The problem with this text is that it lends itself to two possible interpretations. It could mean a continuous 14-cubit wide terrace encircling the entire length of the outer court wall; or the intention might have been a short terrace constructed only in front of the entrance-way to each of the gates, the double-door 'gate-openings'. No such terrace is mentioned in any of the relevant sources, and so we have no guide as to which of the two the author had in mind. However, the second interpretation seems the most likely, for it will be recalled that these 'gate-openings' – which were indeed the 'entrances of all the gates' – were also 14 cubits wide. The terraces would thus serve as the landings which 'the children of Israel' would reach after climbing the twelve steps, and 'enter into my temple' through the doors. The recent discoveries by Professor Binyamin Mazar of magnificent steps with intervals of terraces at the southern wall of the Temple Mount would also appear to favour this possibility. But we cannot know for certain, and it may well be that the author's prescription called for an all-encompassing terrace.

Girdling the terrace and the steps, as the last protective belt at the approaches to the Temple compound, was the fosse, a dry moat, and its excavation and purpose are clearly prescribed. 'And you shall make a fosse around the temple ... one hundred cubits wide' in order to 'separate the holy temple from the city', and so that the people 'may not come suddenly to my temple and desecrate it. They shall consecrate my temple and fear my temple for I dwell among them.'

So end the scroll's commands for the construction of the Temple with all its courts and structures, as issued directly by God.

Solution to an archaeological riddle?

When the scroll's instructions on the plan of the Temple with its three courts had been deciphered, it appeared that they held a possible solution to the tantalizing riddle of the pattern on the linen coverings in which a number of the Dead Sea scrolls had been wrapped. It was a pattern of three quadrangles, carefully woven in blue linen thread.

The late Mrs Grace Crowfoot, in the publication of her study of these fabrics found at Qumran, noted that she had been able to identify this pattern on sixteen of the linen sheets. A thorough examination of the weaving methods had convinced Mrs Crowfoot that the weavers had taken great pains over this pattern of three quadrangles, one inside the other. Despite the simplicity of its form, the task was technically complicated and required considerable skill and concentration. The central figure was rectangular, while the outer two became progressively more square; this may have been occasioned by the need to take the edges of the wrapping sheets into account so that in effect all three were virtual squares.

In view of the immense difficulty in weaving a pattern of this kind in blue linen thread for both warp and crossing weft, Mrs Crowfoot drew the following discerning inference:

The question arises whether this rectangular pattern has perhaps some religious significance. Reference has been made to the difficulty of either

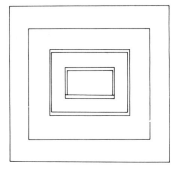

The concentric rectangles woven in purple on the 'kerchiefs' covering the scrolls found in Cave 1. It is suggested that they are a schematic representation of the plan of the Temple as depicted in the Temple scroll.

weaving or embroidering this pattern, and I find it hard to believe myself that people could take so much trouble over a rather uninteresting design unless it had some traditional meaning for them. The obvious suggestion is that the rectangles represent the ground plan of some religious building. The Tabernacle is represented by a simple rectangular figure in the Codex Amiatinus, but our figure does not really agree with this or with the description of the Temple or Ezekiel's temple.

I have no doubt that Mrs Crowfoot's deductions are correct, but it represents the plan of the Temple as conceived by our sect! Though this solution still fails to explain satisfactorily certain details, it holds enough to attest to the central role in the life of the sect of the Temple described in our scroll. Moreover, having the pattern of the Temple on the wrappings of their sacred writings was, in its way, like safeguarding the holy books inside the Temple – which was the practice in the actual Temple in Jerusalem.

16 The Sources

It will have been noticed that while the scroll offers much information on the plan of the Temple structures and courts, it provides very little on the main Temple building itself, the Sanctuary. What there is shows that the author based himself largely on those biblical sources, scant though they are, that yielded descriptions – not ordinances – of Solomon's Temple as well as of the Second Temple rebuilt by the returning exiles from Babylon under Zerubbabel.

The paucity of detail about the Sanctuary indicates clearly that this was not the author's major concern. His primary interests were the Temple courts, their installations, and the rituals specified for each 'house' and court. Thus, the uniqueness of the Temple plan in our scroll finds expression mostly in the plan of the courts and their relationship to the main Temple building.

The descriptive pattern in the biblical sources is the reverse of the one in the scroll. The Bible gives far more information on the Sanctuary than it does on the courts. The one exception is a passage in 1 Chronicles 28, mentioned earlier, in which David commands Solomon to build a Temple and gives him in writing the word of God about its plans. The emphasis in those instructions is on the courts, chambers, vestibule and the service of the priests and the Levites.

Before going further into this subject, it is important to bear in mind that the pagan temples in antiquity, as well as the Jewish Temple of Jerusalem, were not places where people gathered for prayer, as are the synagogues, churches and mosques of today. Among the pagans of the ancient Near East, their temple was the

house of their god in the tangible form of an idol. The Jewish Temple
was also called the House of God in the Bible, though of course there
was no image. Some of the main rituals in the Jewish Temple, with
the participation of the public, were performed outside the House,
namely, in the courts. Though there are several mentions of courts in
the Bible, varying in detail and number, we are told very little about
them. It was precisely for this reason that the author of the scroll
could enlarge upon them and issue his commands, and thereby fill an
important gap.

It should also be remembered, when we deal with the sources which
may have influenced the author, that when we talk of the Temple of
Jerusalem we are really considering three Temples: the Temple built
by Solomon in the tenth century BC, commonly known as the First
Temple; the rebuilt Temple under Zerubbabel towards the end of the
sixth century BC, known as the Second Temple; and the one reconstructed by Herod towards the end of the first century BC. As biblical
sources we might also include the future Temple as envisioned by the
prophet Ezekiel.

The Temple of Solomon is briefly described in 1 Kings and the
parallel text in 2 Chronicles. The post-exilic Temple by Zerubbabel,
erected when the Persian emperors Cyrus and Darius gave permission
to the Jewish exiles to return and rebuild Jerusalem, is also recorded
in the Bible, mainly in the Books of Ezra and Nehemiah. But the
description is so short that very little indeed is known about it,
though it is possible that our author may have used one of the dimensions noted in the account in Ezra – the 60-cubit height of the
House.

The structure of which most is known is the one built by Herod,
for that has the most detailed descriptions both in the Mishnah and
in the works of Josephus. This Herodian Temple replaced the modest
previous Temple, which in its day had replaced the then ruined
Solomonic Temple, and which had been reinforced and renovated from
time to time, particularly during the second century BC Maccabean
period.

Which of the various descriptions of these Temples had influenced
the author of our scroll? Though I am anticipating, I deem it best to
state right away that the one that comes closest to the plan in the
scroll is the description of Solomon's Temple by Josephus. His is quite
different from the accounts in any other source, and it is my belief
that he gleaned his information from the Essene sect. He says explicitly in his autobiography that he spent several years as a young man
with the Essenes for the purpose of studying their laws, and the
description he ascribed to Solomon's Temple may well have been
based upon what he had learned from them about the Temple plan
as decreed in the Temple scroll.

I arrived at this conclusion after a careful examination of all the biblical and post-biblical sources. The most important, of course, were the biblical accounts of Solomon's Temple in 1 Kings 6 and 2 Chronicles 3. These contain enough detail to make possible a plausible reconstruction of the House itself, the Sanctuary; but there is barely a reference to the Temple courts. There is mention of an inner court, and on occasion of an outer court, but without any indication of plan, dimension or location. To our author, on the other hand, it is the courts that are all-important, and so he devotes little space to the House and many columns to the courts. If not Kings and Chronicles, what then could have been his main biblical source – again, if any?

The visionary temple of Ezekiel

One would have expected it to have been the Book of Ezekiel, with the prophet's vision of the future Temple. It is there that we find the most explicit ordinance concerning the Temple: 'Behold, this is the law of the temple' (43:12), as well as a full and detailed description, including certain measurements, of its inner court, outer court, gates and chambers. Surely our author would have relied heavily on a biblical Book that could be said to have provided a ready-made Torah on the Temple and its courts.

But this is not the case. True, there are many similarities between the commands in the Temple scroll and the text – and the very terminology – in Ezekiel. Our author was without doubt intimately familiar with the Book of Ezekiel, and employed terms and descriptions taken from that Book. Moreover, most of the commands in Ezekiel, as in our scroll, are applied to the courts and not to the House. And in both Ezekiel and the scroll, the square is the dominant architectural feature in the design of the courts. Yes, similarities abound. Yet there are radical differences between the two plans, and in each plan there are items that do not appear in the other.

In the scroll, for example, there are three courts, in Ezekiel only two, an inner and an outer one; and some of the laws in Ezekiel concerning the outer court are applied in the scroll to the middle court.

In Ezekiel, the altar is in the inner court; in the scroll, both the altar and the House are in that court.

The number of the gates in the courts differs. The scroll's inner court has four gates, Ezekiel's three; the outer court in the scroll has twelve gates, in Ezekiel again there are only three. The names of the gates are not quite the same. Nor is the form of their structure, those in the scroll protruding both within and outside the courts, while in Ezekiel the gates of the outer court are on the inside and of the inner court on the outside. The two plans also differ in the number and system of location of the chambers. As for elements which appear in one plan and not in the other, an example is the total absence in Ezekiel of the various installations prescribed for the inner court by the scroll, such as the House of the Laver and the House of the Utensils.

The question that comes to mind is why the author of the scroll did not follow meticulously the plan of the Temple in Ezekiel. Why the changes? Why the innovations? It might be argued that the deviation by the author may not be as great as it would appear, for we are comparing the text of the scroll with the texts of Ezekiel in Hebrew and in the early Greek translation which are known to have gaps and distortions. The author, for his part, may have had a different text, the original Ezekiel text, which may conceivably have been closer to his own. But this argument is hardly tenable, for the striking differences to which we have drawn attention occur mostly in that section of the traditional masoretic text of Ezekiel which is unanimously considered to be uncorrupted.

I confess that I have no unequivocal answer to the question of why the author should have departed so radically from the Ezekiel plan, but can only suggest that the explanation may lie in the different purposes of the two Temples. The one in the scroll purports to be the Temple which the Children of Israel are commanded to build. The one in the vision of Ezekiel is the Temple of the future which the Lord himself will create. The two, therefore, need not be identical. And the author could find backing in the fact that in certain significant details Ezekiel himself departs from the plan of Solomon's Temple as depicted in Kings and Chronicles.

This may also help to explain why the gates in the middle and outer courts are named after the twelve sons of Jacob rather than according to the naming pattern of the city gates in Ezekiel, thereby

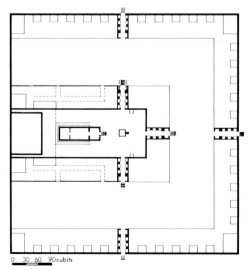

0 30 60   90 cubits

Plan of the Temple envisaged by the prophet Ezekiel at the 'End of Days' (after Professor M. Haran). The similarities and differences between this Temple and the one in the Temple scroll are discussed in the text. Note, for example, the three gates in the inner court as against the four in the scroll.

symbolizing that the Temple was to be an integral part of the Temple city. I believe our author also added a court, and transferred to the middle court certain of the bans and rituals relating in Ezekiel's plan to the outer court, thus providing a further protective ring to safeguard the purity of the Temple compound within the precincts of the city.

A non-biblical source

I disclosed earlier that of the descriptions of Solomon's Temple in the non-biblical sources that have come down to us, the only one bearing any relationship to the plan in our scroll is that of Josephus in his *Antiquities* (8:61ff.). Josephus, of course, was living during the final years of the Temple constructed by Herod, and he wrote a detailed description of that Temple. But he also wrote about Solomon's Temple, and although most of his information on that structure and its furnishings is based on the Greek translation of the Bible, there are many differences in his account, and a number of additions that are not to be found in any biblical source. Most scholars have tended to explain such differences and additions by arguing that he was interpolating into the description of Solomon's Temple some of the features of Herod's structure; or that Josephus misunderstood the biblical texts; or that he recorded details drawn from his imagination. However, if we disregard these hypothetical arguments, take the text of Josephus at its face value, and compare it with the text we now have of the Temple scroll, though they are not identical, there is a striking similarity between the two, particularly as far as they concern the Temple courts. Here is the relevant extract from Josephus:

He [Solomon] also surrounded the Temple [the House proper] with a parapet ... which he raised to a height of three cubits; it was to keep the multitude from entering the sacred precinct and to signify that entry was permitted only to the priests. Outside of this he built another sacred precinct in the form of a quadrangle and erected great and wide porticoes (stoas) which were entered by high gates each of which faced one of the four quarters [the four points of the compass] and was closed by golden doors. Into this precinct all the people who were distinguished by purity and their observance of the laws might enter. But wonderful and surpassing all description, and even, one might say, all sight was the [third] sacred precinct which he made outside of these, for he filled up with earth great valleys, into which, because of their immense depth, one could not without difficulty look down, and bringing them up to a height of four hundred cubits he made them level with the top of the mountain on which the Temple was built; in this way the outer precinct [namely, the outer court], which was open to the sky, was on a level with the Temple. And he surrounded it with double stoas supported by high columns of native stone, and they had roofs of cedar which were smoothly finished in panels. And all the doors which he made for this sacred precinct were of silver.

It seems evident to me that in this account of Solomon's Temple, Josephus is describing three concentric square courts, just as our author prescribes in the Temple scroll. By contrast, in his account of the Herodian Temple, the courts are not concentric but are adjacent to one another. Adjacent courts are also recorded in the mishnaic references to Herod's structure. Therefore, to my mind, Josephus could not have been injecting this feature of the Herodian Temple into his account of Solomon's Temple. However, those scholars who take the opposite view can claim that the above Josephus text on Solomon's Temple does not categorically exclude the possibility that the three courts were alongside one another rather than one inside the other. I confess that the text lends itself to either interpretation. But I am bound to add that the differences between Josephus's own descriptions of both Solomon's and Herod's Temples are so wide and numerous as to render untenable the argument that he used Herod's plan as the basis for his account of Solomon's structure.

I return to my conjecture that in describing Solomon's Temple Josephus drew upon the information in the Temple scroll, though he may well have included some details of the Temple of his own day. He may not have read the text of our scroll, but during the time he spent with the Essenes in his youth, as he says in his autobiography, he acquainted himself with their doctrines, and something of what he had learned lingered in his memory, and emerged years later when he came to write his historical works.

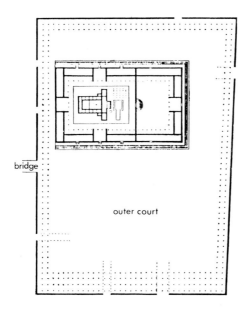

bridge

outer court

Plan of Herod's Temple, based on the descriptions in Josephus and in the Mishnah. Its dissimilarity to the Temple of the scroll is immediately apparent: its courts are not concentric; and the number of its gates and the overall measurements are also different.

To sum up, it seems that the sources upon which our author drew were the descriptions of the Solomonic Temple in Kings and Chronicles; certain elements of the future Temple in Ezekiel; the little that appears in Ezra on the Second Temple; and perhaps other writings on the Temple which have not come down to us but which may have been known to the author. It is my belief, however, that the Temple plan in the scroll is mainly his own creation, an original work in which the author suited his Temple concept to the disposition of the Tribes of Israel round the Tabernacle in the wilderness of Sinai. And it is this creation that may have influenced Josephus in his description of Solomon's Temple.

An interesting footnote to this section is an enigmatic story told by Josephus which I feel may be linked to his knowledge of the Essene plan of a square temple. Describing the capture of Jerusalem and the destruction of the Temple in his *The Jewish War* (6:310ff.), Josephus quotes statements which he claims were made on the eve of the destruction by people whom he terms 'false prophets'. These utterances, he says, helped to delude the people, and were even a factor in the loss of the Temple. He adds a further observation and a related incident at the end of the chapter:

Reflecting on these things one will find that God has a care for men, and by all kinds of premonitory signs shows his people the way of salvation, while they owe their destruction to folly and calamities of their own choosing. Thus, the Jews, after the demolition of the Antonia [the fortress north of the Temple] reduced the Temple to a square, although they had it recorded in their oracles that the city and the sanctuary would be taken when the Temple should become four-square.

What was 'recorded in their oracles' was not known to any of the scholars, and even such specialists in the works of Josephus as H. St J. Thackeray, who translated parts of them, has a footnote against this passage which says 'authority unknown'. There is of course no reference to it in any of the Jewish sources, either in the Bible or in the rabbinical writings. Can it be that the answer is to be found in the scroll, in the context of its absolutely square plan of the Temple with its concentric square courts which, as we have indicated, Josephus may have gleaned from Essene writings or their noted oracle-like commentaries – or perhaps from our very Temple scroll? He may have arrived at the notion that what they had said or written contained the hint that before the Lord would create his Temple 'at the end of days', the earthly Temple had to be square, as set forth in our scroll. This may have been suggested in one of their sectarian texts he had come across, or he may have so interpreted what he had read or heard. We cannot know. What we do know is that the coincidence – if indeed it is a coincidence – is certainly intriguing.

PART FIVE

PURITY

17 The Temple City

The section that follows the account of the outer court contains the ordinances to ensure the purity and sanctity of the city in which the Temple stood. It is one of the most important texts in the entire scroll, for its sectarian character is more pronounced than any other part of the document, revealing the deep rift between normative Judaism, the religious concept crystallized by the rabbis of the Mishnah, and the extremist views of the Essenes.

The biblical source for both sides was the command in Numbers (5:2, 3) to 'put out of the camp every leper, and every one having a discharge, and every one that is unclean ... that they may not defile their camp ['their camps' in the original Hebrew (and in the King James English version)], in the midst of which I dwell'.

This was the starting-point for both. The Essenes, following the plain and straightforward meaning of the Pentateuchal text, held that the ordinances on ritual purity had applied to the entire wilderness camp, with its three components: the divine camp (the Tabernacle) in the centre, the camp of the Levites around it, and the camp of the tribes of Israel around the Levites. They therefore maintained that these very laws were applicable in their own day to the Temple (the divine camp), the Temple precincts (the Levitical camp) and the Temple city (the camp of Israel). This strict approach finds expression in our Temple scroll, so that all the bans are applied also to the Temple city, including, for example, the ban on sexual intercourse.

The approach of the rabbis, on the other hand, cardinal in all their rulings (though it was never said in so many words), was to give a more lenient interpretation to certain laws in the Pentateuch so as to make them easier to live with in conditions very different from those in the wilderness. How were they to do this with the laws on purity? They did so by basing themselves on the mention of the plural form, 'their camps', in the above quotation in Numbers. This enabled them to interpret the rules on uncleanness as referring not necessarily to all three components of the entire camp but in some cases to one specific camp, in others to two of the camps and in yet others to all three. They then decided that most of the biblical strictures on the various categories of uncleanness were to be applied to the divine and Levitical camps and to the priests and Levites alone, while others, dependent on the circumstances in each case, were to be applicable also to the Temple city and to all the people.

To my mind, the rabbis may be said to have been the reformers of those days, as compared with such an extreme sect as the Essenes. Their approach in interpreting the biblical text, so different from its straightforward meaning, reflects the greatness of these sages of old, and disproves the widely held belief that they sought always to favour the strict literal letter of the biblical law. Their modified interpretations were based on what they called 'oral tradition', Halachah, and therein lies the kernel of all the discussions and rulings of the Talmud.

This rabbinical approach was presented diplomatically but very clearly by a great Jewish scholar, the late Professor Gedaliah Alon, in his *Studies in Jewish History*:

It is generally accepted that the Pentateuchal laws of purity applied, in the halachic tradition, only to priests, entry into the Temple and eating of holy things. The halachah reinterprets the literal meaning of these biblical passages that seem to refer to uncleanness outside the Temple or to the ban of uncleanness from any source, even for ordinary priests.... Even the Tannaitic [i.e. mishnaic] interpretation of those sections of the Pentateuch that concern the expulsion of unclean persons from the camp as referring only to Divine and Levitical camps bears little resemblance to the simple sense of the verses.

A holy city

Our scroll, and the Essene sect which followed its rulings, took the opposite view. The biblical 'camp' was all-embracing. Thus, all the ordinances concerning cleanliness and uncleanliness were operative not for the Temple alone but also for the city of the Temple. The city was to be holy and clean, not only in name but also in practice.

For this, our author could claim the authority of the Prophets, if not of the Pentateuch. He was certainly as familiar as we are today with Isaiah 52:1: 'Awake, awake, put on your strength, O Zion; put on your beautiful garments, O Jerusalem, the holy city; for there shall no more come into you the uncircumcised and the unclean.' He could also find backing from the prophet Joel (3:17): 'So you shall know that I am the Lord your God, who dwell in Zion, my holy mountain. And Jerusalem shall be holy and strangers shall never again pass through it.'

The author follows this approach to the letter, banning the entry into the city of the Temple all who are unclean. He also excludes 'the afflicted', such as the blind. He then deals at length with the strict procedure of their purification, all with the single aim of ensuring that the city is to be pure for it is the holy city, the city in which the Temple is to be built, the city in which God dwells. The author repeats this theme time and again, speaking as God in the first person, with such commands as: 'And you shall not defile the city in which I settle my name and my Temple.' And 'the city which I shall hallow . . . shall be holy and clean of any unclean thing . . . everything that is in it shall be clean.'

Indeed, so strict is the author that he demands purity in whatever city the Jews dwell, though the ordinances are not as stringent as those for the Temple city. He also extends certain laws of uncleanness and purity, which the biblical text directs to the priests alone, to all Israel, for fear that it would otherwise be impossible to maintain the purity of the Temple city and other cities.

Sexual 'uncleanness'

The categories of 'impurities' with which the scroll begins this section are those concerned with sexual matters. The first deals with what it calls 'nocturnal emission':

And if a man has a nocturnal emission, he shall not enter into any part of the temple until he will complete three days. And he shall wash his clothes and bathe on the first day, and on the third day he shall wash his clothes and bathe, and when the sun is down, he may come within the temple. And they shall not come into my temple in their menstrual-like uncleanness and defile it. (Col. 45:7-10)

It is clear from the language in which this ban is couched that the author based himself on Deuteronomy 23:9-11, with its commands to the Israelites when encamped against their enemies to keep themselves 'from every evil thing':

If there is among you any man who is not clean by reason of what chances to him by night, then he shall go outside the camp, he shall not come within the camp; but when evening comes on, he shall bathe himself in water, and when the sun is down, he may come within the camp.

This very prohibition in Deuteronomy was interpreted in the following way in another of the Dead Sea scrolls, The War of the Sons of Light against the Sons of Darkness, which I published some years ago:

Any man who is not pure with regard to his sexual organs on the day of battle shall not join them in battle, for holy angels are in communion with their hosts. (7:5, 6)

Our author prescribes that such 'unclean' people not only be kept out of the Temple but also outside the Temple city, and even the other cities in Israel, until they have cleansed themselves. The ordinance for the city of the Temple is specific:

And you shall make three places to the east of the city, separated one from another, into which shall come the lepers and the people who have a discharge and the men who have had a nocturnal emission.

It will be noted that the scroll goes further in its stringency than does Deuteronomy, which calls for one day of purification while the scroll prescribes three days. Why three? This will be better understood in the course of our discussion of the following more severe regulations concerning sexual intercourse:

And if a man lies with his wife and has an emission of semen, he shall not come into any part of the city of the temple, where I will settle my name, for three days. (Col. 45:11, 12)

I find this prohibition of special interest, both because it may explain the origin of religious celibacy, and also because it bears a striking similarity to a ban found in another Dead Sea scroll, the Damascus Covenant, and shows without doubt a connection between the two.

Though the source of this prohibition is Leviticus 15:18, the differences are significant. The biblical verse states: 'If a man lies with a woman and has an emission of semen, both of them shall bathe themselves in water, and be unclean until the evening.' The scroll again prescribes three days of purification as against the biblical one day; it extends the biblical ban on the entry to the city of the Temple of anyone who has not purified himself for three days after intercourse anywhere outside the city; and, by implication, it prohibits intercourse in any part of the Temple city.

What is implicit in our scroll is specified in the parallel passage of the highly sectarian Damascus Covenant document: 'No man shall lie with a woman in the city of the Temple, to defile the city of the Temple with their menstrual-like uncleanness.' The two texts may be said to complement one another. Our scroll deals with the purification procedure after intercourse outside the city before entry is permitted. The Damascus document is concerned not with the purification but with the prohibition. Thus, the two passages taken together may be said to present the laws of the sect roughly as follows: No man shall lie with a woman in the Temple city.... And if a man lie with his wife in any other city ... he shall not come into any part of the Temple city for three days, after purification.

It follows from this that, under the laws of the sect, all males residing in the Temple city must abstain from sexual intercourse therein. It seems to me that this ban is tantamount to a direct ordinance for complete celibacy. Such abstinence, of course, was practised by most of the Essenes, according to the descriptions of Josephus and Pliny. Similar prohibitions appear in the War scroll, where women and children are forbidden to enter the battle camps. Moreover, in our scroll, women during their menstrual period and immediately after confinement are not given places in the city of the Temple, as they are in other cities. This confirms that the doctrine of the sect banned women from permanent residence in the Temple city. Therein, perhaps, lies the distinct source of the development of Essene celibacy, and eventually Christian monasticism.

As for the three days prescribed by our scroll for purification, where the Torah calls for only one, the author clearly sought the strictest possible measures to safeguard the sanctity of Jerusalem, the holy city of the Temple. He therefore resorted to another biblical source, the procedure demanded by Moses of the Israelites before they approached Mount Sinai, as recorded in Exodus 19:10–15:

And the Lord said to Moses, 'Go to the people and consecrate them today and tomorrow, and let them wash their garments, and be ready by the third day; for on the third day the Lord will come down upon Mount Sinai in the sight of all the people. And you shall set bounds for the people round about, saying, "Take heed that you do not go up into the mountain or touch the border of it; whoever touches the mountain shall be put to death...."' So Moses went down from the mountain to the people.... And he said to the people, 'Be ready by the third day; do not go near a woman.'

By evidently basing himself on this passage, our author secured not only the more severe three-day wait but also a certain parallel between Mount Sinai and the Temple Mount and city, by applying to them the commands on the approach to Sinai.

The scroll decreed that anyone suffering from gonorrhoea – the usage in the Bible and in the scroll is 'discharge' – had to cleanse himself for seven days before being permitted to enter the city of the Temple:

And any man who cleanses himself of his discharge shall count for himself seven days for his cleansing and wash his clothes on the seventh day, and bathe his whole body in running water. Only then he shall come into the city of the temple. (Col. 45:15–17)

The injunction is based on Numbers 5:2, 3, referred to earlier, commanding the people of Israel to 'put out of the camp ... every one having a discharge ... you shall put out both male and female ... that they may not defile their camp ...'.

Here again the author's decree differs from the rabbinic ruling. The scroll puts the entire city of the Temple out of bounds to them. The rabbis, on the other hand, followed their principle of the three camps and interpreted 'camp' in this case as referring only to the Levitical camp, namely, the Temple Mount. They therefore banned anyone with this disease from the Temple precincts, but not from the city.

Our scroll's prohibition against entering the city of the Temple apparently followed a very old tradition, and it is of special interest to us that Josephus, writing of those who were denied entry into Jerusalem, echoes the approach of the scroll and not that of the rabbis. According to him, not only lepers were excluded – on this, all were agreed – but also those suffering a discharge: 'Persons afflicted with gonorrhoea or leprosy were excluded from the entire city' (*War* 5:227). And in *Antiquities* 3:261, he writes that Moses 'banished from the city alike those afflicted with leprosy and those with gonorrhoea'. Many scholars have concluded from these two verses that Josephus was describing a custom that was current during the Second Temple years before the decrees of the later rabbis. But the possibility cannot be discounted that Josephus may have been drawing upon his re-collections of what he had heard or read of the Essene writings, particularly of a scroll such as ours.

The blemished

The scroll decrees that 'No blind man shall enter the city of the Temple'. This is a classic example of how our author takes a biblical prohibition affecting only priests, and only the Temple compound, and extends it to include all the people of Israel and the entire Temple city. (The term 'blind' in this context is intended to cover all those with physical disabilities.)

The biblical basis of this ordinance is God's injunction to Moses recorded in Leviticus 21:17–23:

Say to Aaron, None of your descendants throughout their generations who has a blemish may approach to offer the bread of his God. For no one who has a blemish shall draw near, a man blind or lame, or one who has a mutilated face or a limb too long, or a man who has an injured foot or an injured hand, or a hunchback, or a dwarf, or a man with a defect in his sight or an itching disease or scabs or crushed testicles; no man of the descendants of Aaron the priest who has a blemish shall come near to offer the Lord's offerings by fire; since he has a blemish, he shall not come near ... the veil or approach the altar, because he has a blemish, that he may not profane my sanctuaries; for I am the Lord who sanctify them.

Though the essence of this text is to ban a 'blemished' priest from officiating at the sacrificial offerings, the explanation for it, 'that he may not profane my sanctuaries', gave our author the opportunity of applying it more widely to persons and places.

Why this stigma on the afflicted? It was widely accepted in ancient times, and not only by the Essenes, that physical disability was a divine punishment for people who were sinful, and therefore not 'pure'. It is noteworthy that the verse following the account of David's capture of Jerusalem (in 2 Samuel 5:8) – 'Therefore it is said, "The blind and the lame shall not come into the house [the House of God]"' – is interpreted in some of the earliest biblical commentaries and translations as reflecting an ancient tradition that held the handicapped to be 'sinful and guilty'.

In addition to the explicit passage in our scroll, other sectarian writings also emphasized, though in different contexts, that the ban in question as understood by the sect had indeed to be applied to all Israel and to the entire city of the Temple, and not exclusively to the priests and to the Temple precincts. The War scroll, for example, in its battle regulations, decrees that:

Any one halt or blind or lame, or a man in whose body is a permanent defect, or a man affected by an impurity of his flesh, all these shall not go forth to battle with them. All of them shall be volunteers for battle and sound in spirit and flesh, and ready for the day of vengeance.

Thus, the ban applying to the Temple priests is here extended to all warriors. They, too, must be 'sound in spirit and flesh'. Another sectarian document, a scroll known as the Messianic Rule, describing an assembly to be held during the messianic period, disqualifies all persons 'with a defect' from 'entering into the congregation'.

Lepers – and a Jesus episode

'And any one unclean through contact with the dead shall not enter it [the city of the Temple] until he cleanses himself.' This too is based on Numbers 5:2. And here, again, the scroll's stringent decree is diametrically opposed to the ruling of the sages, which is best summed up by Maimonides in his *Code* 'Laws Concerning Entrance into the Sanctuary':

It was permissible for one unclean by the dead, and even the dead corpse itself, to enter the Temple Mount. For it is said: 'And Moses took the bones of Joseph with him' (Exodus 13:19); that is, 'with him' into the Camp of the Levites.

The scroll prohibits 'any leper or diseased person' from entering the city of the Temple 'until he cleanses himself, and when he has been cleansed, he shall sacrifice. . .'. This also accords with rabbinic law.

It is of interest, however, that our author goes on to decree that 'in every city you shall allot places for those afflicted with leprosy or with plague or with scab, who may not enter your cities and defile them'. As for the Temple city, the scroll adds that the lepers must be kept outside it – 'east of the city' (Col. 46:16–17).

There can be no doubt that the stress here and in another passage that lepers were to be isolated in a separate place east of the Temple city was prompted by the belief that this disease was contagious and was carried by the wind. Since the prevailing winds in Jerusalem are westerly, the areas east of the city, particularly the eastern slopes of the Mount of Olives facing the Dead Sea, would have been considered least likely to endanger the people in the Temple and city of Jerusalem.

There is support for this view in a rabbinical Midrash, Leviticus Rabba 16, as well as in the Talmud. In the Midrash we read:

Rabbi Yohanan said: One is not permitted to pass within four cubits to the east of a leper. Rabbi Simon ben Lakhish said: Within a hundred cubits. There is no contradiction. The one who said 'within four cubits' meant when there is no wind blowing; and the one who said 'within a hundred cubits' meant when there is a wind blowing.

And in Baba Batra 3:9;13 of the Palestinian Talmud, we find the following: 'Rabbi Mana would walk with people afflicted with boils. Rabbi Abbaya said to him: "Do not walk east of him, but rather to the west of him."'

There are indeed a number of rabbinic regulations ordering that workshops, such as tanneries, that give off unpleasant odours should not be established west of the city because of the prevailing westerly winds. Here in the scroll, however, we learn for the first time that there were special places of isolation for lepers east of the city.

This may shed significant light on the celebrated New Testament account of Jesus, on his way to Jerusalem 'two days before the Passover', stopping off at Bethany: 'And while he was at Bethany in the house of Simon the leper, as he sat at table ...' (Mark 14:3). Bethany is situated at the eastern edge of Jerusalem, on the eastern slopes of the Mount of Olives, and would fit the requirements of an isolation centre for the sufferers of leprosy. If my suggestion is correct, this would prove that Jesus had not happened by chance to find himself in the house of a leper, but had deliberately chosen to spend the night before entering Jerusalem in this leper colony, which was anathema both to the Essenes and the Pharisees.

18 The 'Hand', the Corpse, the Sacrifice

The 'hand' is the literal translation of the Hebrew word used in the scroll (and in the Bible) for a privy, latrine or lavatory. The ruling in the scroll prohibits 'hands' not only within the Temple compound, and not only within the Temple city, but also anywhere they might be visible within a distance of fifteen hundred yards from the city:

And you shall make them a place for a hand outside the city, to which they shall go out, to the north-west of the city – roofed houses with pits within them, into which the excrement will descend, so that it will not be visible at any distance from the city, three thousand cubits. (Col. 46:13–16)

This injunction is remarkable, apart from its extreme severity, for the information that reveals the link between this scroll and the Essenes, as well as details of the structural features and location of the privies that were to serve the scroll's Temple and city communities.

The prohibition and most of the phraseology employed by the author of the scroll undoubtedly are based on the text of Deuteronomy 23:9–14:

When you go forth against your enemies and are in camp, then you shall keep yourself from every evil thing.... You shall have a place [a 'hand'] outside the camp and you shall go out to it; and you shall have a stick with your weapons; and when you sit down outside, you shall dig a hole with it, and turn back and cover up your excrement. Because the Lord your God walks in the midst of your camp, to save you and to give up your enemies before you, therefore your camp must be holy, that he may not see anything indecent among you, and turn away from you.

The War scroll of the Essenes also has a prescription on latrines when the men are encamped against their enemies, but it contains no details beyond the distance they must be located from the camps: 'There shall be a space between all their camps and the place of the hand about two thousand cubits, and no unseemly evil thing shall be seen in the vicinity of their encampment.'

Our scroll imposes the ban on the entire city of the Temple, in line with its extreme interpretation of all the bans concerning 'the camp' in the Pentateuch, so that 'outside the camp' becomes 'outside the Temple city'.

This interpretation, of course, finds absolutely no support in rabbinic law. On the contrary, according to the normative halachah, excrement was not considered ritually unclean. Here, for example, are some of the sayings of the sages in the characteristic style in which they appear in the Mishnah: 'Is excrement impure? Is it not for purposes of cleanliness?' (Pal. Talmud Pesahim 7:11;35b). In another tractate we find the definition of a rich man: 'He who has a convenience near his table' (Bab. Talmud Shabbath 25b). And yet another tells us that 'a scholar should not reside in a city where the following ten things are not found ...'; one of them is 'a convenience' (BT Sanhedrin 17b).

The problem that needs discussion is whether the severe rules on public conveniences in the scroll, assuming, as I believe, it was a Torah, a book of the law of the Essenes, were in fact observed by them. After all, having to go out of the city and walk almost another mile in order to relieve oneself was a considerable hardship. On this point, I discovered what may appear to be a remarkable coincidence but which I think is further proof of the definite link between the Dead Sea scrolls and the Essenes, confirming the theory accepted by most scholars but never before proven.

The Essenes and their privies

Our scroll decrees that the 'hand' was to be located not less than 3,000 cubits outside the city, while the War scroll, referring to battle-field conditions, prescribes 2,000 cubits from the encampment. In either case, the 'hand' had to be beyond the Sabbath limits. (The Sabbath limits in normative Judaism were also 2,000 cubits.) According to one of the sect's laws, it was not permitted on the Sabbath to 'walk more than one thousand cubits beyond his town', while another ordered that 'No man shall walk more than two thousand cubits after a beast to pasture it outside his town'. Thus, if the Essenes practised their laws, they would be unable to relieve themselves on the Sabbath day! Was this indeed the case?

What Josephus has to say on this very topic shows that it was because of the laws in the Pentateuch requiring the digging of a hole, that the Essenes refrained from relieving themselves on the Sabbath. He writes:

...they do not venture [on the Sabbath day] ... even to go to stool. On other days they dig a trench a foot deep with a mattock ... and wrapping their mantle about them, so that may not offend the rays of the deity, sit above it. They then replace the excavated soil in the trench. For this purpose they select the more retired spots. And though this discharge of the excrements is a natural function, they make it a rule to wash themselves after it, as if defiled. (*War* 2:147-9)

They evidently trained themselves, or ate special foods, to enable them to have no recourse to a privy on the Sabbath, and on other days to retire to a far spot – beyond the minimum distance at which they would not defile the sanctity of where they lived and, in the case of the city of the Temple, 3,000 cubits north-west of the city.

We now come to the final step in the process of discovering whether or not there is proof of a connection between the Essenes and the Temple scroll. We do so by approaching the problem from another angle. We know from Josephus that, apart from the community in Qumran, some of the Essenes were also living in Jerusalem, the city of the then existing Temple. If it can be shown that these Jerusalem-ite Essenes did indeed observe the decrees set out in our scroll, that would put the seal on proof of the link. For this, we revert once again to Josephus.

The 'Essene Gate'

In his description of the wall of Jerusalem, Josephus makes a single mention of 'the Gate of the Essenes'. He is the sole authority for the existence of such a gate. It appears in no other source. What and exactly where was this Essene Gate? And what bearing can it have on our problem?

Tracing the course of the city wall, Josephus starts from the north-west corner, from the tower of Hippicus (near the present Tower of David), and proceeds eastwards: 'Beginning at the north, at the tower called Hippicus, it extended to the Xystus, and then joining the council-chamber terminated at the western portico of the Temple.'

The direction is clear. He is describing the north wall, from west to east, towards the Temple. He then goes back to the north-west corner to describe the west wall, and here I believe our scroll can solve what has always been a puzzle in his account. Starting again at Hippicus and proceeding from north to south, Josephus writes that this west wall 'descended past the place called Betsoa to the gate of the Es-senes'; then turned along the south 'above the fountain of Siloam; thence it again inclined ... to the east'; and after passing the Ophel, 'finally joined the eastern portico of the Temple' (*War* 5:144–6).

Thus 'the place called Betsoa' and the Essene Gate were both in the western section of the city wall and both were close to each other, Betsoa near Hippicus in the north-west and the Essene Gate further south. Both were puzzling, but if one could not tell what 'Gate of the Essenes' represented, at least the meaning of the words was clear. Betsoa, however, long defied explanation. What did the word mean?

Not until the nineteenth century did two scholars come up with an ingenious suggestion. They were the American Edward Robinson and Rabbi Joseph Schwartz of Jerusalem, celebrated explorers of ancient Israel. With scholarly intuition they proposed that Betsoa could be

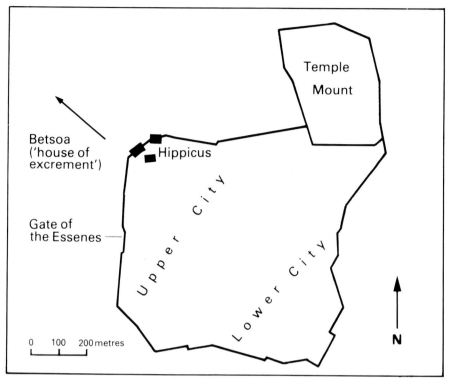

Suggested locations of 'Betsoa' (lavatory) and the 'Gate of the Essenes' according
to the description by Josephus of the walls of Jerusalem. The starting-point in his
account is Herod's Tower of Hippicus (today's 'Tower of David'), which in his day
stood at the north-west corner of the city wall.

the transliteration of two Hebrew words, 'beth', which means 'house
of', and 'tzoa', meaning 'excrement'. Both these words are used with
those very meanings in the passage of the scroll under discussion.

The suggestion of Robinson and Schwartz prompted some scholars
to attribute to Josephus's Betsoa a meaning similar to that of the
gate normally translated from the Hebrew as the Dung Gate (though
the Hebrew word for 'dung' could also mean 'quiver'). And because
of this similarity, there was a tendency to ignore the directions in
Josephus and conclude that the Essene Gate, whatever it might have
been, was close to the Dung Gate of today – in the southern wall of
the city. The text in Josephus, however, is quite clear: both the
Betsoa and the Essene Gate were on the western side of the city, with
the Betsoa nearer to the north-western corner – in line with the
location of the 'hand' in the scroll – 'to the north-west of the city'.

What of the Gate of the Essenes? What could it have been, and
why the name? We have seen that there were Essenes living in Jerusalem; that they observed the decrees in our Temple scroll; and that
the Essene Gate, mentioned only in Josephus and nowhere else, must
have been unlike any of the other, well-known gates in the city wall.

It is therefore feasible to conclude that it was a kind of wicket gate on the west side used by the local Essenes to get to the latrine, the Betsoa, the 'house of excrement', located outside and to the north-west of the city.

It is possible, therefore, that this strange phenomenon of the Essenes going outside the city wall to relieve themselves and using this small gate as the quickest exit to reach the 'hand', may have prompted the people of Jerusalem to nickname it the Gate of the Essenes. It may also be that the Essenes in Jerusalem chose to live in the area closest to the gate leading to the latrine so as to get there more quickly, and in the course of time the gate might have been popularly named after the Essene residents of the quarter.

Contact with the dead

Of the remaining laws in the scroll to safeguard the purity of the Temple city (as well as other cities), the strictest are those concerning 'uncleanness' through 'contact with the dead'. They, too, are dealt with at length, taking up several columns.

All matters pertaining to the handling of a corpse, the house in which death occurred, and the place of burial were also treated in detail in the Pentateuch and in rabbinic teaching, the more restrictive ordinances, of course, directed to the priests. The author of the scroll, however, is far more extreme. His prescriptions are more rigorous than any to be found in the rabbinic literature, and at times go beyond what is called for in any apparent source in the Scriptures.

His general approach, as we have seen in other cases, is to apply to all the people of Israel the restrictions set out for priests alone, and to make the Pentateuchal laws related to the circumstances of a tented encampment in the wilderness equally applicable to the dwelling conditions of a settled population in towns at the time he was writing the scroll. Thus, where the Bible (Numbers 19:14) declares that 'when a man dies in a tent ... every one who comes into the tent ... shall be unclean seven days', the scroll substitutes 'house' for 'tent'; and, to make certain of its intention, adds the words 'in your cities', using the command governing the desert camp in biblical times to cover populated cities in the author's time. Accordingly, the scroll's counterpart sentence reads: 'And when a man dies in your cities, every house in which a dead man died shall become unclean seven days ... and every one who comes into the house shall become unclean seven days' (Col. 49:5–7). The author's further addition in this command about the house itself being unclean will be considered later when we deal with the scroll's rigorous ordinances on the purification of a house of death, contrary to the more lenient rabbinic rulings.

Of the ordinances concerned with the dead, three are of intrinsic interest, and also exemplify our author's rigidity and his differences with the decisions of the sages. One of them deals with burial.

Burial

The scroll's command reads:

And you shall not do as the nations do: everywhere they bury their dead, even within their houses they bury. For you shall set apart places within your land in which you shall bury your dead; between four cities you shall allot a place to bury in them.

The main prohibition here is directed against the custom, that must have been current at the time the scroll was composed, of burying a dead person in his home. There is also the implied prohibition against burial within a city in the instruction to set aside one burial place to serve every four cities.

The rabbinic authorities prohibited burial within walled cities, but were less strict with open cities, where a graveyard was allowed, albeit with certain restrictions. (Incidentally, this total ban on burial in a walled city, on which all were agreed, and certainly within the walled city of Jerusalem, is at the root of the scholarly controversy over the authentic site of the Holy Sepulchre. The Church of this Sepulchre is now within the city walls, but the question is whether the course of the walls in the time of Jesus included or excluded the site of the grave. If, at that time too, it was within the walls, this could not have been the Holy Sepulchre because of the strict ban accepted by all.)

We have seen that with open cities the rabbis were more lenient, but there are varied measures of lenience in the rabbinic literature. One allows graveyards if they are at least 50 cubits away from the city limits (Tosefta Baba Batra 1:11). Another goes even further, stating that 'In a field containing a lost grave a house may be built and an upper storey thereon' (Oholoth 17:5). It is evident that people used to bury anywhere, even inside houses in settled areas. The author of the scroll angrily challenges this custom. He is particularly wrathful against burial within a house, and is also against graves within any city, as well as random burial in the country as it 'defiles the land'. There should be a special place for a cemetery, one for every four cities.

Of special interest in this context is the fairly recent archaeological discovery of a large cemetery in the vicinity of the ruins at Qumran of the settlement of the Dead Sea sect with more than 1,100 graves. It is possible that this may have been the 'allotted place' prescribed in the scroll as the central burial site for all the Essene settlements in the neighbourhood of Qumran.

The house of death

The second example worthy of attention is the scroll's severe ordinance on the purification of a house in which a person had died. We have seen that holding the 'house' to be unclean, like the 'tent' in Numbers, the author of the scroll is at odds with the leniency of the rabbis. The rabbinic decisions are best expressed by Maimonides in two brief passages in his *Code*. Concerning the difference in the application of uncleanness between priests and non-priests, he writes that 'scripture warns none but the sons of Aaron ... against incurring uncleanness from a corpse, thereby implying that for all other people it is permissible'.

As for the abode in which the corpse has lain, Maimonides says that if it be a tent, it 'incurs seven-day uncleanness on the authority of the scripture'. This, he says, applies only to a tent, whether it be of cloth, sacking, wood or leather. Then comes this key addition: 'Needless to say, *if it is a building, it is not susceptible to uncleanness.* For wherever it is said "the house is unclean", only persons and utensils throughout the house are meant.'

Giving the contrary ruling that the building *is* unclean, our author then prescribes how it is to be purified, and here he goes even beyond the biblical injunctions, setting out new and original procedures. Numbers 19:18 orders that when a man dies in a tent, which thereupon becomes unclean,

then a clean person shall take hyssop, and dip it in the water, and sprinkle it upon the tent, and upon all the furnishings, and upon the persons who were there . . . .

And here are the rigorous instructions in the scroll for purifying the house of the dead:

They shall sweep the house of any defiling smirch of oil and wine and moisture of water; they shall scrape its floor and its walls and its doors, and they shall wash with water its locks and its doorposts and its thresholds and its lintels. On the day on which the dead body will leave it, they shall purify the house and all its vessels.

The woman with a dead foetus

The third example of special interest among the ordinances relating to the dead is the case of a woman with a dead foetus in her womb. Apart from demonstrating a conflict with the rabbinic ruling, with our author displaying his characteristic extremism, the text on this topic in the scroll is in fact an 'additional Torah', expressed as God speaking in the first person and using the style in Numbers, but not based on anything known to us in the Scriptures.

Of further importance is the fact that precisely such a case is dealt with in the Mishnah, which uses the same language and terminology, but arrives at the opposite conclusion. This shows that the rabbis and the various breakaway Jewish sects all drew from a common stock of legal cases at the time, with the Dead Sea sect the most extreme and the rabbis the most lenient.

The scroll says explicitly: 'If a woman is pregnant, and her child dies in her womb, all the days on which it is dead inside her, she is unclean like the grave, and every house she comes into is unclean.'

By contrast, the rabbinic ruling on the same case, preserved in the Mishnah in Tractate Hullin (4:3), states: 'If the young of a woman died in its mother's womb . . . the mother remains clean until the child comes forth.'

The polemical nature of the scroll's harsh ordinance is well manifested by the extremely detailed prescriptions on the purification procedures for anyone and anything 'contaminated' by a woman with a lifeless foetus in her womb. These are far more detailed, for example, than those prescribed for purifying the house in which someone has died. I have found throughout the scroll that the author usually resorts to detailed treatment of the subject of an ordinance when he is challenging the prevailing rulings or customs. In the case of this woman, he seeks to emphasize that for as long as the dead child is within her, she carries and distributes uncleanness as 'a grave' wherever she goes.

Thus, any house 'she comes into' is unclean for seven days, as are its furnishings, and the instructions on purification are the same as those for the house of a dead man. But the scroll adds that anyone who touches the house shall be 'unclean until evening'; and 'if he enters the house with her he shall be unclean seven days. And he shall wash his clothes and bathe himself on the first day', and 'on the third day he shall sprinkle and wash his clothes and bathe himself', and on the seventh day, as in the case of the house of the dead, 'he shall sprinkle himself for the second time and wash his clothes and bathe himself and with the going down of the sun he will become clean'.

Comparing these ordinances in the scroll with their counterparts as crystallized in the rabbinic writings, one can sense that the author of the scroll and those who originated the laws that were later codified in the Mishnah each knew of the other's ruling; and though both forbore from mentioning the fact, they were consciously engaged in fierce controversy – and used much the same language to reach opposite conclusions.

Sacrificial slaughtering in the Temple city

The central feature in the Mosaic ritual of divine worship were the sacrifices. These were to be offered in 'the place which God shall choose', and that, as understood by the Jewish people, was Jerusalem. However, the name of Jerusalem is not mentioned in the Pentateuchal terminology, and it is for this reason that our author omits Jerusalem from the scroll as otherwise his text would appear anachronistic, since it is presented as God speaking to Moses. Instead, our author uses the term 'the city of the Temple'.

The Temple is thus the central element in the character of the city, and the sacrifices are the kernel of the ritual inside the Temple. Accordingly, the city must be absolutely pure, and the rules regarding sacrifices in the city and its environs must be clearly delineated in the scroll. Here, again, many of the decrees are unique. Some, like others of our author's prescriptions, may have been based on practices in the earlier part of the Second Temple period which may already have been forgotten or abandoned by the time the rabbinic halachah had crystallized.

It is characteristic of the author's style that when he lays down basic laws that are not directly rooted in the text of the Scripture as we know it, or when his interpretation enlarges on a biblical text that has not been clearly defined, he substantiates it with unduly repetitive reasoning. He does this with the ordinances to safeguard the holiness of the Temple city.

This trait is particularly conspicuous in his preface to a group of prohibitions that have a decided polemical overtone. They deal with the skins in which wine, oil and other foodstuffs were brought into the city of the Temple. The essential point in the scroll's commands is that these provisions are to be brought only in containers made from the hides of animals that have been ritually slaughtered within the Temple. The reason, repeated three times within a single column, is to preserve the purity of the hallowed city. It is presented in the words of God. We first read (in Col. 47:3-5): 'And the city which I shall hallow by settling my name and my temple within it shall be holy and clean of any unclean thing with which they may be defiled.' Five lines further comes the exhortation not to 'defile the city in which I settle my name ...'. And finally (lines 17, 18): 'and you shall not defile my temple and my city ... *with the skins of your abominations.*'

Here, our author is taking sharp issue on a basic principle with the prevailing view that allowed any foodstuffs to be brought into the Temple city in the skins of ritually clean animals even if they had not been slaughtered in that city.

To make even clearer his prohibition of the skins of clean animals slaughtered outside the Temple city, our author states unequivocally:

All skins of clean animals that will be slaughtered within their cities, they shall not bring into the Temple city; but in their cities they may do with them their work for all their needs; and into the city of my temple they shall not bring them.

He justifies this in an explanatory passage in which one can sense the controversial overtones:

For according to the degree of cleanness of its flesh is the degree of cleanness of the skins. If you slaughter it in my Temple, the skin will be clean for my Temple; but if you slaughter it in your cities, it will be clean for your cities. And all the purity of the Temple [namely, the offerings] you shall bring in Temple skins.

It is possible, of course, that the reason behind so severe a ban so heavily emphasized by repetition may have been to protect the vested interests of the Temple priests, for the public was thereby compelled to 'redeem' by payment the skins of the animals. This is probably true, as it is of many of the rules on sacrifices in the Pentateuch. But if it is, it cannot be the only reason. At all events, our author makes no mention of it, and the prime reason must surely be sought through an analysis of his own explanations justifying his decree.

This brings us back to the question of whether this decree, for which no support can be found in the plain text of the Scriptures, represented simply the wish of the sect or of the author, or whether it was based on an earlier practice which may have been abolished later. If there had been such a practice, and it was common knowledge at the time of the author, this would account for his insistence that it be reintroduced.

Unexpected parallel to the author's decree

The fact is that there are echoes of a strict prohibition against bringing animal skins considered unclean into the Temple city in the writings of Josephus. He tells a story in *Antiquities* (12:146) about Antiochus III (Antiochus the Great) who reigned from 223 to 187 BC. This Seleucid emperor in the year 217 BC suffered a grave defeat near Rafiah, south of Gaza, at the hands of the Egyptian ruler, Ptolemy IV, in one of the fiercest battles of the Hellenistic period. In his subsequent successful struggle to reverse his fortunes, Antiochus received support from the Jews, and in reward he showed them favour, permitting 'members of the nation to have a form of government in accordance with the laws of their country'. Josephus records the concessions he granted to the Jews, among them one that is strikingly similar to the ordinance in our scroll:

And out of reverence for the Temple he [Antiochus III] also published a proclamation throughout the entire kingdom, of which the contents were as follows: '... nor shall anyone bring into *the city* the flesh of horses or of mules or of wild or of tame asses ... or, in general, of any animals forbidden to the Jews. *Nor is it lawful to bring in their skins* or even to breed any of these animals in *the city*. But only the sacrificial animals known to their ancestors and necessary for the propitiation of God shall they be permitted to use.' [The italics are mine. YY]

Thus, not only does the Josephus record stress the holiness of the entire Temple city, but it also contains the explicit ban on bringing into it the skins of animals forbidden for sacrifice. The laws in our scroll extend the ban – apparently current during the Maccabean period – by including in that category the skins of clean animals that have been slaughtered outside the Temple.

Profane slaughtering and the Temple city

Certain restrictions on slaughtering in the Temple city and its environs throw additional light on the objective of our author in his prescriptions for the important ritual of sacrifices. The main biblical basis for his bans is Deuteronomy 17:1 prohibiting the sacrifice of 'an ox or a sheep in which there is a blemish, any defect whatever'.

This is an isolated verse, related neither to what follows nor to what has come before. Our author therefore takes the opportunity of dealing not only with the subject of animals unfit for sacrifice, which was hardly in dispute, but also, and mainly, with the controversial restrictions on slaughtering any animals, even clean, let alone profane, in and around the Temple. These passages in the scroll show that the author was primarily concerned with defining the areas outside the Temple city where the slaughter for meat of both unblemished and blemished animals was permitted, while emphasizing at the same time that within the city of the Temple 'you shall not eat the flesh of an ox or a sheep or a goat ... which is not to enter my Temple', namely, which was not slaughtered in the Temple. This is an unqualified ban on butchering animals for food in or near the Temple city.

Only when he has completed the text of these restrictive injunctions does our author continue with the main laws set forth in Deuteronomy on permitted and prohibited meat for food. Here, in his customary manner, he not only assembled the various laws on the same subject scattered in different parts of Deuteronomy and Leviticus, but above all wove them into a unified code and, while so doing, set additional limits and reservations, and 'resolved' clear contradictions in the Pentateuchal sources.

Pregnant animals

A good example of this is his ordinance on pregnant animals. After citing the Deuteronomy ban on a blemished animal, he adds this typical modification: 'And you shall not sacrifice to me an ox or a sheep or a goat that is pregnant, for they are an abomination to me.'

His purpose is to make absolutely clear, contrary to the rabbinic ruling, that a pregnant animal is to be considered in the same category as an animal with a blemish, and offering it for Temple sacrifice would be 'an abomination'.

This ban in the scroll is of particular interest, as a similar law is to be found in the writings of Philo (*De Virtutibus* 137), roughly a contemporary of Josephus, as well as in the (later) laws of the Karaites, for whom this was a matter of grave importance. Indeed, it became a central issue in their dispute with the 'rabbinites' (the term they used for other Jews), so much so that one of the conditions in the marriage contract between a Karaite woman and a rabbinite groom stated specifically that among those things that the husband was forbidden to bring into the home was 'the flesh of an animal which had conceived' or 'of a pregnant one'.

Clean animals

The scroll next deals with 'clean' animals, both blemished and unblemished, including the procedure and the places for slaughtering and consuming them. A clean blemished animal is one that is fit for eating but not for sacrifice. An unblemished clean animal is fit for sacrifice, but the scroll lays down the circumstances under which it must be used solely for Temple sacrifice, and those in which it may be slaughtered and eaten by the general public.

The opening command states:

And you shall not slaughter a clean ox or sheep or goat in all your towns, near to my Temple within a distance of a three-days' journey; nay, but inside my temple you shall slaughter it, making it a burnt offering or a peace offering, and you shall eat and rejoice before me at the place on which I shall choose to put my name. (Col. 52:13–16)

As for clean but blemished animals, the scroll commands:

And every clean animal which has a blemish, you shall eat it within your towns, far from my Temple thirty stadia around it; you shall not slaughter near my Temple, for it is foul flesh.

These two cases dealt with in the scroll, clean and fit for sacrifice, and clean but blemished, are the subjects of complicated and conflicting laws in the Pentateuch, and the sages already had difficulty in harmonizing some of them and enabling them to be lived with. The author of the scroll, however, with his unswerving and strict adherence to the letter, ordains categorically that a clean but blemished animal cannot be slaughtered or eaten within 30 stadia (4 Roman miles) of the Temple; that a clean unblemished animal owned by someone living within a distance of a three-days' journey from the Temple must be slaughtered in the Temple and sacrificed as a burnt or peace offering (except for certain parts, a peace offering was eaten by the priests and the sacrificer); and that a clean unblemished animal may be slaughtered for food only if the owner lives beyond a three-days' journey from the Temple.

This distance of 'a three-days' journey' is the same as the distance specified in another section of the scroll relating to the consumption of the second tithe. It is clearly based on God's directive to Moses on what he should say to the Pharaoh, recorded in Exodus 3:18: 'The Lord, the God of the Hebrews, has met with us; and now, we pray you, let us go a three days' journey into the wilderness, that we may sacrifice to the Lord our God.'

Thus the author stresses that the commands pertaining to the uniqueness and purity of the Temple must also be observed within the entire area surrounding the Temple up to the distance covered by a three-days' journey. This is in addition to his earlier prescriptions against doing anything in any other city that may vie with the Temple city: 'you shall not purify a city of your cities to be my city'.

As for the slaughtering of clean but blemished animals, we have seen that the author prohibits this as well as the eating of their meat within a distance of 30 stadia from the Temple. Thirty stadia was a common definition in the Second Temple period for the distance from a city to the boundary of its environs, and in an earlier chapter we gave the example of a prescription in the Mishnah on pigeon trapping: 'They may not set snares for pigeons unless it be far thirty stadia from an inhabited place.' It will be recalled that this was mentioned when we explained that the word for 'stadium' both in the Mishnah and in the scroll was 'ris', and that this was a further indication that the scroll was composed, at the very earliest, during the Hellenistic period.

The major ban

It is evident that our author's main concern on this topic was the banning of profane slaughtering in the city of the Temple, and this was to him a matter of major importance. Indeed, all his previous prescriptions led up to it; for after ordaining that blemished clean animals are not to be slaughtered 'within the limit of a three days' journey', and fixing the boundaries for slaughtering animals unfit for the altar, the author sets forth this main command:

You shall not eat flesh of an ox or a sheep or a goat within my city which I shall consecrate to put my name there which is not to enter my Temple; and they shall slaughter it there and throw its blood on the base of the altar of burnt offerings; and its fat they shall burn.

Thus within the boundaries of the city of the Temple, no one may eat any flesh that has not been properly slaughtered in the Temple. This meant that no ordinary flesh could be eaten within the Temple city.

This law was ultimately not accepted by normative Judaism. Here is what the great biblical commentator Nachmanides has to say about the injunction in Deuteronomy 12:21 about slaughtering 'if the place which the Lord your God will choose to put his name there is too far from you':

The phrase 'too far' cannot be understood as permitting ordinary flesh to be eaten only on the strength of the distance of the place from the Temple, for if so, ordinary flesh would be forbidden to residents of Jerusalem.

Certain circles among the Karaites, however, took the same view as the author of the scroll, and Karaite law, indeed, forbids the eating of meat within or in the proximity of Jerusalem. And one of the Karaite religious codifiers dealt with this problem in the following way:

And you shall know that it is forbidden to slaughter cattle and sheep in Jerusalem [in a marginal note are the words 'in the time of the Exile'] and its proximity since it is permitted only to slaughter sacrificially in it and its proximity, not profanely, and for those who reside a distance from the chosen place, it is permitted.

Here again, when a Karaite girl marries a rabbinite groom, the Karaite marriage contract specifically obliges the groom to undertake 'not to eat the meat of cattle and sheep in Jerusalem until the establishment of God's altar'.

PART SIX

STATUTES OF THE KING

19 The Royal Guard, the Council and the King's Consort

One of the most original and provocative texts of 'additional Torah' in the scroll is a code of laws which I have called the Statutes of the King, covering some four columns (56-59) towards the end of the document. Apart from the intrinsic interest of the subject-matter, ranging from military organization to polygamy, divorce and capital punishment, it reflects the political patterns of the period in which the scroll was composed or finally edited, and also has a direct bearing on some of the doctrines of Christianity.

What triggered the inclusion of such a 'Torah', with God speaking in the first person singular, was, I believe, similar to that which prompted our author to devise an 'additional Torah' on the Temple itself – the lack or paucity of a Torah on the subject in the Bible. I am convinced it was his belief that what he was offering in the scroll was a part of the Torah that had somehow been lost, and had been divinely revealed to him.

As against his Temple 'Torah', he was on firmer ground with his Statutes of the King, for there are clear hints in the Pentateuch that there had indeed once been a Torah on this theme. In 'revealing' it he could – and did – present it in a manner which deliberately emphasized the doctrines of the sect.

His main biblical source is the brief passage on future kingship in the Promised Land recorded in Deuteronomy 17:14-20, which begins:

When you come to the land which the Lord your God gives you, and you possess it and dwell in it, and then say, 'I will set a king over me, like all the nations that are round about me'; you may indeed set as king over you him whom the Lord your God will choose.

What follows are short statutes that deal only with certain aspects of the royal activities. This section of the scroll opens with the quotation of these Deuteronomy verses, with typical changes by the author. Before considering these changes, we must mention an additional biblical 'authority' on which our author relied – a further hint in the Bible of the existence of a Torah concerning the king. It appears in 1 Samuel 10:25, recording events in the days of the prophet Samuel when the first king in Israel was installed: 'Then Samuel told the people the rights and duties of the kingship; and he wrote them in a book and laid it up before the Lord.'

What were the statutes and the regulations governing royalty that receive little more than passing mention in the Scriptures?

The second Torah

Of the changes introduced by the author into the Deuteronomy passage quoted in the scroll, so that it differs somewhat from the masoretic text that has come down to us, some are in the nature of glosses – the insertion of words to explain the text. For example, one of the Deuteronomy statutes orders that the king shall not 'cause the people to return to Egypt' (Deut. 17:16). Our author adds: 'for war'.

Other changes, however, are more fundamental, and have the clear purpose of laying down a law different from that of the masoretic text. A good example is verse 18 in this chapter of our masoretic Deuteronomy: 'And when he sits on the throne of his kingdom, he shall write for himself in a book a copy of this law, from that which is in charge of the Levitical priests.'

Instead of 'he shall write for himself . . . a copy', the scroll has 'they shall write for him the law in a book'. To understand the full significance of this change, a little background on the Hebrew text is essential. The original Hebrew words which were translated into English as 'a copy of this book' are 'Mishneh Ha'Torah'. These were translated in the Septuagint as 'Deuteronomion', Greek for 'the second law'. Indeed, it was this Greek word which gave the name Deuteronomy to the entire fifth Book of the Pentateuch in many translations of the Bible. It is not called that in the Hebrew Bible. The name there is 'Devarim', Hebrew for 'words', which appears in the opening verse of the Book. But some of the ancient Jewish sources also called the Book 'Mishneh Ha'Torah', which can be translated as 'the second law' or as 'the copy of the law'.

We can now tackle the different version in the scroll of Deuteronomy 17:18: 'And when he sits on the throne of his kingdom they shall write for him the law in a book.' A little later, the scroll states: 'And this is the law [Torah] which they shall write for him.' What follows is the main 'additional Torah' with the statutes of the king.

Thus, not only does our author command, in God's words, that the Levitical priests shall write the law for the king, instead of 'he shall write for himself', but he also drops the word 'second' or 'copy' altogether. Had his version been accepted as the authentic text of the original, the name Deuteronomy for this Book of the Pentateuch would never have come into existence. And there would have been none of the scholarly controversy, that has continued from early to modern times, over whether the 'second law' referred to the whole of the Pentateuch, to Deuteronomy alone, or simply to this chapter.

The main significance of our author's omission of the word lies in his purpose of presenting the statutes of the king not as a second or a copy but as the original law. And to remove any doubt, he added specifically: 'And this is the law [Torah] which they shall write.'

So, according to our author, there was no 'deuteronomy', and we now follow him as he sets forth the 'original' law which the Levitical priests, by their ancient tradition, wrote for the king, prescribing his obligations and the general statutes of kingship.

The military organization and the royal guard

'On the day on which they make him king', he is to perform two duties. He is to order a census in all the cities of Israel of all the male children of Israel from the ages of twenty to sixty, according to their battalions. And he is to appoint military commanders of thousands, hundreds, fifties and tens. The interesting aspect of this injunction is not only that this is the first obligation of the king, but that he himself is to appoint the commanders. It is in fact a royal prerogative. This is doubtless based on 1 Samuel 8:12: 'and he will appoint for himself commanders of thousands and commanders of fifties'. (This was the warning of the prophet when he was trying to discourage the people who were clamouring for a king.) It was put into effect by David as recorded in 2 Samuel 18:1 when he 'mustered the men who were with him, and set over them commanders of thousands and commanders of hundreds'. So far, then, our author is on firm biblical ground.

It is when he comes to prescribe the composition of the royal guard that we are struck by unusual features in the text. While some of its sources are to be found in various places in the Bible, the very organization of this body, its character, and the emphasis given to it in the scroll clearly reflect, to my mind, the political circumstances in the country at the time the scroll was composed.

This guard is to be made up of 12,000 'chosen men', 1,000 from each tribe. Their duty – and this already sets the political background to this section – is to be with the king, lest he fall into the hands of foreign nations. This is given further stress in a subsequent statute: 'And they shall always be with him, day and night. They shall guard him from every sinful thing and from a foreign people, lest he be taken by them' (Col. 57). More interesting, and one would have thought somewhat challenging even in those days, was the calibre demanded of the soldiers who were to form the royal guard. They were to be 'men of truth, God-fearing, hating unjust gain, and mighty men of war'. One can only hope there were enough men at that time with all four virtues.

This data provided by the scroll shows clearly how our author worked. The number of guardsmen is based on Numbers 31:3–5, even though that reference is to a totally different situation:

Moses said to the people, 'Arm men among you for the war, that they may go against Midian ... send a thousand from each of the tribes....' So there were provided, out of the thousands of Israel, a thousand from each tribe, twelve thousand armed for war.

As for the character traits of the guardsmen, these were drawn from the advice on organization and administration given by Jethro to his son-in-law Moses, as recounted in Exodus 18:21–25: 'Moreover, choose able men from all the people, such as fear God, men who are trustworthy and who hate a bribe.... So Moses ... chose able men out of all Israel....'

The author of the scroll also seems to have heeded the words of Jethro by demanding that members of the royal guard should possess the highest qualities among all the children of Israel.

But there was more behind our author's demand for qualifying criteria in the selection of guardsmen. One can detect between the lines of the scroll hidden criticism of what was happening in the country at the time he was writing. In this very context, what Josephus has to say of several of the Hasmonean monarchs may be of considerable significance. Of John Hyrcanus I – mentioned in an earlier chapter as the king who installed rings in the Temple slaughterhouse – Josephus writes that he was 'the first of the Jews to keep an army of mercenaries' (*Antiquities* 13:249). Aristobulus I, the son of Hyrcanus, 'was the first to place a diadem on his head' (13:301), proclaiming himself king in addition to being High Priest. With him, too, Josephus emphasizes the role of his mercenary guards. (Incidentally, it is in this chapter of *Antiquities* that Josephus makes his first mention of an Essene, writing of a certain 'Judas of the Essene group, who had never been known to speak falsely in his prophecies' [13:311].)

Most telling, perhaps, in the light of the scroll's words on the required character and duties of the royal guards, and their need to protect the king 'lest he be taken by' his enemies, are the remarks of Josephus about Alexander Jannaeus. He succeeded his brother Aristobulus in 103 BC, and many scholars associate some of the Qumran commentaries with acts and incidents in which he was involved during his twenty-eight-year reign. Jannaeus, writes Josephus, 'also maintained foreign troops of Pisidians and Cilicians, for he could not use Syrians, being at war with them' (13:374). And in his battle with the Nabatean king Obodas, Jannaeus 'fell into an ambush ... and barely escaped with his own life, fleeing from there, came to Jerusalem' (13:375).

I do not claim that it was precisely these particular circumstances recounted by Josephus that prompted the author of the Temple scroll to write as he did. But I do believe that events of the early Hasmonean period, more than those of any other, may have been much in his mind, and may well explain the motives behind some of his writings. We mentioned earlier the association of John Hyrcanus with the rings in the Temple slaughterhouse. This was the period – the second half of the second century BC – when the Temple was being renovated, giving rise to sharp controversy on many matters and problems relating to the Temple ritual as well as to its installations and architecture.

Furthermore, the Hasmonean high priests were increasingly anxious to extend their power by including the power of a monarch, becoming kings, and surrounding themselves with bodyguards consisting of foreign mercenaries. This was the usual custom of the kings in the region, who felt safer with foreigners: they were considered less likely to become involved in internal intrigues. It could well have been to stop this practice – which may have begun soon after the initial Maccabean successes – that our author insisted in his ordinance that the royal guard should be drawn only from among the Children of Israel and should comprise men of the highest integrity.

The judicial council

The text on the king's bodyguard is immediately followed by the scroll's prescription on the formation, structure and function of a judicial council. This, however, was very much more than an exercise in public administration. It had a definite purpose: to curtail the power of the king, and make him subject to the decisions of a council in which the priests and the Levites held a commanding majority! Again, in my judgement, the historical setting of these ordinances would appear to have been the period when Hasmonean leaders were moving towards absolute rule, with the ruler less dependent on the priests and other Temple officials.

The commands in the scroll on this council and on the status of the king read:

And the twelve leaders of his people shall be with him, and of the priests twelve, and of the Levites twelve. They shall sit together with him for judgment, and declare the decisions of the law, that his heart may not be lifted up above them, and that he may not do anything by any counsel apart from them. (Col. 57:11–15)

The scroll's phrase 'twelve leaders of his people' evokes, among other sources, the verse in Numbers 1:44: 'the leaders of Israel, twelve men, each representing his father's house'. These twelve lay readers were to sit with twelve priests and twelve Levites on this judicial council, and together with the king make decisions. The king cannot decide anything without them, and he cannot overrule them: 'his heart may not be lifted up above them'.

This last phrase is clearly based on Deuteronomy 17:20 on the enthronement of a king: 'his heart may not be lifted up above his brethren'. But it was not through inadvertence that our author wrote not 'above his brethren' but 'above them', namely, the council.

With whom lies the decision to take the country to war? This crucial question is dealt with in a column (58) devoted entirely to military matters, and the scroll makes a clear distinction between what the sages called a 'war of duty' and a 'war of choice'. There is a prescription I shall be discussing later which gives the king the power to mobilize if the country is in imminent danger of invasion. If, however, he seeks to initiate an attack and launch a war of choice, he must first secure the approval of the high priest. As the ordinance puts it:

he shall not go out until he comes before the high priest, who shall inquire for him by the judgment of the Urim and the Thummim. At his word he shall go out, and at his word he shall come in, both he and all the people of Israel with him; he shall not go out by the counsel of his heart . . .

Here, in limiting the king's power to take military action when there may be no enemy threat, our author, in characteristic manner, has drawn on, and applied to this special case, a biblical source (Numbers 27:21) which deals with a totally different situation – the ordination of Joshua as leader of Israel:

And he [Joshua] shall stand before Eleazar the priest, who shall inquire for him by the judgment of the Urim before the Lord; at his word they shall go out, and at his word they shall come in, both he and all the people of Israel with him . . .

Incidentally, to hark back to the composition of the council, the Temple scroll is the earliest Jewish source attaching special importance to the number 36, and prescribing that number for a body with a unique function. This number may also have had some bearing on the determination of the size of the Sanhedrin. It consisted of seventy-one members, making a majority decision of thirty-six to thirty-five the minimum required for a legally binding verdict. And later in Judaism, in a homiletical interpretation of a verse in Isaiah, one of the sages said: 'The world must contain not less than thirty-six righteous men in each generation who are vouchsafed the sight of the countenance of the *Shechinah* [the visible glory of God].'

The king's consort

Among the most interesting rulings in the Statutes of the King are those that concern the royal consort. They follow directly after the passage on the judicial council, and they impose upon the king one obligation and two prohibitions: he must not marry a Gentile; he is obliged to take to wife not any Israelite woman but only one belonging to his father's tribe and family; and bigamy and divorce are forbidden to him.

The first ban is non-controversial. Other Jewish sects as well as the rabbis were all agreed on the prohibition of marriage to a Gentile. The obligation and the second ban, however, reflect the deep differences between the teaching of our author and the doctrine as finalized in rabbinic law. The ban on bigamy and divorce is also of special importance for our understanding of certain rulings in Christianity.

The full text of these ordinances in the scroll is brief. It reads:

And he shall not take a wife from all the daughters of the nations, but from his father's house he shall take unto himself a wife, from the family of his father. And he shall not take upon her another wife, for she alone shall be with him all the days of her life. But should she die, he may take unto himself another wife from the house of his father, from his family. (Col. 57:15–19)

The ban on marriage to a Gentile was not controversial because it is explicitly ordained in the Bible: 'You shall not make marriages with them [the other nations], giving your daughters to their sons or taking their daughters for your sons' (Deut. 7:3). But the author presumably included it together with the other two rulings in this passage as a polemical move against a custom prevalent at the time. This is what Nehemiah did in an earlier part of the Second Temple period, and he was able to enforce his ordinances:

And I contended with them and cursed them and beat some of them and pulled out their hair; and I made them take oath in the name of God, saying, 'You shall not give your daughters to their sons, or take their daughters for your sons or for yourselves.' (Neh. 13:25)

Nehemiah follows this with an interesting comment of relevance to the scroll's ban on a Gentile consort for the king:

Did not Solomon king of Israel sin on account of such women? Among the many nations there was no king like him, and he was beloved by his God, and God made him king over all Israel; nevertheless foreign women made even him to sin. (Neh. 13:26)

A wife from the house of his father

The scroll's command that the king's wife must come from the tribe and family of his father is clearly polemical in character. The rabbinical law on this subject, as preserved in Tosefta Sanhedrin 4:2, states that the king 'chooses for himself wives from wherever he wishes: the daughters of priests, Levites or Israelites'.

Our author disagrees totally, and from the wording in the scroll it is evident that he drew on Abraham's instruction to his servant whom he sent to seek a wife for his son Isaac, as recounted in Genesis 24:37, 38: 'You shall not take a wife for my son from the daughters of the Canaanites ... but you shall go to my father's house and to my kindred, and take a wife for my son.'

Once again, the scroll's command may reflect certain circumstances during the period when the scroll was composed, and that might well have been the period when the priestly rulers of the Maccabean or Hasmonean dynasty were also the lay rulers. The law on the High Priest in Leviticus 21:14 states that 'he shall take to wife a virgin of his own people'. The rabbis took 'of his own people' to mean 'the people of Israel'. Curiously enough, however, the Septuagint translation, after the words 'in her virginity' (verse 13), adds 'of his own family'. This is also the interpretation of Josephus, and it is based on a different translation of the Hebrew word that is given in English as 'his own people'. It can also mean 'his father's family', and that presumably is how it was interpreted by our author.

Incidentally, if we go back to the time of Aaron the High Priest, it would seem that the command in the scroll is more severe for the king than it is for the priest, for Aaron of the tribe of Levi married 'Elisheba, the daughter of Amminadab', who was of the tribe of Judah (Exodus 6:23).

Bigamy and divorce

The ban on bigamy and divorce is unequivocal in the scroll's command that the king's wife alone shall be with him all her life and that he can take another only when she dies. How and why our author came to issue this prohibition can best be understood by examining its source and comparing it with other writings of the sect on this subject. It is also illuminating to see how it relates to the corresponding rabbinic laws – and to the teaching in the New Testament.

The language of the scroll indicates that the source of the scroll's ban is Leviticus 18:18: 'And you shall not take a woman as a rival wife to her sister, uncovering her nakedness while her sister is yet alive.' Thus the scroll interprets the Bible's 'her sister' to mean not a blood sister but 'another woman', the 'sister' simply serving as a term to define the gender; and so our author forbids the taking of 'another wife' while the first wife is alive. The rabbis, on the other hand, followed the straightforward meaning of the biblical command: 'sister' was a blood sister, and the ban applied to her alone and not to a non-relative.

It is interesting that the Karaites held the same view as our author on this matter, possibly influenced by the scrolls discovered in the Middle Ages. In his noted polemic against the Karaites that appears in his late eleventh-century Midrash on the Pentateuch, Tobias ben Eliezer wrote: 'How great is the error of the Karaites who said' that the phrase in Leviticus '"and thou shall not take a woman to her sister" refers to two women! It is clear from the Bible that the Israelites used to marry two [unrelated] women.'

A twin passage from the Damascus Document

The same subject is dealt with in a passage in the Damascus Document which, as we have seen, is similar in many respects to the Temple scroll, and may have been influenced by it. This passage gave rise to a scholarly controversy that has gone on for decades over the ambiguity of a crucial word in the text. I think our Temple scroll now settles that argument once and for all.

The relevant passage in the Damascus Document opens as follows:

They [the opponents of the sect] are ensnared by two: by fornication, taking two wives during their lifetimes, but the foundation of the creation is 'male and female he created them' [Gen. 1:27]. And they who came into the Ark, 'two and two . . . went into the ark'. (Gen. 7:9)

The crucial word is 'lifetimes' (the plural form is called for by the grammatical context, not by the content), and the question was, whose lifetime, the husband's or the wife's? The Hebrew for 'during their lifetime' is a single word, and in the Damascus Document it has a masculine ending. Many scholars long ago suggested that this had been a literal error, and that it should have had the feminine ending *khayehen* instead of the masculine *khayehem*, namely, during the wife's and not the husband's lifetime. Opposing scholars held to the masculine ending, the husband's lifetime, which would mean not only that he could divorce his wife but also that if she died or if he divorced her he could not remarry. In the absence of supporting proof for either theory, scholars of both sides had a field day. The Temple scroll now clinches the argument. Both texts have the same meaning: 'during the lifetime of the wife', the husband was to take no other wives. No bigamy and no divorce.

The rabbinical view

We have already indicated that the prohibition in our scroll, as in the Damascus Document, forbidding even the king to take more than one wife, is in direct contradiction to the rabbinic law, which allows the king to marry as many as eighteen women! As for the injunction in Deuteronomy 17:17 that the king 'shall not multiply wives for himself, lest his heart turn away', the Mishnah quotes this comment: '"Nor shall he multiply wives to himself" – eighteen only. Rabbi Judah says: He may multiply them to himself provided that they do not turn away his heart' (Tractate Sanhedrin 2:4). Another saying appears in Tosefta Sanhedrin 4:5: 'Nor shall he multiply wives to himself like Jezebel, but like Abigail [one of David's wives] it is permissible, says Rabbi Judah.'

Here, then, was a basic rift. Normative Judaism, based on the rabbinical interpretation of biblical law, held to the view, and applied it in practice, that a man, including the king, could have more than one wife. The pattern of 'eighteen wives' was set by King David. (Just as well King Solomon had not been taken as the model!) The Dead Sea sect, for its part, insisted on monogamy for king and commoner, and banned divorce.

The Christian doctrine

The Temple scroll's ordinances on bigamy and divorce, and the arguments in the Damascus Document based on the Genesis quotations 'male and female he created them' and 'two by two' going into the ark, call to mind the words of Jesus on this subject which became a fundamental issue in Christianity, particularly within the Catholic Church. The position taken by Jesus appears in the accounts of Matthew (19:3–9) and Mark (10:2–9), and they are worth comparing with the passages in the Temple scroll and the Damascus Document quoted above. The Mark version records that when the Pharisees asked Jesus whether it was lawful for a man to divorce his wife, Jesus replied that 'from the beginning of creation, "God made them male and female." "For this reason a man shall leave his father and mother and be joined to his wife, and the two shall become one flesh." ... What therefore God has joined together, let not man put asunder.'

The special relevance of this New Testament text is that long before the birth of Jesus, the decree against bigamy and divorce – the first such Jewish decree – appeared in both the Temple scroll and the Damascus Document, and must assuredly have influenced the early Christians.

Another relevant fact with a link to Christianity is that among the Pharisees of the first century BC there were two views on divorce. The usually liberal School of Hillel allowed a husband to divorce his wife for any reason whatsoever – even for spoiling the dinner! The School of Shammai, however, in general more severe in its judgements, held that a husband could divorce his wife only if he found her 'unchaste'. Interestingly enough, in the Matthew account of the dialogue between Jesus and the Pharisees, after forbidding divorce, Jesus adds 'except for unchastity' (19:9). Thus, Matthew's version follows the School of Shammai. The version of Mark, banning divorce outright, follows the rule set by the Temple scroll and the Damascus Document.

Mobilization of the army

I have left one important statute of the king to the last, for in presenting it I cannot forbear from mentioning my personal feelings when I first deciphered it – though these feelings of mine are of no scientific significance whatsoever. This was a statute prescribing the duties of the king when the land of Israel was in danger of invasion (unlike the prescription discussed earlier for a 'war of choice').

It was soon after the Six Day War in June 1967 that I pored over the text in this section of the scroll and began to read the instructions to the king on the action he was to take when the country was threatened, matching the size and stages of mobilization with the magnitude of the imminent peril.

It may be recalled that Israel did well in those six days, and the country was in victorious mood when I was able to return to my studies. But the mood had been very different in the weeks before the opening shot was fired. Egypt had suddenly started moving large concentrations of troops into Sinai, their numbers swelling day by day as they came steadily closer to our southern border. The situation in Israel was tense. We are a small country with a small population, and though vastly outnumbered by our potential enemies, we cannot afford a large standing army. Our defence is based on what is virtually a people's militia, a comparatively small regular force backed by an army of reservists – the able-bodied population called up in an emergency.

As that emergency became daily more acute, with the enemy strength increasing and approaching our gates, there was steady pressure to increase the mobilization of our reservists to meet the growing danger. I do not think I am divulging military secrets when I say that what happened to us then in Israel, and the action we took, was almost identical with the prescription for such a situation in the statute of the king in the Temple scroll. It reads:

When the king hears of any nation or people who seek to rob of everything that belongs to Israel, he shall call the commanders of thousands and the commanders of hundreds, who are stationed in the cities of Israel, and they shall send with him a tenth of the people to go out with him to battle over their enemies and they shall go out with him; but if many people shall come to the Land of Israel they shall send with him one fifth of the warriors; but if a king and chariots and horses and many people shall come they shall send with him one third of the warriors and two thirds shall watch their cities and boundaries lest a band may come into the midst of their land, but if the battle be too strong for him they shall send him half the people, the men of war, but half the people shall not be cut off from their cities.

There is, of course, military logic in these rules; and the wording in the Hebrew text shows that here, too, our author has drawn on various verses scattered throughout the Bible, given them his own interpretation, and woven them into harmonious statutes. One of the most conspicuous is the ordinance dealing with the division of the spoils of battle, which we discussed in chapter 5.

A curse and a blessing

The Statutes of the King end with what reads like a form of covenant between God and the king, with warnings of catastrophe should the statutes be ignored, and the promise of good fortune if they are respected.

The text lists an alarming catalogue of disasters that will befall the people and the king if he fails to follow the laws of God as prescribed in the Torah. Among other dire punishments,

their cities will become a waste, a hissing and a desolation, and their enemies will devastate them. And in the land of their enemies they [will] groan and cry out because of a heavy yoke, and they will call, and I will not hear; and they will cry and I will not answer.

Fortunately, this chapter ends with the blessing:

But if he [the king] will walk in my statutes, and observe my commandments and will do what is right and good in my sight, a man of his sons shall not be cut off from sitting on the throne of the kingdom of Israel for ever, and I will be with him and deliver him from the hand of those who hate him and from the hand of those who seek to take away his life. And I will give up all his enemies before him and he shall rule over them according to his will, and they shall not rule over him. And I will make him tend upward, and not downward, the head, and not the tail, so that he may continue very long in his kingdom, he and his sons after him.

On the face of it, there would seem to be nothing unusual in these curses and blessings. Behind them, however, as we shall see, lies a definite purpose in the mind of our author not unrelated to certain events that may have occurred when he was composing the scroll.

20 'To Hang Alive upon a Tree'

There is a long passage towards the end of the scroll, in Column 64, that deals with a certain form of capital punishment. It is of considerable significance on several counts. It specifies particular crimes that are to carry the death penalty; it prescribes the method of execution; it sheds light on – or adds fuel to – a scholarly controversy on the attitude of the Essenes and other Jewish sects towards this mode of execution, as well as on the true interpretation of a puzzling text in another Dead Sea scroll; and it is one of the few sections in the Temple scroll, apart from the Statutes of the King, that may reflect the political situation in the country during the period it was written.

The views expressed in the scroll differ from those prevailing at the time, and they can best be understood if we first present the position taken by the sages. The prime biblical source for both are two key verses, 22 and 23, in chapter 21 of Deuteronomy:

And if a man has committed a crime punishable by death and he is put to death, and you hang him on a tree, his body shall not remain all night upon the tree, but you shall bury him the same day, for a hanged man is accursed by God; you shall not defile your land which the Lord your God gives you for an inheritance.

The rabbinic interpretation

The first of these two verses, more than any other in the Pentateuch, served the rabbis as a guide for their interpretation as to how this punishment was to be carried out. The culprit was to be put to death quickly, by strangulation, and the body then hanged until evening. (The rabbis adopted the same approach towards two other slow-death methods of execution of the four ordained in the Pentateuch, stoning and burning. The fourth was beheading.) It was the humane rabbinic purpose to hasten the execution rather than prolong it by the primitive ancient procedures called for by a more rigid interpretation of the Mosaic law.

An example of how the rabbis argued to support their more lenient application of the Deuteronomy command is to be found in Tractate Sanhedrin 46b:

Our rabbis taught: Had it been written, 'If he has sinned, then you shall hang him', I could have said he is hanged and then put to death, as does the State [i.e. the alien ruler]. Therefore Scripture says: 'and he is put to death, and you shall hang him' – he is first put to death and afterwards hanged.

Sifre, an important halachic document on Deuteronomy, states that, lest it 'be interpreted that he is to be hanged alive ... therefore it is written: "and he is put to death, and you hang him on a tree".' Similarly, the Palestinian Targum, the Aramaic translation which also embodies interpretation, reads that 'if one is condemned to death, he is to be put to death by stoning, and afterwards they may hang him on a tree'.

What is the point, in this rabbinic interpretation, of hanging the man when he is already dead? Well, there is an ambiguity in the original Hebrew of the phrase in Deuteronomy 21:23 that, as we have seen, is translated in the Revised Standard Version as 'for a hanged man is accursed by God'. In Hebrew, the phrase could also mean 'he cursed God'. The rabbis were much perplexed by this ambiguity, and finally resolved to apply both meanings. This is well demonstrated in another passage from Tractate Sanhedrin, quoted above, where the sages are discussing the capital punishment of stoning. Rabbi Eliezer held that 'All that have been stoned must be hanged.... But the Sages say: None is hanged save the blasphemer and the idolater.'

Thus, the final rabbinic ruling is that these are put to death for the crime of blasphemy or idolatry – for cursing God. The corpse is then hanged as a further penalty.

It is interesting that the same verse in Deuteronomy, as understood by Paul – and as translated in the Septuagint – is the source for the phrase in his letter to the Galatians about Jesus: '... for it is written, "Cursed be every one who hangs on a tree"' (3:13).

A final source of rabbinical perplexity over these Deuteronomy verses was the absence of any specification of the crimes carrying the penalty of death by hanging. All that is said is 'if a man has committed a crime punishable by death'. This, of course, also became the subject of much controversy.

The clear overall conclusion from their discussions and rulings is that the rabbis were firmly against punishing a man condemned for a capital offence by hanging him alive. Execution was to be quick, by strangulation, and the corpse hanged as an additional punishment.

The scroll's interpretation

The position taken by our author is quite different. The text on this subject in the scroll contains extensive quotations from Deuteronomy chapter 21 and the beginning of chapter 22. But immediately after quoting verses 18 to 21 in chapter 21, at the point where the key biblical verses begin, our author interpolates the following remarkable passage which defines the exact form of execution, and also fills in the gap in the Pentateuchal ordinance by specifying the crimes which incur this penalty:

If a man informs against his people, and delivers his people up to a foreign nation, and does harm to his people, you shall hang him on the tree, and he shall die.... And if a man has committed a crime punishable by death, and has defected into the midst of the nations, and has cursed his people and the children of Israel, you shall hang him also on the tree, and he shall die. (Col. 64)

Before analysing the rulings inherent in this passage, it is worth noting that the crimes specified by our author are all of a political nature, coming under the heading of treason: transmitting information to the enemy; causing or intending to cause the surrender of his nation to the enemy; evading the judicial process for a capital offence, fleeing to enemy territory, and there cursing his own people.

The relevance of these specific crimes to historical events – and to certain texts in other Dead Sea scrolls – will be considered later in greater detail. But it is evident that the nature of the crimes and the way they are described in the scroll point to a contemporary situation in which such treasonable acts were not unusual.

The mode of execution

Even a quick comparison of the text in the scroll with that in Deuteronomy reveals a subtle but basic difference in the directive of how the death penalty was to be carried out. Where Deuteronomy says the condemned man 'is put to death, and you hang him on a tree', our author, using similar wording but deftly changing the word order, writes: 'you shall hang him on the tree, and he shall die'. (He repeats this in the punishment of the escapee who has defected to the enemy: 'you shall hang him also on the tree, and he shall die'.) Thus, our author decreed that the culprit was to be hanged alive, and his death brought about by the hanging – as against the final Pharisaic halachah which held, as we have seen, that death was to precede the hanging. The arguments in the talmudic passages from Sanhedrin quoted earlier were not part of an idle homiletic exercise but grounds

The controversial command in the Temple scroll concerning capital punishment, reflecting the political situation in the country at the time: 'If a man informs against his people, and delivers his people up to a foreign nation, and does harm to his people, you shall hang him on the tree, and he shall die. . . .'

for a sober rabbinic ruling – perhaps prompted by the very different view expressed in the scroll. It was to give substance to this view that the penalty should be hanging alive that our author deliberately changed the word order of Deuteronomy. (Incidentally, the Syriac translation of Deuteronomy 21:22 shows a close relationship to the interpretation in the scroll: 'He is hanged on a tree and is put to death.')

It is possible, of course, that hanging alive goes back to the Second Temple period as the legitimate interpretation of the Bible's command to execute by 'hanging', and that it was only the later Pharisaic halachah which gave a different interpretation, and condemned the practice of stringing up a condemned man while still alive. There is in fact proof of this in the Aramaic Targum (of a sentence in Ruth) which dwells on the four methods of carrying out judicial sentences of death. It affirms that the fourth type, which is strangulation in rabbinic terminology, is indeed 'hanging on a tree'. And the late Israeli scholar Professor J. Heinemann pointed out that this Targum preserves an ancient pre-Tannaitic (i.e. before the mishnaic sages) tradition of punishment by actual hanging – namely, with hanging as the cause of death. There may already in those distant days have been a difference of opinion over a law of that kind. At all events, traces of such a penalty all but disappeared from halachic or religious judicial literature.

The revelation in this passage of our scroll that the Essenes adopted the plain meaning of the Deuteronomy text on hanging – or so interpreted it – as hanging alive, and applied it to persons found guilty of the political crimes detailed in the scroll, is of general importance for our understanding both of this form of execution and of the prevalence of treasonable acts in the Second Temple period. Of immediate interest, however, is its relevance to what has heretofore proved one of the most baffling texts in another Dead Sea scroll known as the Nahum Commentary.

Pesher Nahum – a sectarian commentary on the Prophet Nahum

Very characteristic of the Dead Sea sect's writings, as noted in an earlier chapter, is a type of commentary on the prophetic works. The term in Hebrew for this type is *pesher*, commonly translated as 'commentary'; but it is far more than that, and does not lend itself to a single-word translation in English. It is a combination of interpretation, commentary, and the elucidation of the hidden significance of the prophetic text, and its application to specific contemporary events. The writer seeks to convey some conceived meaning in the prophecies known only to a select few.

The most celebrated *pesher* is the Habakkuk Commentary. It was, in fact, one of the four Dead Sea scrolls I had the privilege of acquiring in the United States for the Shrine of the Book in Jerusalem. From that commentary, we learned that the dominant external power in the region, and the enemy of Israel at the time, were the people called 'Kittim' (believed to refer to the Romans) both in the commentaries and in the Scroll of the War of the Sons of Light against the Sons of Darkness. We also learned – and its relevance will become apparent later – that the founder of the Dead Sea sect was a man they called 'The Teacher of Righteousness', and that the arch-enemy of the sect was 'The Wicked Priest'. The Habakkuk Commentary went on to say that the Wicked Priest sought to kill the Teacher of Righteousness on Yom Kippur. Now, however wicked he may have been, it is inconceivable that a priest of Jerusalem would travel outside the Temple on the most solemn Day of Atonement, let alone for the purpose of killing someone. However, since we now know that the

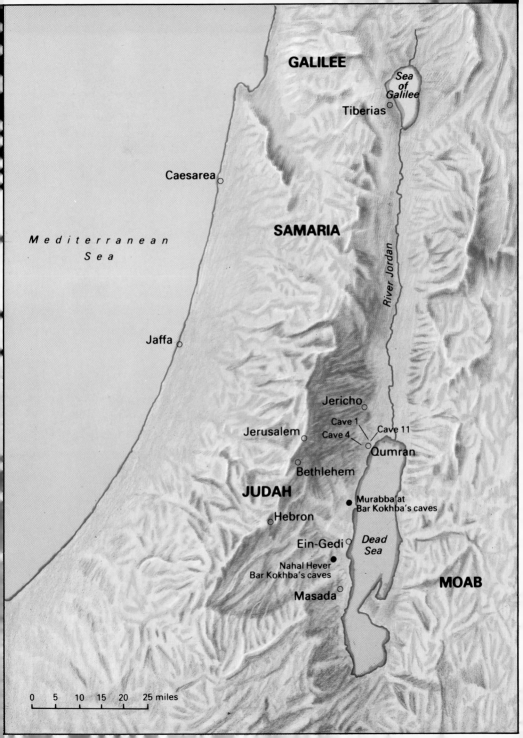

GALILEE

Sea of Galilee

Tiberias

Caesarea

SAMARIA

*M e d i t e r r a n e a n
S e a*

River Jordan

Jaffa

Jericho

Cave 1

Cave 11

Jerusalem

Cave 4

Qumran

Bethlehem

JUDAH

Murabba'at
Bar Kokhba's caves

Hebron

*Dead
Sea*

Ein-Gedi

Nahal Hever
Bar Kokhba's caves

MOAB

Masada

0   5   10   15   20   25 miles

The 'Tower of David' and the western city wall of Jerusalem: the view from the

The Herodian Temple, as reconstructed by the late
Professor M. Avi-Yonah in a model that stands in the
gardens of the Holyland Hotel in Jerusalem.

General view of Qumran and the Dead Sea as seen from a cave in the cliffs
(© *David Harris*).

Essenes followed a calendar different from the calendar of normative Judaism, it is clear that the Habakkuk Commentary referred to the Day of Atonement as observed by the Essenes – which would have been an ordinary working day to a non-sectarian Jew. And the Wicked Priest may have chosen that day to venture forth precisely because it was the Yom Kippur of the Essenes according to their different calendar.

Fragments of other commentaries on various prophets have been found at Qumran. But the most important one, and the one that pertains directly to the topic of execution by hanging alive, is the commentary on the Prophet Nahum. It contains a text on this form of capital punishment which has been the subject of serious controversy among scholars, for unfortunately it has many gaps, and there are divergent views on how it is to be reconstructed. But the particular interest in this passage is that it is the only Qumranic document of its kind which mentions known historical figures, and this helps to date the composition of these commentaries.

Because of its outstanding importance, I propose to quote this passage verbatim, noting the gaps, and see what light can be thrown upon it by the text from our Temple scroll that we have been discussing. I should add that the method of presentation followed by the authors of this and the other commentaries, as we have seen in an earlier chapter, is to quote a verse from the prophetic work, and add immediately 'Its *pesher* is'. I have thought it best to translate this as 'Its hidden interpretation concerns. . . .'

The passage deals with chapter 2, verses 11 and 12, of the biblical Book of Nahum, and where these verses are quoted in the text I have put them in italics. It should be noted that the language in the copy of Nahum used by the author of the commentary differs somewhat from the masoretic text, and accordingly the English translation will not be quite the same as that in the Revised Standard Version of the Bible.

Gaps in the text are indicated by dots within square brackets, except where the reconstruction is obvious, in which case square brackets alone are used enclosing the reconstructed words.

The entire oracle of the prophet is devoted to the fall of Nineveh, but the author, as is usual in such commentaries, has transferred the scene to Jerusalem, and the events and personalities to those of his own time:

... *Whither the lion, the lioness, the lion's cub [and none to terrify*. Its hidden interpretation concerns Deme]trius King of Greece, who sought to enter Jerusalem by the counsel of the seekers of smooth things. [And God did not surrender Jerusalem into] the hands of the kings of Greece from Antiochus until the rise to power of the rulers of the Kittim; but afterwards [the city] shall be trodden down. [. . .] *The lion tears sufficiently for his cubs and strangles prey for his lioness.* [Its hidden interpretation] concerns the Lion of Wrath who strikes by means of his great men and the men of his counsel. [*And he filled with prey*] *his cave and his den with torn flesh*. Its hidden interpretation concerns the Lion of Wrath [...] death unto the seekers of smooth things and who hangs men alive [...] in Israel as of old since the hanged one is called ....

This imperfectly preserved passage from the Dead Sea sect's scroll of Pesher Nahum prompts several questions, the answers to which are of considerable historical importance. Who is Demetrius? And who is Antiochus? There were several Seleucid emperors with these names. Who are 'the seekers of smooth things'? To what historical incidents does the commentary refer? And – of direct concern to our discussion of a particular form of execution – how are the gaps to be filled in the verses which tell of the 'Lion of Wrath' who 'hangs men alive'?

Many scholars have concluded that the 'Lion of Wrath' in this passage is none other than the Hasmonean king Alexander Jannaeus; that 'the seekers of smooth things' are the Pharisees, who rebelled against him; and that Demetrius is the Seleucid monarch Demetrius III (Eukairos). The main reason for these conclusions is that the actions to which this scroll alludes are strikingly similar to the account by Josephus of certain events that occurred during the reign (103–76 BC) of Alexander Jannaeus. Josephus tells us that some of the Pharisees rebelled against Jannaeus and sought the intervention of Demetrius (96–88 BC) to help them in their struggle. Later, when their uprising failed, Jannaeus took cruel revenge upon them.

For our examination of the views of the above-mentioned scholars, I think it best to give the highlights of the Josephus story in the following excerpts from *The Jewish War* (1:90–8):

After escaping an ambush in his unsuccessful engagement with the Nabatean king Obodas, Alexander Jannaeus returned to Jerusalem, where

he provoked the multitude, which hated him before, to make an insurrection against him. ... However, he was then too hard for them; and in the several battles that were fought on both sides, he slew not fewer than fifty thousand of the Jews in the interval of six years. Yet had he no reason to rejoice in these victories, since he did but consume his own kingdom; till at length he fell off fighting, and endeavoured to come to a composition with them, by talking with his subjects. But this mutability and irregularity of his conduct made them hate him still more. ... [And] they invited Demetrius, who was called Eukairos, to assist them; and as he readily complied with their request, in hopes of great advantages, and came with his army, the Jews joined with those their auxiliaries.

Josephus then describes the rival armies, both of which comprised mercenaries and Jews. Demetrius was aided by the Jewish rebels who had sought his aid, and Jannaeus had with him 'that part of the Jews which favoured him'. Demetrius's forces outnumbered those of Jannaeus. Before the battle,

the kings made proclamation, and endeavoured to draw off each other's soldiers, and make them revolt; while Demetrius hoped to induce Alexander's mercenaries to leave him, and Alexander hoped to induce the Jews that were with Demetrius to leave him.

Both failed in their pleas, and battle was joined. The fighting was bitter, and Alexander, outnumbered, was in retreat.

Yet did the upshot of this battle prove different from what was expected, as to both of them; for neither did those that invited Demetrius to come to them continue firm to him, though he was the conqueror; and six thousand Jews, out of pity to the change of Alexander's condition, when he was fled to the mountains, came over to him. Yet could not Demetrius bear this turn of affairs; but supposing that Alexander was already become a match for him again, and that all the nation [of Jews] would at length run to him, he left the country, and went his way.

However, the rest of the [Jewish] multitude did not lay aside their quarrels with him [Jannaeus], when the foreign auxiliaries were gone; but they had a perpetual war with Alexander, until he had slain the greatest part of them, and driven the rest into the city of Bemeselis; and when he had demolished that city, he carried the captives to Jerusalem. Nay, his rage was grown so extravagant, that his barbarity proceeded to the degree of impiety; for when he had ordered eight hundred to be hung upon crosses in the midst of the city, he had the throats of their wives and children cut before their eyes. ... Upon which so deep a surprise seized on the people, that eight thousand of his opposers fled away the very next night, out of all Judea, whose flight was only terminated by Alexander's death.

The Nahum Commentary and the Temple scroll

Before the discovery of the Temple scroll, all scholars took it for granted that the attitude of the Essenes on execution by hanging was the same as that expressed in the rabbinic literature. Thus, according to them, the sectarian author of the Nahum Commentary had denounced the 'Lion of Wrath' – whoever he was – for hanging people alive, even though the victims were the Pharisees, the 'seekers of smooth things', who were the principal ideological enemies of the Essenes themselves. However, in the light of the text on hanging in our Temple scroll, the common interpretation of the Nahum Commentary passage needs to be re-examined, with possibly far-reaching results.

In the first place, it could be said that the two treasonable crimes for which the capital punishment of hanging alive is decreed in the Temple scroll may also be an allusion to this very episode involving Jannaeus, Demetrius and the Pharisees. The crime of informing

against one's own people and seeking to deliver them up to a foreign
nation well fits the words of Josephus: 'they invited Demetrius, who
was called Eukairos, to assist them'. This meant going over to the
Seleucid king and passing on information which led to the ensuing
disaster. The second crime in the Temple scroll – the escapee who
defects to the enemy – could also be a reference to the aftermath of
the revolt when 'eight thousand of his [Alexander Jannaeus's] opposers', who had fought with Demetrius against Alexander, 'fled away
the very next night, out of all Judea, whose flight was only terminated by Alexander's death'.

I confess that this interpretation is possible but indefinite, for incidents of this nature had occurred even before the reign of Alexander
Jannaeus, notably during the turbulent period preceding the Maccabean uprising, and later with the establishment of the Hasmonean
dynasty. What is clear, however, is that our author, according to
the injunctions in our scroll, would certainly have considered that
the 'seekers of smooth things', who invited Demetrius to come to
Jerusalem and joined him in his war against Israel, deserved capital
punishment by hanging.

As to the argument by some scholars that the 'Lion of Wrath' who
'hangs men alive' refers to Alexander Jannaeus, I think this is most
unlikely. The sect would hardly have chosen 'lion' as an apt description of Jannaeus. Other scholars have sought to identify this wrathful
lion with the arch-enemy of the sect, the Wicked Priest – and of these
scholars some maintain that the Wicked Priest was Jannaeus (who
was both king and high priest). But this, too, is improbable, for the
same reason. My own view – based on the biblical usage of these
words – is that 'Lion of Wrath' more appropriately fits God's instrument for inflicting punishment: the sect is not necessarily criticizing
whoever it was who hanged the 'seekers of smooth things'. These
seekers, in the sect's view, by inviting Demetrius and joining him in
a war against Israel, deserved that punishment.

We finally come to the intriguing mystery of the missing words in
the final verse of the passage in the Nahum Commentary, where there
is a gap immediately after 'who hangs men alive' and before the
words 'in Israel as of old'. Again, before the discovery of the Temple
scroll, to all scholars, myself included, the missing words probably
conveyed the sense of 'which was not done'. The sentence would then
have read: 'who hangs men alive [on the tree which was not done] in
Israel as of old'. Now, however, the gap could well be filled by words
conveying the opposite sense: 'who hangs men alive [on the tree as is
the law] in Israel of old'. This, indeed, would fit the Hebrew terminology and grammar even better.

The most difficult phrase to understand is the last one in the quoted
passage – the one immediately following 'in Israel of old' – which has
been translated 'since the hanged one is called'. No satisfactory ex-

planation has been offered for this phrase on the basis of the concept that the sect was against 'hanging alive'. Now that we have seen that the object of this passage is to corroborate their view that this form of punishment was the law – at least in certain cases – in Israel as of old, in my opinion this phrase should be interpreted as stressing that the 'hanged man' of Deuteronomy 21:22, 23 means one who has been hanged alive. This needed to be emphasized because it was already disputed at the time the commentary was written. I would therefore translate the last words in the passage – and the original Hebrew lends itself to this translation – as: 'since the hanged one is called hanged alive on the tree'.

I hope it is clear that a distinction should be made between what the Temple scroll says on this subject – the text is clear and I have nothing to add – and the interpretation I have offered on the enigmatic passage in the Nahum Commentary that was prompted by the revelations in our scroll, and which became a controversial subject among scholars when I published my proposal some time ago. Some very distinguished scholars accept my interpretation, among them Professor Martin Hengel, a great authority on Jewish life during the Hellenistic and Roman periods, who wrote a book on hanging and crucifixion, and Professor Joseph A. Fitzmayer SJ, who is also a noted expert on the Hebrew and Aramaic of the Dead Sea scrolls and on the history of the period. Scholars no less distinguished, such as Professor A. Dupont-Sommer and the Russian Jewish expert Dr Amusin, do not. It is only fair that the reader should know this.

My interpretations provoked controversy on another issue. Some took them as indicating that both the Temple scroll and the commentary on Nahum allowed crucifixion, which could fall within the definition of hanging alive. While this is possible, I did not suggest it, though I doubt that the members of the sect at Qumran differentiated between hanging alive at the end of a rope and crucifixion.

I conclude this unsavoury subject with a final word on the sages. However lenient they were in their rulings on the execution procedure, condemning hanging alive, when it came to describing the way in which sinners are punished in Hell, their accounts are filled with gruesome details – drawn from the methods used by the Romans to put people to death. One example will suffice. It concerns the 'slanderer', the term for a person who gave information to the enemy. Such traitors, who broke the command 'You shall not go up and down as a slanderer' – the very words used in the Temple scroll – faced hanging by their tongues in Hell. This is recounted in a document evoking a vision of the prophet Isaiah:

He [Isaiah] entered a second house [in Hell] and found there two people hanging by their tongues, and he said to the Holy One, Blessed Be He: 'Reveal the secrets, reveal this secret to me!' He said to him: 'These are people who have slandered and were so sentenced.'

PART SEVEN

DATE AND STATUS OF THE SCROLL

21 Time and Place

This chapter and the two that follow deal with the place given to the Temple scroll by the members of the sect, and with the relationship of the scroll to the beliefs of the various Jewish sects in the Second Temple period, including the early Christians. They are different from the earlier chapters in one vital respect. So far, I have presented objective factual data on the major themes in the scroll, interspersed of course with my own interpretation of baffling passages and my proposed reconstruction of missing text which may be open to question. I think the reader should know that in these three final chapters, while there is much that is factual, the element of conjecture, though based on textual material, is more pronounced. I shall offer the subject-matter in a way that I hope will make clear in each case what is hard fact and what is conjecture.

Date of composition

The exact dating of all the Dead Sea scrolls is fraught with the most difficult problems involved in their study, and there has been much research in the quest for a solution. The method in such an investigation is to seek clues in a variety of factors that fall broadly into one of two categories, a hint of which was provided in an earlier chapter. One type enables us to determine that a scroll could not have been composed later than a particular date or period. An example of this would be the date when the scrolls were hidden in the Dead Sea caves – about AD 70, when the Romans destroyed the Qumran centre. They could certainly not have been written later than that. That they must have been written at a much earlier date was

established by a major factor in this category – paleography, identifying a script characteristic of a particular time in the oldest copy of
a given scroll.

The second category of factors are those that tell us that a scroll
could not have been composed earlier than a given time. Among the
most important ones are language – choice of words, style – and the
mention of known historical events or personalities, as in the commentary on Nahum. Another example in this category, involving
language, is the use of a particular word, referred to in an earlier
chapter, which had not entered the Hebrew language before the Hellenistic period.

This method of time-bracketing, determining the upper and lower
limits, from 'not earlier than' to 'not later than', provides the time-
frame within which the scroll must have been composed. But that
frame is usually wide, and the goal of every scroll scholar is to pinpoint the particular period within those time limits. Data for such
pinpointing are meagre in all the Qumran scrolls, and one always has
to remember that different parts of a scroll might have been composed
at different times. In general, determining the exact period can only
be inferred from the special emphasis placed on a particular subject.

It is upon such factors and data that we must depend when we
tackle the problems of dating the Temple scroll. We shall first try to
establish the 'no earlier and no later than' time-frame when the scroll
or parts of it were written, and only then attempt to pinpoint the
likeliest period.

Dating by script

If the main copy of our Temple scroll, the one I had acquired, were
the only one to have been found, we would most likely have fixed the
latest possible date of its composition at the beginning of the first
century AD or the end of the first century BC, and we discussed this
in chapter 4. This dating was based on the meticulous paleographic
studies by Professors Cross and Avigad of the Qumran scripts. Fortunately, as mentioned earlier, a few fragments exist of an essential
part of an older copy of this scroll, discovered in Qumran Cave 4 and
now in the Rockefeller Museum. These are written in what the
paleographers call the Hasmonean semi-formal script, not unlike the
complete Isaiah scroll, dating back to roughly the last quarter of the
second century BC (c. 125–100 BC) or the very beginning of the first
century BC. Thus, in our effort to determine the 'no later than' date,
we can disregard the script of our main copy and refer only to the
earliest fragments, particularly as these contain important sections of
the 'Torah' of the Temple included in the scroll. To set this paleo-

graphic bracketing in its historical framework, we could say that, based on these criteria alone, the scroll was – or its main parts were – composed no later than the reign of John Hyrcanus I (135–104 BC), or the very beginning of the reign of Alexander Jannaeus (103–76 BC).

Dating by language

An analysis of the language of the scroll shows that there are not enough data to determine the precise limits for its composition within the period of the Second Temple. However, it is clear that the composition in its present form did not precede the second half of that period. Furthermore, several linguistic features, especially words and expressions typical of mishnaic Hebrew, present obvious evidence that the scroll could not have been composed before the Hasmonean period. And nothing has been found in the language to warrant a dating later than the time limits set by the script of the earlier copy.

Dating by content

Independently of the above conclusions, it is necessary to examine the contents of a scroll for any data that may aid in the more precise dating of the composition, and which may confirm, or refute, the general chronological limits suggested by the script and language. Is there, then, anything in the contents of our scroll that can help to pinpoint the time of its composition?

In my view, the very preoccupation with such subjects as the plan of the Temple, the obsession with problems of impurity, the festivals, the Statutes of the King, the composition of the army and the royal guard, and treasonable activities and defection to the enemy, all fit very well into the pattern of the second half of the second century BC. These were the very formative decades of the Hasmonean period, when the Temple was being reconstructed, giving rise to renewed concern with questions involving its plan and the mode of worship; and this was also the period when the princes of the Hasmonean dynasty, holding the position of high priest at first, were gradually assuming the title and status of king as well. These factors, and others, seem to me to point to this period – roughly from the middle to the end of the second century BC. This, too, roughly matches the paleographic findings.

A few scholars think this date is somewhat too early, and consider a later period – the almost three-decade reign of Alexander Jannaeus – more likely. Others think my proposal sets too late a date, and would prefer a period earlier by fifty years or more. I spare the reader the highly technical reasons behind the various views, which can be dealt with only at considerable length, by saying simply that having read them all, I still believe my own proposal accords best with the known facts.

Pinpointing

Can we, with the data at our disposal, narrow the time-frame even more and fix a definite time for the composition of the scroll? Well, there is one subject dealt with by our author which may help to pinpoint the date. I think it does, though I should add that the very elements upon which I draw to prove my thesis may be interpreted differently in order to prove the opposite. I shall present the arguments of both sides.

The subject I refer to is the set of commands in the scroll involving the system of rings and wheels in the slaughterhouse used to fasten the animals for sacrifice in the Temple's inner court, which we have already described and considered in chapter 14. Our author's preoccupation with these rings might not in itself have been of decisive importance in the dating of the scroll had it merely bespoken a custom contrary to that prevailing in the Temple during the Herodian period, as attested by the codified rabbinic laws. But this is not the case, for there *were* rings in the slaughterhouse of the Herodian Temple. However, all the rabbinical sources and talmudic tradition attribute the installation of rings to fasten the animals to Johanan the high priest – John Hyrcanus I – and so we may reasonably draw upon this fact for our present discussion.

The question arises, of course, as to how to use this item of information. Was our author describing an existing situation, with the rings already in use in the Temple in his time? If so, this would be a highly important pointer to the dating of the scroll to the period *following* John Hyrcanus. Or was he, as in other instances, preaching for a change in the practice prevailing in his time by urging the installation of rings? This would put back the date of composition of the scroll to the reign of Hyrcanus, or slightly before.

The first alternative is possible, of course, and one or two scholars hold to it. But I think it unlikely, as our author as a rule dealt with commands and subjects that ran counter to contemporary practice. Indeed, the more detailed his descriptions and injunctions, the more polemical is his style, which indicates that he was calling for something new rather than echoing what was already in existence.

For this reason I favour the second possibility, and prefer the suggestion that it was the commands in our Temple scroll – or the doctrine behind them held by the author and his sect – that influenced John Hyrcanus to make the changes in the Temple. It is my assumption that Hyrcanus was aware of that doctrine.

My suggestion is supported by a fact related by Josephus that John Hyrcanus turned his back on the Pharisees and their religious doctrines and openly went over to the camp of the Sadducees. (Sadducees in this case, I believe, was a general term for priestly groups to whom, in certain respects relating to the Temple cult, the Essenes were close.) As Josephus wrote: 'He [John Hyrcanus I] joined hands with the Sadducees and left the sect of the Pharisees and nullified and cancelled the religious rules which the Pharisees fixed for the people.' (*Antiquities* 13:296) Of special importance for our discussion is the emphasis by Josephus on the nullification by Hyrcanus of fixed religious practices and the introduction of new ones, including, as the Mishnah tells us, the installation of rings in the Temple.

These are the facts. The reader may make of them what he will. It is my opinion, as I indicated at the outset, that both paleography and content put the composition of significant parts of the scroll at not later than the third quarter of the second century BC, namely, the first years of the reign of John Hyrcanus or slightly earlier.

The status of the scroll

A more fundamental question about the scroll is its status among the writings of the sect to the members of the sect. Did they regard it as a 'Torah', on a par in holiness and authenticity with the Books which were eventually included in the canon of the Scriptures? Or did they consider it a kind of commentary, a 'Midrash', an interpretation of the Pentateuch, its laws, though binding, drawing their authority exclusively from the belief that the author of the scroll, by divine inspiration, had truly construed the Pentateuchal commands?

In our quest for the answer, which is of the utmost importance, we must be careful to avoid being misled by the general attitude towards the masoretic text of the Pentateuch. We have all tended to accept this text as the sole canonical Pentateuch of all Israel at all times. The fact is, however, that the discovery of biblical texts among the Dead Sea scrolls had already shown, for the first time, the existence in certain periods of different textual versions of the canonical works among various sects, and the main concern of most scholars was the study and analysis of the variant texts. Now, however, with the

discovery of the Temple scroll, a book of the Law of the Qumran sect, •
it seems possible that other 'scriptures' were regarded as equally 'canonical' by the sectarians, the two side by side being equally respected.
This has now become a central problem in studies on the evolution of
the biblical canon.

My friend and colleague Professor M. Goshen-Gottstein, a very distinguished biblical scholar, must be credited with having presented
the acuteness of this problem in so far as it concerned the Psalms
scroll, a Psalter from Qumran Cave 11, when it was published by
Professor James A. Sanders in 1965, which we mentioned in chapter
2. The claim by Sanders that the Psalter represented a parallel canonical text to the accepted biblical Book of Psalms provoked strong
reactions. Goshen-Gottstein, for example, wrote among other things
that 'our whole picture of the completion of the growth of the various
books of the Bible accepted as "canonical" may be wrong ... we must
doubt whether any other view we hold with regard to questions of
"canon" is more than the result of lack of information'. In a further
argument against Sanders's claim for the 'canonical' status of the
Psalms scroll, Goshen-Gottstein wrote (and it has a direct bearing on
our discussion):

To be sure, were there anything to compel us to assume that the collection
[the Psalter] was meant to be 'canonical', we would be forced at the same
time to admit that our scroll also proves the existence of a variant 'canonical'
collection, specific to the Qumran Covenanters.... *Since nothing specifically
'Qumranic' has been discovered so far with regard to Bible texts*, this would be
a result of far-reaching consequences. [The italics are mine – YY]

Goshen-Gottstein, of course, was writing before the discovery of the
Temple scroll, and the fear of such 'far-reaching' conclusions
prompted him to add that if we accepted the supposition that there
were indeed books which had been composed with the intention of
their being 'canonical', then 'a far-reaching restatement of our theory
with regard to the state of the Bible text at that time would become
necessary'.

Now we have the Temple scroll, proving that in Qumran there
actually *were* specific biblical works, with rulings different from those
in the accepted canon, all claiming to be canonical as spoken directly ☞
by God.

I should add that when I first lectured on the discovery of the
Temple scroll, outlined its contents and suggested that it might have
been regarded as 'canonical' – for reasons I shall soon explain –
Goshen-Gottstein revised his views somewhat, saying that 'the new
scroll is a basic innovation in the literary works of the Qumran sect
in our possession today and in the body of works from the Second
Temple period known so far'. However, he found it inconceivable that
the author of the scroll would consider presenting a canonical text of

the Torah, or, in his words, that the author 'was of the opinion that this is a text of the Torah or that others would accept it from him'.

Posing the problem in this way is not necessarily the only approach to its solution, for the existence of the Temple scroll does not, in itself, indicate that the Qumranites, i.e. the Essenes, denied the authenticity of the canonical Pentateuch, rejected it and replaced it with the Temple scroll. The question is whether they considered this scroll to be 'canonical', but of a different nature. To find the answer, I thought it might be fruitful to search in other writings of the Dead Sea sect for a possible mention or hint of the existence of this scroll, and, if there were such a reference, whether it contained any indication of how it was regarded.

Before offering my findings, I think it pertinent to recall an outward indication in the text of the scroll itself which may serve as circumstantial evidence, though admittedly not decisive, to support the thesis that the Qumranites considered it a holy scripture. This was the fact, mentioned in chapter 5, that the divine name, the tetragrammaton, appears in the text in the same square script as the rest of the scroll, exactly as in the canonical Books of the Bible found at Qumran, whereas the common practice of the Qumran scribes was to use the more ancient palaeo-Hebrew script for the tetragrammaton in commentaries and other scrolls which they did not consider canonical.

Mention of the scroll in other sectarian writings

Whatever our conclusions regarding the 'canonical' status of the Temple scroll within the sect – and it must be clear by now that I believe it was held to be holy scripture by the sectarians – there can be no doubt that its members treated it as a document of major importance. It is the only one in our possession that deals comprehensively with some of the cardinal religious rulings concerning the Pentateuchal commands, and the painstaking labour invested by the sectarians in making copies of so lengthy a scroll is evidence of how much it meant to them. Is it likely, then, that so basic a book should not have been mentioned, quoted or referred to in some way in the other sectarian scrolls found at Qumran? Or can it be that there *are* references to it but they are difficult to identify?

There are several such possibilities that are worth probing. These are the mention in a few Dead Sea scrolls of unknown works, and our Temple scroll may well be one of them. Indeed, some of these mentions may all be an allusion to the same scroll but in different terms. After all, none of the scrolls was given an original title by the composer as far as we know. They are now known by titles usually given them by the scholars who deciphered, studied and published them – like my title for this Temple scroll. Thus, one must try to identify these unknown works, referred to in different ways in the various scrolls, by studying the quotations from their contents and seeing whether they bear any relationship to a known work in our possession, such as the Temple scroll. Doing so, of course, may be embarking on a wild-goose chase, as it is equally possible that none of these unknown works is our scroll. However, the following seem the most promising. I shall present the facts and allow the reader to make his own judgement.

The Book of *Hagu*

The first possibility that comes to mind is a book referred to in the Damascus Document, in the Manual of Discipline, and in the Messianic Rule, as the Book of *Hagu*. The root of the Hebrew word *hagu* is translated in the English Bible as 'meditate', as in the injunction in Joshua 1:8: 'This book of the law shall not depart out of your mouth, but you shall meditate on it day and night.'

Ever since the discovery of the Damascus and Manual scrolls, scholars have been trying to identify this Book of *Hagu*, for it is one of the few mentioned explicitly in the literature of the sect as being fundamental. It was mandatory, as one reference to it states, for a man to know and understand it before he was considered fit to act as a judge of the congregation. And we learn from another reference that 'every citizen in Israel' was required to study this book in his youth.

Of the following four quotations which refer to the Book of *Hagu* (or *Hagi*), the first three are from the Damascus Document and the fourth is from the Messianic Rule:

And this is the rule for the Judges of the Congregation: ... They shall be learned in the Book of the *Hagu* and in the constitutions of the Covenant. (10:4–6)

And in a locality of ten there shall never be lacking a priest learned in the Book of the *Hagu*; they shall all be ruled by him. (13:2, 3)

And the priest who enrols the many shall be ... learned in the Book of the *Hagi*. ... (14:6, 7)

And this is the rule for all the hosts of the Congregation, for every citizen in Israel: From his youth they shall instruct him in the Book of the *Hagi*. ... (1:6–8)

Scholars are divided in their views about this book. Some believe the reference is to the 'canonical' Law of Moses. I find this improbable, for in these very Dead Sea writings there is frequent mention of that

'canonical' Law and it is called by that name, the Law of Moses. All
agree, however, that the Book of *Hagu* is a book of Divine Law of
sorts.

I favour the opinion that the allusions here are to a veritable Book
of Law, also because of the link between its name and the injunction
in Joshua. Can this book be our Temple scroll? It is difficult to give
a decisive Yes; but neither can the possibility be summarily dismissed.
The fact is that our scroll deals with such fundamental issues as the
laws of the Festivals and the Temple, purity and polygamy, and all
the commands of Deuteronomy in a manner different from that revealed to all Israel in the 'canonical' Pentateuch, and it was for this
reason that the 'Judges of the Congregation' had to be well-versed in
this book.

The 'Book of the Second Law (Torah)'

Two other references in the writings of the sect, albeit fragmentary,
deserve close scrutiny, as they may contain explicit allusions to the
Temple scroll. Both are taken from commentaries, and both refer to
a second 'Torah'. The first appears in the *pesher* on Psalm 37:32: 'The
wicked watches the righteous, and seeks to slay him.' The commentary to this verse reads: 'Its hidden interpretation concerns the
Wicked Priest, who watched the Teacher of Righteousness and sought
to slay him [. . .] and the Law which he sent to him.' (The Hebrew
word used for 'the Law' is 'Torah'.) It is clear from this that one
reason why the Wicked Priest tried to put to death the Teacher of
Righteousness, the founder of the sect, was the 'Torah' the latter had
sent him. This could not possibly have been a reference to the 'canonical' Pentateuch, as that would not have given cause for wishing to
kill the sender. It seems to me that here we have a definite hint that
the founder of the sect had sent a certain 'Torah' which had so infur-
iated the Wicked Priest that he 'sought to slay him'.

This assumption of mine finds corroboration in another *pesher*, a
commentary called The Chain of Peshers (*Catena*). This document
deals with commentaries on various biblical Books, and the one that
interests us is a commentary on Hosea 5:8: 'Blow the horn in Gibeah,
the trumpet in Ramah.' In the 'hidden interpretation' of this verse,
the following lines are preserved, with the missing text indicated by
dots followed by reconstructed words or letters, where they are obvious, within square brackets:

'Blow the horn in Gibeah': 'the horn' is the book of [. . . and the trumpet is]
the Book of the Second Torah which [. . . m]en of his counsel, but they spoke
rebelliously against him and [. . .]

As usual, the gaps occur in the most inconvenient places, but it is evident, from the characteristic method of the commentary author, that the 'horn' (*shofar* in Hebrew) is the book of the first Law, the 'canonical Torah', while the trumpet, as the preserved original words state, refers to the 'Book of the Second Law', which was 'revealed' by the Teacher of Righteousness to the 'men of his counsel'. It would seem that this Book of the Second Law was the very Book of the Law that the Teacher of Righteousness sent to the Wicked Priest.

It is my conjecture, upon which I shall soon elaborate, that the author of the Temple scroll might have been none other than the Teacher of Righteousness himself. But for the moment, I offer the submission that the references to 'the Law' sent by the Teacher of Righteousness in the first commentary, and to the 'Book of the Second Law' in the second, may possibly be actual references to the Temple scroll. Again, the probability is there, but there is no definite proof.

The third reference in the sectarian writings is the most intriguing – and the one most likely to have alluded to the Temple scroll. It may be recalled that when we discussed the scroll's ban on the king from taking more than one wife – the way the ordinance put it was to prohibit his taking another wife while his wife was still alive – we mentioned a similar ban in the Damascus Document. But this Document went on to explain, in somewhat apologetic terms, how it was that, in the light of such a ban, King David had had so many wives. (King Solomon, it will be remembered, was not mentioned!) In the Damascus text that follows, its author was clearly trying to vindicate the king of Israel:

As to the prince [i.e. the king], it is written: 'He shall not multiply wives unto himself.' [Deuteronomy 17:17 – the very passage that is quoted at the beginning of the Statutes of the King in the Temple scroll.] But David read not in the Book of the Law that was sealed which was in the Ark [of the Covenant]. For it was not opened in Israel from the day of the death of Eleazar and Joshua, and the elders who worshipped Ashtoreth. And it was hidden and was not revealed until Zadok arose. (5:1–5)

Thus, David was to be excused, as he was unaware of the ban on bigamy, since this was written in the sealed Book of the Law that had not yet been revealed in his time.

It is almost the unanimous view of scholars that this passage refers to the Book of the Law discovered by Hilkiah, the high priest in the Temple at the time of King Josiah, recorded in 2 Kings 22:8: 'And Hilkiah the high priest said to Shaphan the secretary, "I have found the book of the law in the house of the Lord."' This is generally taken to have been the Book of Deuteronomy. Furthermore, the reference to the ban in Deuteronomy 17:17 'he shall not multiply wives for himself' appears to support the accepted interpretation that the book in question is indeed none other than Deuteronomy.

Even before the discovery of the Temple scroll, scholars were aware of certain snags in this theory. If the reference was to the book found by Hilkiah, why would the Damascus Document have mentioned the 'sealed book' found by Zadok? One of the greatest Talmudists of his time and commentator on the Damascus Document, Professor Louis Ginzberg, sought to overcome this difficulty by suggesting that this Zadok was the grandfather of Hilkiah, according to the lists in 1 Chronicles 9:11. This is an ingenious interpretation, but the fact remains that the Damascus Document ascribed the discovery of the sealed book to Zadok and not to Hilkiah, and it can be taken for granted that the author of the Damascus Document well knew what is written in 2 Kings 22:8.

The second snag is that even if the author did imply that King David was unaware of the existence of the Book of Deuteronomy and its command not to 'multiply wives for himself', this in itself is not enough to prove that there was indeed a ban on the king's taking more than one wife. The Damascus Document author was well aware of the other interpretations in this connection that were current at the time in Jewry, for, after all, the Deuteronomy command says only that the king shall not '*multiply* wives', the plain meaning of which does not prohibit him from taking more than one wife.

It seems to me that the author intended to convey something like the following in the Damascus passage quoted above:

And if you say, 'He shall not multiply wives for himself', our answer is that the real meaning of this command [namely, the ban on taking more than one wife] was not known to King David, as it was written in the sealed Book of the Law: and this sealed book was not revealed until the time of Zadok.

Now, with the discovery and decipherment of the Temple scroll, we have for the first time a clearcut injunction by the same sect, avowedly based on their interpretation of Deuteronomy, prohibiting bigamy, and this ban appears as a divine command only in the Temple scroll. I therefore suggest the possibility that the sealed Book of the Law referred to in the Damascus Document is our very Temple scroll, where this prohibition is explicitly set forth. If the allusion in the Damascus Document can be so interpreted, then what the passage in that Document is saying is that the Temple scroll was not known, of course, to King David, as it was revealed only in the days of Zadok.

Who, then, is Zadok? It will be recalled that the Qumran community called themselves the sect of The Sons of Zadok or The Followers of Zadok, and their founder is called The Teacher of Righteousness. The Hebrew word for 'righteousness' is *zedek*, and springs from the same root as Zadok. It therefore seems to me possible, perhaps even probable, that our Temple scroll was composed by none other than the founder of the sect, whose name was Zadok.

Summing up

If, as I believe, there is substance to my above arguments and suggestions, it could mean that the Temple scroll was in fact the basic
'Torah' of the Essenes, and was referred to by them as the Book of
Hagu – which had to be 'meditated upon' and in which all had to be
'instructed' – or as the Second Torah, a Book of the Second Law
which had been revealed only to the sect, and which was considered
by them accordingly as 'canonical'. The revelation had come to the
founder of the sect, Zadok. It would be legitimate, then, to suggest
that our scroll was really the hidden 'Torah' of the Essenes, as holy
to them as the canonical Torah. It is, as we have seen, a 'Torah' that
spans all the subjects of the religious rulings in the Pentateuch, including Deuteronomy itself.

The numerous references to the Teacher of Righteousness in the
sect, and the qualities attributed to him, seem to me to justify these
assumptions. It was to the Teacher of Righteousness that God made
known the 'hidden interpretation of the writing of His servants, the
prophets' (Habakkuk Commentary 7:4, 5). Or, as Professor Geza
Vermes put it,

the Teacher's interpretation alone propagated by his disciples offered true
enlightenment and guidance; but what remains important is that the very
knowledge of the true law and its interpretation was also a gift of God which
the Teacher and the members of the sect were given.

What better describes this than the following hymn from the Manual
of Discipline (in the translation by Vermes) which may have been
written by the Teacher himself:

> From the source of His righteousness
> is my justification,
> and from His marvellous mysteries
> is the light in my heart.
> My eyes have gazed
> on that which is eternal,
> on wisdom concealed from men,
> on knowledge and wise design
> [hidden] from the sons of men;
> on a fountain of righteousness
> and on a storehouse of power,
> on a spring of glory
> [hidden] from the assembly of flesh.
> God has given them to His chosen ones
> as an everlasting possession,
> and has caused them to inherit
> the lot of the Holy Ones. (Col. 11)

An historical paradox

One of the most startling findings of the study of the Temple scroll is the undeniable fact, which I believe was already apparent, that the Dead Sea scrolls sect – considered to be the Essenes – clung tenaciously to the most rigorous interpretation of the Law of Moses in general, and in particular to the ordinances on the Temple and its rituals, festivals and sacrifices alike. Yet it was this very sect, of all the Jewish sects, that had the most profound influence on the beliefs, practices, organization and even the phraseology of early Christianity. Christianity eventually strove to detach itself from the Law of Moses. How was it, then, that this most extreme and orthodox Jewish sect had this impact on Jewish Christianity which was subsequently to fight against the legalistic and rigid interpretation of the Law of Moses, and finally to reject that Law?

To understand and explain this paradox, certain relevant issues need to be examined.

The scroll and the Qumran sect

The primary question is whether it can be established beyond doubt that our Temple scroll is sectarian in the narrowest sense of that term, namely, that it was composed by members of this particular Dead Sea sect at Qumran. True, it was discovered in one of the Qumran caves, and, together with other copies, it was part of the library of this sect. But it could be argued that, like such other writings as the biblical books, it was not a product of the sect but a book of learning written by others which the sect thought worthy of study.

Some scholars have so argued; but to my mind most of the topics covered by the Temple scroll and the rulings it gives point unmistakably to its being a product of the sect itself, like the other sectarian Dead Sea scrolls. And the subjects dealt with, the ordinances on those subjects, and the terminology, too, in the Temple scroll are all akin to those in these other sectarian scrolls.

The most important of those scrolls, in itself and in its relationship to the Temple scroll, is the one called the Damascus Document or the Damascus Covenant. Although it was first found in a late medieval copy in the Cairo Geniza fifty years before the 1947 discovery of the Qumran caves scrolls, it was considered from its contents to be part of the library of the Dead Sea sect. It is now known to have been a fundamental composition of the sect, and several fragmentary copies have been found in the caves.

The kinship between this Damascus Document and the Temple

A facsimile of the Damascus Document text prohibiting bigamy. It absolves King David on the ground that he was unaware of the 'hidden Torah' (the Temple scroll?) which imposes this prohibition, and which was revealed, says the Damascus Document, 'to Zadok', most probably the 'Teacher of Righteousness', founder of the Qumran sect.

scroll on basic points has been demonstrated throughout this presentation. To mention the most notable examples, both documents – and only these two – use the terminology 'the city of the Temple'. Both have the rulings, almost in the same words, banning bigamy and divorce. This is also true of the prohibition on sexual intercourse in the city of the Temple, and the rigorous rules of purification following sexual intercourse anywhere. And it is in both these documents that we find the strict laws of purification from uncleanness contracted from the house of a dead person. It must also be remembered that the Damascus Document is a composite scroll which deals with a number of subjects concerning the sect, including the reference to two of its basic concepts: the expectation of two Messiahs – one from Aaron and one from Israel; and the sect's belief in its founder, the Teacher of Righteousness. These two concepts also appear in other sectarian scrolls.

In general, therefore, we can say that the connection of the scroll with the writings of the Qumran sect is perceptible from the nature of the laws contained in it, as well as from the employment of terms peculiar to the sect, and that the inspiration of the scroll is especially noticeable in the Damascus Document. There is also a definite relationship between the laws of the scroll concerning the purity of the camp and those in the War of the Sons of Light scroll.

No less important is the fact that the Temple scroll is based on the unique calendar followed by the Dead Sea scrolls sect. It is true, as we have indicated earlier, that this special calendar is also the calendar of the Books of Jubilees and Enoch, two of the so-called pseudepigraphal works. This fact, I believe, supports the theory, which more and more scholars have come to accept, that Jubilees and similar pseudepigraphal writings are compositions embodying the teachings of a wider movement from which the Qumran sect developed in the course of time, if not compositions of the sect itself.

It is my considered view that the Temple scroll is undoubtedly a literary and religious product of the Dead Sea scrolls sect. And if I am right in my interpretation of the evidence I have brought in this book to support this view, then there can be equally no doubt that this scroll was perhaps the most important of all the sect's writings, containing as it does what both author and sect believed to be the hidden law given by God to Moses and revealed and known only to the founder of the sect and his followers.

22 The Qumran Sect and the Essenes

The next point that requires examination is whether the Temple scroll can help us identify the Dead Sea scrolls sect at Qumran. Most scholars now agree that they were none other than the Essenes, one of the small though dominant breakaway Jewish sects in the latter part of the Second Temple period described by Josephus, Philo and Pliny the Elder.

While it would be beyond the scope of this book to marshal all the evidence for such identification, it may be noted that, despite some understandable discrepancies, the account by Josephus of the organization, practices and rituals of the Essenes, coupled with some remarks by Philo, fit remarkably well what we know today of the Qumran community from the Dead Sea scrolls, mainly the Manual of Discipline and the Damascus Document. No less important is the information supplied by Pliny (AD 23-79) in the following passage from his *Naturalis Historia* (5:73):

On the west side of the Dead Sea, but out of range of the noxious exhalations of the coast, is the solitary tribe of the Essenes, which is remarkable beyond all the other tribes in the whole world, as it has no women and has renounced all sexual desire, has no money, and has only palm trees for company. Day by day the throng of refugees is recruited to an equal number by numerous successions of personnel tired of life and driven thither by ways of fortune to adopt their manners. Thus, through thousands of ages (incredible to relate) a race in which no one is born lives on forever; so prolific for their advantage is other men's weariness of life. Lying below the Essenes was formerly the town of Engedi, second only to Jerusalem in the fertility of its land and in its growths of palm trees, but now, like Jerusalem, a heap of ashes. Next comes Masada, a fortress on a rock, itself also not far from the Dead Sea. This is the limit of Judea. (Translation by H. Rackham)

Of the utmost significance in this passage is the specific geographic location of the Essene settlement. It is on the western shore of the Dead Sea, and 'lying below' it is En-Gedi. This of course could mean that the Essenes lived in the hills above En-Gedi, as scholars in the past believed; or, as most scholars agree today, that En-Gedi lay to the south of the Essene centre. The latter is the more likely, for Pliny goes on to say 'Next comes Masada', showing that he was proceeding from north to south. And the site of the Essenes in his description is exactly the spot where the Qumran community dwelt – the ruins of their settlement may be seen to this day. Moreover, the pattern and principles guiding the lives of the Essenes, in Pliny's account, albeit over-simplified and idealized, match those, as we have seen, of the Qumran sect.

The negative factors

The question of concern to us is whether there is anything in the Temple scroll that strengthens – or negates – this identification of the Dead Sea scrolls sect with the Essenes. Let us deal first with the negative factors, namely, those rulings in the Temple scroll which, on the face of it, would appear to be contrary to the principles and practices of the Essenes as these were conceived in early studies of the Dead Sea scrolls. The most prominent of such apparently divergent views was over the attitude of the sect towards Temple sacrifice.

We have drawn attention on more than one occasion to the fact that the main theme of the Temple scroll and the cardinal subject with which its author was concerned was the cult of the Temple, with the installations, the vessels, and the whole procedure of the sacrifices. And he was dealing not with a spiritual Temple but with the physical Temple in which sacrifices were to be offered on the various festivals in exactly the way in which he prescribed them in the scroll.

In the works of Josephus and Philo, which are the main sources for our knowledge of the Essenes, there are references which could have been, and were in fact, interpreted as indicating that the Essenes were opposed to sacrifices in principle. But a careful examination of these references shows that no such categorical conclusion can be drawn from them.

Citing Josephus would appear to be somewhat complicated since there exist two conflicting versions of his report on the subject of sacrifices. One version reads:

When the Essenes send their gifts to the Temple, they do not offer sacrifices owing to a difference in the rites of purity which they practise, and therefore, being excluded from the common precinct [of the Temple], they offer sacrifices by themselves. (*Antiquities* 18:19)

The other version has it that 'they do offer sacrifices'. However, it is clear from either version that they did not object to sacrifices. For even in the version which records that they did not offer sacrifices in the Temple, it is evident that this was not because they were opposed to sacrifices in principle but only because they practised different 'rites of purity'. This is very similar to what may be deduced from the Temple scroll.

As for the report by Josephus that 'they offer sacrifices by themselves', this is an obscure point on which there are no hard facts. The Temple scroll does not tell us what was the practice in Qumran where they were cut off from the Temple. It is possible, however, that there was a hint in an earlier chapter that certain rites, such as the Days of Ordination, which involved offerings, may have been carried out in Qumran. But this is not definite, and in any case it is not a matter that is essential to our present discussion.

All in all, therefore, I think it is fair to say that the Josephus report does not rule out identifying the sect of the Temple scroll with the Essenes. And if it emphasizes that the Essenes were against sacrifices in the Temple at that time only because they practised different rites, we may add that this was not the only feature of the Temple to which they objected. They regarded the whole concept, plan and conduct of the contemporary Temple as wrong, and, in addition, they followed a different calendar, so clearly they could not participate in its ritual.

The reference to the Essenes and sacrifices in Philo, who sought to idealize this sect, is associated with what he calls 'their extraordinary devotion to God'. This, he says, is manifested 'not by sacrificing animals, but by determining to render their own minds holy'. This in itself, however, as has already been shown by scholars, does not indicate that the Essenes were in principle opposed to sacrifices. It simply echoes the ideas expressed long before by the Hebrew prophets. As Samuel put it, 'Has the Lord as great delight in burnt offerings and sacrifices, as in obeying the voice of the Lord? Behold, to obey is better than sacrifice, and to hearken than the fat of rams.' (1 Samuel 15:22)

Even before the discovery of the Temple scroll, it was evident from the scroll of The War of the Sons of Light against the Sons of Darkness that the sect was not in principle opposed to sacrifices. In that scroll, we are told how the members of the sect, the Sons of Light, were to prepare themselves for 'the last days', after they had overcome the Sons of Darkness and could return to Jerusalem, there to resume the whole Temple cult of sacrifices as prescribed by the Law of Moses. Now, in the Temple scroll, this point is made quite clear. And I submit that the references to the Essenes in the only sources extant on their attitude towards sacrifice do not negate this view. What they were opposed to, and wished to have no part of, was the whole cult of the Temple in Jerusalem as practised in their times. And this is in keeping with what we learn from the Temple scroll.

The positive factors: identifying the Qumran sect with the Essenes

In addition to the emphasis on the laws of purity and the strict ritual pertaining to cleanness that were common to both the Temple scroll and the Essenes, there is another factor which to my mind indicates even more clearly that the Temple scroll is an Essene composition. This is the siting of the latrine – the 'hand' – outside the city, and quite a distance from it, almost a mile. This is presented in the scroll as a divine ordinance, to keep the Temple city free of impurity.

When we discussed this subject in chapter 18 we quoted the account by Josephus on the Essene forbearance from relieving themselves on the Sabbath, since that entailed work – digging a hole – and work on the Sabbath day was prohibited by the Law of Moses. But Josephus had added that whenever and wherever they relieved themselves on other days, they did so in a remote place because, as he explains in a tone of surprise, they considered excrement to be impure from a ritualistic point of view. I think this is telling proof of the close connection between the doctrines of the Temple scroll and those of the Essenes.

Finally, the general attitude in the scroll towards marriage and to 'impurity' conveyed by sexual relations is much the same as that of the Essenes, from all we know about them. Most of them were celibate.

To sum up, the Temple scroll, a product to my mind of the Dead Sea scrolls community of Qumran, strengthens, if not confirms, the proposition that this community is to be identified with the Essenes.

Josephus, the Essenes and the Temple scroll

Of special interest is the fact, to which I have often referred, that Josephus occasionally mentions certain Jewish laws as though they were the accepted laws of what might be called the 'normative' Judaism of the time, but which in fact have no parallel in the Jewish sources. Some of them, as we have shown, can be traced to the text in the Temple scroll. One example, which we presented in detail, was the scroll's prohibition on the entry into the Temple city of persons suffering 'a discharge'. There is no parallel in the Jewish legal code, yet Josephus records it as though it were accepted common law. How is this to be explained?

It is evident that Josephus had knowledge of traditions that were contrary to rabbinic law, which he had acquired from different sources. The most probable primary source, in my opinion, which I have expressed more than once in other contexts, were the Essenes themselves. He had become familiar with their traditions early in his life when he had lived among them and studied their teachings. Many years later, when he was writing his works and recalling the customs and laws of Israel, the differences between the doctrines of the Essenes and those of non-sectarian Judaism at that time may, on occasion, have become blurred in his mind so that they emerged as one, lumped together as 'Jewish law'.

The sect of the Temple scroll and other Jewish groups

If our identification of the Qumran sect with the Essenes is to be watertight, we must face the problem of whether or not there may be a similar identity between the views of the sect and those of other Jewish sects or groupings. This problem has become more challenging in the light of the laws, and their phrasing, in the Temple scroll. Is there, to go from the general to the particular, a direct relationship between the laws of the sect and those of the early Pharisaic teachings, the doctrines of the Sadducees, and the rulings finally formulated in the rabbinic literature?

I hope I have shown that a study of the innumerable laws on almost every relevant subject that are interwoven in the Temple scroll leaves no doubt that it presents a codex of laws absolutely contrary to the rabbinic statutes. This we have established because we have long known a great deal about these statutes – the rulings of Pharisaic Judaism as crystallized in the rabbinical writings – and because we now know so much more than we did, thanks to the Temple scroll, of the views and rulings of the Essenes. But what of the early Pharisees? And what of the Sadducees? Is there not perhaps a similarity between their views and those in the Temple scroll?

This is not easy to answer, as very little is known of the Pharisees at the beginning of their movement in the final centuries BC beyond the fact that their laws on purity, tithing and certain Temple rituals were stricter than those that emerged under the more liberal development of rabbinical Judaism. And as for the Sadducees, almost nothing can be gleaned of their doctrines from the brief mentions in Josephus and the few references to them in the Mishnah – if indeed the term 'Sadducees' used by the rabbis always applied to them and not indiscriminately to all sectarian groups. We know only that most of the Sadducees belonged to the priestly stream of Judaism, and therefore held strict views on all aspects of the Temple ritual, particularly the detailed procedures of the sacrifice.

Thus, there would appear to be similarities between the teachings of the Temple scroll and certain elements in the early Pharisaic and Sadducean practices. However, this does not mean that either the Pharisees or the Sadducees might possibly be identified with the Essenes. We have too little data to determine the exact relationship of early Pharisaic law to the counterpart Essene laws as they appear in the Temple scroll. And as for the Sadducees and the Essenes, ranged against their similarity of views on the rigid interpretation of the Pentateuch is the wide disparity between the two. The Sadducees accepted the Temple plan and its ritual and followed the 'normative' Jewish calendar. The Essenes rejected all three, replacing them with a new Temple plan and ritual devised by the author of the Temple scroll, and a calendar of their own. On no account can the Sadducees be identified with the Essenes.

The ordinances of the scroll and other halachic doctrines

Two further questions worth considering, and conclusions worth seeking, arise out of the similarity of language in certain notable instances between the writings of the sect and the talmudic sources. Does this denote the influence of the one upon the other, and the possible existence of a written codex of law upon which all halachists, 'normative' and dissident, drew? And does it shed special light on the nature of talmudic discussion?

There are two striking examples in the ordinances of the Temple scroll with which we have dealt at length earlier in this book, but one aspect of which is relevant to our present examination. One example concerns the degree of uncleanness of a woman with a dead foetus. It will be recalled that the Mishnah judges the woman to be clean as long as the foetus is in her womb. The scroll ordains that she is unclean as long as the foetus is inside her – exactly the opposite. Yet the legal situation is presented in both works in almost the same phraseology. The texts in the Mishnah and the scroll are virtually identical.

The second example is the case of the 'seduced' and the 'seized' woman. Again, we discussed earlier the basic difference between the ruling in the rabbinic literature and that in the scroll. But when the author of the scroll decrees that the man must marry the young woman, he adds the qualifying phrase: provided that 'she is fit for him according to the law'. The talmudic sources add the same qualification in the same phraseology: the woman must be 'a wife that is fit for him' – fit, of course, from the legal point of view.

How is this similarity of terminology in both these examples to be explained? I think it is safe to conclude that each school of thought in this Second Temple period well knew the opposing views; but in arguing with their opponents and setting forth their own decrees, its members studiously avoided all mention of the names of their adversaries. The similar and at times identical phrasing signifies, to my mind, that the author of one set of ordinances had studied the written rulings of the other; and/or that both had drawn upon a third written source, which had provided a common legal Hebrew terminology to which all 'doctors of the law' of that period had recourse, with each reaching his own conclusions. As to whether there was such a third source, the subject requires more detailed study before a definite conclusion can be reached. And this also holds for any conclusion about the influence of one sect upon its adversary.

The second major question – to which, unlike the first, a definite answer can be given – involves the nature of talmudic discussion. I refer to the numerous instances in which halachic issues are treated at considerable length even though there is no difference of opinion among the sages taking part. Such characteristic talmudic discussions have often been called *pilpul*, the Hebrew term meaning hair-splitting casuistry, for not always was there a recognition of their intent. However, I found after a cursory examination that, for the most part, these lengthy discussions in the Talmud were precisely on those points on which the ordinances of the Temple scroll and many other religious rulings of the sect were the direct opposite of the decisions by the sages.

It is evident that the sages were well aware of these contrary sectarian laws but did not wish to mention the names of the dissidents. Nevertheless, these sectarians and their views had to be combated, and so some of the sages served as devil's advocate, ostensibly arguing against the accepted halachah by introducing the very reasoning of the breakaway sectarians, solely in order to provide the opportunity for its rebuttal.

I think this opens a fruitful avenue for study. A careful analysis of the arguments at these talmudic discussions by sages posing as opponents of the halachah in question might enable us to reconstruct the varied views of the different Jewish sects, particularly the Essenes, during this period of the Second Temple.

23 The Scroll and the New Testament

In the early phase of the study of the Dead Sea scrolls, shortly after their discovery in 1947, it became apparent that there were similarities between the teachings of the Jewish sect, the Essenes, as expressed in these scrolls, and certain writings in the New Testament. This came as a shock to some scholars, both Jewish and Christian, who, though well aware of the fact that Christianity had sprung from Judaism and its founders were Jewish, had not given it due emphasis. Today, the relationship between the Jewish sectarian writings and the beginnings of Christianity is one of the central concerns of scroll study – and perhaps explains the universal interest in these ancient documents.

Apart from differences in approach and emphasis, most scholars are in agreement – rightly so, in my opinion – that the influence of the sect's teachings is recognizable in the views, practices, ideology and even the very phraseology of the founders of Christianity. Until the discovery of the Temple scroll, it was feasible to assume that the members of the sect and the early Christians shared an approach that disavowed the Temple and its rituals, and developed new concepts to take their place. Now, with the decipherment of this scroll in which the Temple and the sacrificial ritual have a central place, we are faced more acutely with the earlier mentioned paradox of how it was that the Essenes, who adhered so tenaciously to all the minutiae of the Law of Moses, could have influenced, of all the breakaway Jewish sects, precisely the early Christians whose followers would in due course and in essence reject that Law.

I think a careful study of our Temple scroll reveals the probable explanation for this paradox. Though it is beyond the scope of this book to discuss this fascinating subject in detail, it seems to me appropriate in this concluding chapter to sharpen the focus on both the paradox and its explanation.

We must first be clear, however, about what Christianity we are discussing, for the term 'early Christianity' covers different periods, with concomitant social and religious developments, and variations in its relations with the Dead Sea sect.

John the Baptist

There is now a near consensus that the earliest of such relations emerged in the time of John the Baptist. From all we know through the New Testament – and there is very little, for the stories associated with him are brief, and heavily edited – it seems evident that John himself not only knew the Essenes but may also have been a member of the community for a period. He roamed about in the same area – the eastern edge of the Judean desert close to the river Jordan and the Dead Sea – preaching and practising an ascetic mode of life; and the type of baptism he advocated is in keeping with the texts on baptism in some of the Dead Sea scrolls. (Archaeological remains associated with baptism were excavated at Qumran.) We do not know what additional practices and patterns of behaviour may have infiltrated into Christianity through this contact. One of them may have been the sharing of wealth by the organization of the early community of the primitive church in Jerusalem, although this organization, which was very similar to the Qumran community, might have originated through the influence of the Essenes living in Jerusalem – the ones we mentioned in an earlier chapter in connection with the 'Essene Gate'.

Jesus

The relationship of Jesus to the Essenes must have been far more complex. There can be no doubt that they shared the same views on certain issues; and in the Sermon on the Mount (in Matthew 5), Jesus definitely used phraseology and metaphor that echo the language in the writings of the Essenes, as we now know from the Dead Sea scrolls. The prominent examples in the Sermon addressed to his disciples and to the crowds at the foot of the Mount are: 'You are the light of the world' (Mat. 5:14); 'Let your light so shine before men, that they may see your good works' (5:16); and 'Think not that I have come to abolish the law and the prophets; I have come not to abolish them but to fulfil them ... not an iota, not a dot, will pass from the law until all is accomplished' (5:17, 18). Also in this Sermon text is to be found a parallel not only with the language but also with the practice of the Essenes. For example, the Dead Sea scrolls contain strict bans on oath-taking; and here is what Jesus tells his followers:

Again you have heard that it was said to the men of old, 'You shall not swear falsely, but shall perform to the Lord what you have sworn.' But I say to you, Do not swear at all, either by heaven, for it is the throne of God, or by earth, for it is his footstool, or by Jerusalem, for it is the city of the great King. (Mat. 5:33–35)

Nevertheless, despite these parallels, I am convinced that Jesus was anti-Essene – as I hinted in our discussion of the Days of Ordination and the Herodians. Indeed, his whole approach was anathema to the Essenes, with their rigid legalism and their insistence that their rigorously interpreted laws of purity be carried out to the letter.

It is in the very Sermon on the Mount that scholars have discerned the strongest opposition by Jesus to the teachings of the Essenes. Here is an instructive passage from the Austrian scholar Professor Kurt Schubert, who was the first to elaborate on this theme:*

The key to the religious and historical understanding of broad parts of the Sermon on the Mount ... seems to me to be given in Mat. 5:43f., where we read: 'You have heard that it has been said, "You shall love your neighbour, and hate your enemy." But I say unto you, Love your enemies ...' Who were these listeners, who had heard that they should hate their enemies? Nowhere in the entire Jewish tradition, and still less in the Old Testament, is there any trace of a command to hate one's enemies. Probably, however, such a concept is to be found in the writings of the Qumran sect, which is associated by the majority of investigators, and with good reason, with the Essene movement. There we read: '[It is the duty of members of the sect] to love everyone, whom he [God] has elected, and to hate everyone, whom he has rejected'; '... to hate all sons of darkness, each one according to his sinfulness in the revenge of God'; '... and the Levites curse all men of Belial's lot, lift their voices and speak "Cursed art thou".' [The quotations from the scrolls are in the oath administered to new members upon joining the sect, as recorded in the Manual of Discipline. YY]

There seems to be no doubt that Jesus was referring to the Essenes when he spoke scathingly of those who urged it as a duty to hate one's enemies, and it is my opinion that the people he was addressing were familiar with this Essene injunction, having perhaps been close to the Essene sect and believed in its doctrines, but who had now

*'The Sermon on the Mount and the Qumran Texts', *The Scrolls and the New Testament*, ed. K. Stendahl (New York, 1957)

converted or were about to convert to the views of Jesus, and follow him.

The Christianity of Paul and the Johannine literature

With such divergent teachings of the Essenes and Jesus, how is it that scholars speak of the amazing similarity between the concepts and theology of the Dead Sea scrolls and Christianity? The fact is that the Christianity they have in mind is the Christianity that is given basic expression in the Gospel of John and the Johannine literature, and in the Epistles of Paul. Not that it originated there – some scholars think there was an interim stage between the early Christian Church and the message of those texts; but it is in those texts that we find the striking parallels.

To sharpen what I have called the historical paradox, it is worth examining some of these similarities before tackling the area of comparison that is of prime interest to us – the respective attitudes of the two communities towards the Temple and its cult.

Good and evil, light and darkness, and the 'End of Days'

I shall present five excerpts from two Dead Sea scrolls, which contain some of the fundamental teachings of the Essenes, and follow them with parallel quotations from John and Paul. The first excerpt is from the Manual of Discipline, and the remaining four are taken from The War of the Sons of Light against the Sons of Darkness:

He [God] has created man to govern the world and has appointed for him two spirits in which to walk until the time of His visitation: the spirits of truth and falsehood. The origins of truth are from the source of Light and of the source of Darkness are the origins of evil. The Sons of Righteousness shall be ruled by the Prince of Light ... and in the hand of the Angel of Darkness is the rule of all the Sons of Evil ...

The Sons of Light, ruled by the Prince (Angel) of Light, are the members of the sect. Ranged against them are the Sons of Darkness, who walk in the ways of Belial, the Prince (Angel) of Darkness. (Belial, 'worthlessness' in the literal translation from the Hebrew, became a later connotation for Satan.) The 'End of Days' will be marked by a climactic war between the two groups, and with the help of the Prince of Light and the mighty hand of God the Sons of Light will emerge the victors.

This is how that war will be launched:

The first engagement of the Sons of Light shall be to attack the lot of the Sons of Darkness, the army of Belial ... the Sons of Levi ... of Judah ... of Benjamin, the exiles of the wilderness, they shall fight against them.... Yea, against all their troops, when the exiles of the Sons of Light return from the wilderness of the Nations and encamp in the Wilderness of Jerusalem.

And this is how the War scroll envisages the day of the final battle, 'a day of mighty encounter and carnage before the God of Israel ... a day appointed by Him from of old for a battle of annihilation for the Sons of Darkness'. The passage continues:

That is a time of ... trouble for the people to be redeemed by God.... In three lots shall the Sons of Light prove strong so as to smite the wicked, and in three the army of Belial shall recover so as to bring about the withdrawal of the lot of Light.... But in the seventh lot the great hand of God shall subdue Belial and ... for all men of his lot there shall be eternal annihilation.

In the battle prayer of the Sons of Light, the War scroll repeats the content of our earlier excerpt from the Manual scroll, though in a different manner, about the Prince of Light and the Angel of Darkness:

Thou, O God, didst redeem us ... and into the lot of Light didst Thou cast us for Thy truth. Thou didst appoint from of old the Prince of Light to assist us.... And Thou wast the one who made Belial to corrupt an Angel of Hatred....

This Prince of Light is even identified in the same scroll with the Archangel Michael:

He [God] will send eternal assistance to the lot to be redeemed by Him through the might of an angel. He has magnified the authority of Michael through eternal light to light up in joy the House of Israel ... to raise among the angels the authority of Michael and the dominion of Israel among all flesh. And justice shall rejoice up on high.... But yea ... be ye strong in God's crucible until He shall lift up His hand and shall complete His testing through His mysteries with regards to your existence.

We can now compare these passages from the scrolls with some well-known New Testament verses taken mainly from the Gospel of John, the Epistles of John and the Epistles of Paul, which refer to the dualism of light and darkness as well as the final battle at the End of Days – often in the very terminology of the scrolls.

Here, first, are a few extracts from the Epistles of Paul:

But you are not in darkness, brethren.... For you are all sons of light and sons of the day.... (1 Thess. 5:4, 5)

For what partnership have righteousness and iniquity? Or what fellowship has light with darkness? What accord has Christ with Belial? (2 Cor. 6:14, 15)

Here, Jesus is presented as the Angel of Light, set against his evil counterpart, Belial, Satan, the Angel of Darkness. The theme is underlined further in the same Pauline Epistle:

For such men are false apostles ... disguising themselves as apostles of Christ. And no wonder, for even Satan disguises himself as an angel of light. (11:13, 14)

The dualism reappears in the Epistle to the Romans – night and day, darkness and light:

the night is far gone, the day is at hand. Let us then cast off the works of darkness and put on the armour of light. (13:12)

For once you were in darkness, but now you are light in the Lord; walk as children of light.... Take no part in the unfruitful works of darkness.... (Ephesians 5:8–11)

Striking as are these examples from Paul, scholars have been even more impressed by the similarities in the whole concept of light and darkness between certain texts in the Dead Sea scrolls and such verses in the Fourth Gospel and the Epistles of John as the following:

In him was life, and the life was the light of men. The light shines in the darkness, and the darkness has not overcome it. (John 1:4, 5)

And this is the judgement, that the light has come into the world, and men loved darkness rather than light, because their deeds were evil. For every one who does evil hates the light. (John 3:19, 20)

Again Jesus spoke to them, saying, 'I am the light of the world; he who follows me will not walk in darkness .... (John 8:12)

The most important, perhaps, is this next quotation from the Gospel of John:

Jesus said to them, '... he who walks in the darkness does not know where he goes. While you have the light, believe in the light, that you may become sons of light. (12:35, 36)

Two further examples, this time from the First Letter of John, are also of interest:

God is light and in him is no darkness at all. If we say we have fellowship with him while we walk in darkness, we lie ... but if we walk in the light, as he is in the light, we have fellowship with one another.... (1:5–7)

The Manual scroll's 'two spirits ... of truth and falsehood' is given almost identical expression in another passage from this Epistle of John (4:1–6)

Beloved, do not believe every spirit, but test the spirits to see whether they are of God; for many false prophets have gone out into the world.... Whoever knows God listens to us, and he who is not of God does not listen to us. By this we know the spirit of truth and the spirit of error ....

The main cemetery at Qumran, lying to the east of the community centre. Each grave is marked by a heap of stones (© *David Harris*).

The Dead Sea cliffs in the area of Qumran. It was in the caves of the cliffs that the
ancient scrolls were discovered.

TOP A typical baptismal pool at Qumran (© *David Harris*).
BOTTOM A model of Qumran in the Masada Museum
(at Masada) prepared by the author. The several
baptismal pools and water installations are coloured
blue.

The excavated ruins of the communal buildings of the Dead Sea sect at Qumran
(© *David Harris*).

I conclude this section with a passage from *The Ancient Library of Qumran and Modern Biblical Studies* by Professor Frank Moore Cross, Jr. Discussing the parallels between the scrolls and the Johannine literature, he writes:

These Essene parallels to John and the Johannine Epistles will come as a surprise only to those students of John who have attempted to read John as a work under strong Greek influence. It now turns out – as a small coterie of scholars have long maintained – that John has its strongest affinities not with the Greek world, or Philonic Judaism, but with Palestinian Judaism. Its concepts of truth, knowledge, spirit, and even the Word must be seen, not as rooted in Greek or Gnostic thought, but as concepts emerging precisely out of Sectarian Judaism. So that rather than being the most Hellenistic of the Gospels, John now proves to be in some ways the most Jewish.

The attitude towards the Temple

We have now reached the decisive point in our discussion of the similarities – both those I have quoted and many more – between the teachings of the Dead Sea scrolls and the New Testament. What awaits us now is an examination, in the light of our Temple scroll, of the proposition held so far by many scholars that there is a parallel between the attitude towards the Temple of the Essenes during their settlement in the Judean desert, and the Temple symbolism in the New Testament.

The concept of the Essenes

The Essene attitude is clearly revealed in various Qumran writings, notably the Manual of Discipline, the Damascus Document and the Thanksgiving scroll: the Essene sect was equated symbolically with the Temple (and thus used Temple terms when speaking of itself); and the Temple ritual, including sacrifices, was replaced by pious deeds and behaviour and scrupulous religious orthodoxy. Here are a few examples from the Manual of Discipline (in the translation by Professor Geza Vermes):

They shall atone for guilty rebellion and for sins of unfaithfulness ... without the flesh of burnt offerings and the fat of sacrifice. And prayer rightly offered shall be as an acceptable fragrance of righteousness, and perfection of way as a delectable free-will offering. (Col. 9)

There we find 'prayer rightly offered' and 'perfection' of behaviour serving as substitutes for ritual sacrifice. The concept that the Essene community was to be like the Temple appears in a continuation of the same passage:

At that time, the men of the Community shall be set apart as a House of Holiness for Aaron for the union of supreme holiness, and [as] a House of Community for Israel, for those who walk in perfection. The sons of Aaron alone shall command in matters of justice and property, and every rule concerning the men of the Community shall be determined according to their word.

Thus, the community, like the Temple, is set apart as a 'House of Holiness', and, as with the Temple, the priests, the 'sons of Aaron', are the supreme authority.

Another column in the same scroll repeats the 'House of Holiness' theme. And yet a further passage expands on the concept of the community as being 'separate', set apart, establishing 'the Rule for the men of the Community' that they 'shall separate themselves from the congregation of the men of falsehood'. They are to

unite, with respect to the Law and possessions, under the authority of the sons of Zadok, the Priests who keep the Covenant.... Every decision concerning property and justice shall be determined by them. They shall practise truth and humility in common, and justice and uprightness and charity and modesty in all their ways. (Col. 5)

Members of the community are to embody these virtues, and this is to be their form of 'sacrifice' in place of the conventional Temple ritual.

The concept of the New Testament

We now turn to the New Testament, where we find a similar symbolism of the Primitive Church as the Temple, though with a different attitude towards the sacrifices. Again, the most striking passages appear in the Pauline Epistles, but we shall also offer, after the Pauline extracts, a very telling quotation from Peter.

In Paul's Second Epistle to the Corinthians (6:16), we read: 'For we are the temple of the living God ...' And, like the Qumran community, to achieve the state of being the Temple they must separate themselves from the rest and become pure in spirit and in body. For, the Epistle continues immediately, 'as God said, "I will live in them and move among them.... Therefore come out from them, and be separate from them ... and touch nothing unclean...."' (6:17, 18)

The theme is carried over to the opening sentence of the next chapter: '... let us cleanse ourselves from every defilement of body and spirit, and make holiness perfect in the fear of God.' (7:1)

There is an equally clear statement by Paul equating the Christian community with the Temple in his First Letter to the Corinthians, in which he says: 'Do you not know that you are God's temple and that God's spirit dwells in you? ... God's temple is holy, and that temple you are.' (3:16, 17)

And again, in his Letter to the Ephesians, Paul says:

So then you are no longer strangers and sojourners, but you are fellow citizens with the saints and members of the household of God, built upon the foundation of the apostles and prophets, Christ Jesus himself being the cornerstone, in whom the whole structure is joined together and grows into a holy temple in the Lord; in whom you also are built into it for a dwelling place of God in the Spirit. (2:19–22)

My final New Testament quotation is taken not from the Pauline material but from the First Letter of Peter. It presents very clearly the belief in the Christian community as the Temple, and their belief in spiritual sacrifices. My colleague at the Hebrew University, Professor David Flusser, rightly equates it with a passage in the Manual of Discipline. Here are both quotations, both based on Isaiah 28.

In the Manual of Discipline, Column 8, we read: 'It shall be ... a House of Holiness for Israel, an Assembly of Supreme Holiness for Aaron.... I shall be that tried wall, that *precious cornerstone*, whose foundations shall neither rock nor sway in their place. It shall be a Most Holy Dwelling for Aaron ... and shall offer up sweet fragrance. It shall be a House of Perfection and Truth in Israel that they may establish a Covenant according to the everlasting precepts. And they shall be an agreeable offering, atoning for the Land....'

And this is what we read in I Peter 2:4–8: 'Come to him, to that living stone, rejected by men but in God's sight chosen and precious; and like living stones be yourselves built into a spiritual house, to be a holy priesthood, to offer spiritual sacrifices acceptable to God through Jesus Christ. For it stands in Scripture: "Behold, I am laying in Zion a stone, a *cornerstone chosen and precious*".... To you therefore who believe, he is precious, but for those who do not believe, "The very stone which the builders rejected has become the head of the corner", and "A stone that will make men stumble, a rock that will make them fall".'

The paradox and its probable explanation

It will be evident by now that the many similarities between the Essene writings and the New Testament, of which I have mentioned only a few, are indeed striking. And so we return to our original question: how was it that the early Christians, influenced by such rigid adherents of the Law of Moses and the Temple ritual as the Essenes, should be the very group who would eventually reject Judaism, Mosaic doctrines and the Temple cult? We have seen in our Temple scroll how strict were the Essenes, a sect more extreme in its literal interpretation of the Mosaic Law than the Pharisees; how un-compromising in their obedience to the letter of the Pentateuchal ordinances; above all how central was Temple sacrifice to their wor-ship. And we have also seen their impact on early Christianity in the Epistles of Paul and the Johannine writings. How, then, was this possible?

There were a few scholars who held that the passages I quoted earlier from the Manual of Discipline and the Damascus Document indicated that the Essenes had forsaken their adherence to the material Temple and its sacrifices for ever. If this were so, the beliefs on this subject held by the Essenes and the Christians would be identical.

This opinion, however, was expressed before the discovery and de-cipherment of our Temple scroll, though even then I ventured the suggestion that this was not the case. I felt we had enough evidence from other Dead Sea scrolls to show that the Essenes and the Christians held divergent concepts. The Essene attitude towards the Temple was temporary – it was an attitude towards the Temple that existed in their time, and in whose ritual they were unable and unwilling to participate. But they hoped for their eventual return to Jerusalem at the End of Days when the Temple would be rebuilt and the ritual of Sacrifices reinstituted in accordance with their concept of the Pentateuchal laws. For the Christians, however, the rejection of the entire cult of the Temple was permanent. For them, Jesus was the last sacrifice.

As I say, I held this view even before the revelations of the Temple scroll, finding my main support in the following passage of the War scroll, which I also had the privilege of deciphering, with its dramatic and detailed description of the reinstitution of the Temple cult in Jerusalem after the Sons of Light vanquish the Sons of Darkness:

The fathers of the congregation, fifty-two. The chiefs of the priests they shall dispose after the chief priest and his deputy, twelve chiefs to be serving in the daily burnt offering before God. The chiefs of the courses, twenty-six, in their courses they shall serve. After them the chiefs of the Levites to serve continually, twelve, one to each tribe. And the chiefs of their courses shall serve each man in his *ma'amad* [in his course]. The chiefs of the tribes and the fathers of the congregation after them, to stand perpetually in the gates of the sanctuary. The chiefs of their courses with their subordinates shall stand by on their festivals, on their new moons and on the sabbaths and on all the days of the year, from the age of fifty years upwards. These shall stand by at the burnt offering and the sacrifices, to set up the incense offering of sweet savour for the pleasure of God, to atone for all His congregation, and to bring fat sacrifices before him perpetually on the table of glory.

When I published my findings on this scroll several years ago (*The War of the Sons of Light against the Sons of Darkness*), in a reference to this passage, here is what I wrote (page 201): 'A sect which believed in the Pentateuchal Laws and desired to observe them in every detail was compelled to prohibit its members from participating in the existing sacrificial service, since the priests who then officiated in the Temple of Jerusalem, the only place where sacrifices might be brought, defiled the altar, and their practice was not according to the Pentateuchal Laws as understood by the sect. With the approach of the time described in the War of the Sons of Light against the Sons of Darkness, when legitimate priests again officiate and the Temple service is conducted according to the spirit of the sect, the members of the latter will be able once more to offer up lawful sacrifices. Until that time ... they must content themselves with prayers and special ceremonies at home. These prayers are such as to prove their sincere will to observe the Law since "the prayer of the righteous" is like an offering of delight, preferable to the "sacrifice of the wicked" which is an abomination.' (The quoted phrases are from a Damascus Document paraphrase of Proverbs 15:8.)

Those, it transpired, were not the only reasons for the non-participation by the Essenes in the Temple service. We now know from the Temple scroll that they had an entire concept of their own of the Temple, its plan, the sacrificial procedures, the celebration of the festivals, that was different from that of the Temple establishment in Jerusalem. They also had a different calendar.

They had therefore separated themselves from the rest of the Jewish community and from the normative Judaism of the time, and gone to live on the shore of the Dead Sea at the edge of the Judean desert. There they would await the coming of the End of Days when 'the exiles of the Sons of Light return from the Wilderness of the Nations to encamp in the Wilderness of Jerusalem', when the Temple would be restored. Thus, they say (in the Manual of Discipline, Col. 8), basing themselves on Isaiah: 'they shall separate from the habitation of ungodly men and shall go into the wilderness to prepare the way of Him, as it is written, "In the wilderness prepare the way of the Lord, make straight in the desert a highway for our God"' (Isaiah 40:3).

In the meantime, during this waiting period, they had to contrive an *ad hoc* theology and worship as a substitute for the Temple ritual, hoping and praying for the time when they would be able to carry out the Divine Law in all its meticulous detail as prescribed and revealed to them.

Therein, I think, lies the explanation for the apparent paradox. The very early Christians came into contact with the teachings of the Essenes and were swayed by them at the stage when these sectarians had already evolved their substitute practices. John, Paul in particular, and others could thus 'borrow' from the Essenes an almost ready-made theology of how to be a Jew without the Temple. But what was temporary for the Essenes was final for Paul, and became final for Christianity.

Here was the basic difference on this subject between the Christians and the Essenes – and indeed the rest of the Jews. For after the destruction of the Temple in AD 70, normative Judaism faced the same dilemma as the Dead Sea sect: how to live as a Jew without the Temple. Faithful to the Law of Moses, but having no Temple, the Jews in the interim also found a substitute in prayers, ethical principles and certain rites of worship, also awaiting the day when the Temple would be restored. It was this temporary pattern for the Essenes and for normative Judaism that became, for the Christians, a fixed and permanent canon.

A word to the reader as I end this account of the Temple scroll, the longest and perhaps the most important of all the Dead Sea scrolls discovered so far.

Whether or not one accepts my interpretations, suggestions and conclusions – and I have made an effort to offer the material in a way that would enable the reader to form his own judgement – one thing is clear: this scroll provides us with a 'Torah' of absorbing interest, strange, novel, comprehensive, of one of the Jewish sects in the Second Temple era. This sect of the Essenes was most extreme in its interpretation of the Law, and possibly for this reason eventually went out of existence, but not before it had left its mark on several streams of Judaism, not excluding the sect of the Early Jewish Christians.

It is my hope that further specialist studies on each facet of the teachings of the Temple scroll will draw forth data on the biblical texts, the Hebrew language and the Jewish faith of two thousand years ago, on the eve of the destruction of the Temple by the Romans.

Selected Bibliography

Burrows, M., *The Dead Sea Scrolls* (Secker and Warburg, London, 1956; Viking Press, New York, 1955; new ed. Baker Books, Michigan, 1978)

Burrows, M., *More Light on the Dead Sea Scrolls* (Secker and Warburg, London, 1958; Viking Press, New York, 1958)

Black, M., *The Scrolls and Christian Origins: Studies in the Jewish Background of the New Testament* (Nelson, London, 1961; Scribner, New York, 1961; new ed. Scholars Press, California, 1983)

Cross, F.M., Jr, *The Ancient Library of Qumran and Modern Biblical Studies* (Duckworth, London, 1961; Doubleday, New York, 1958; rev. ed. Baker Books, Michigan, 1980)

Cross, F.M., Jr, and Talmon, S. (eds), *Qumran and the History of the Biblical Text* (Harvard University Press, London, 1976; Harvard University Press, Massachusetts, 1975)

Daniélou, J., *The Dead Sea Scrolls and Primitive Christianity* (Helicon Press, Baltimore, 1958; new ed. Greenwood Press, Connecticut, 1979)

Dupont-Sommer, A., *The Jewish Sect of Qumran and the Essenes* (Vallentine Mitchell, London, 1954; Macmillan, New York, 1956)

Flusser, D., *The Dead Sea Sect and Pre-Pauline Christianity*, in *Scripta Hierosolymitana IV* (Hebrew University, Jerusalem, 1958)

Horgan, M.P., *Pesharim: Qumran Interpretations of Biblical Books* (Catholic Biblical Association, Washington, DC, 1979)

Sanders, J.A., *The Dead Sea Psalms Scroll* (Cornell University Press, New York, 1967)

Schiffman, L., *Sectarian Laws in the Dead Sea Scrolls: Courts, Testimony and the Penal Code*, Brown Judaic Studies (Scholars Press, California, 1983)

Stendahl, K. (ed.), *The Scrolls and the New Testament* (SCM Press, London, 1958; Harper, New York, 1957; new ed. Greenwood Press, Connecticut, 1975)

Sukenik, E.L., *The Dead Sea Scrolls of the Hebrew University* (Hebrew University, Jerusalem, 1955)

Vaux, R. de, *Archaeology and the Dead Sea Scrolls*, Schweich Lectures (OUP for the British Academy, Oxford and New York, 1973)

Vermes, G., *The Dead Sea Scrolls* (Penguin, London, 1962; Penguin, New York, 1962)

Yadin, Y., *The Dead Sea Scrolls and the Epistle to the Hebrews*, in *Scripta Hierosolymitana IV* (Hebrew University, Jerusalem, 1958)

Yadin, Y. (ed.), *The Scroll of the War of the Sons of Light Against the Sons of Darkness* (OUP, Oxford, 1962)

Yadin, Y., *The Temple Scroll*, three vols (published jointly by the Israel Exploration Society; the Institute of Archaeology, Hebrew University; and The Shrine of the Book, Israel Museum, Jerusalem, 1983)

Index